MWA1043230

ALIEN CONTACT

ALIEN CONTACT

John and Anne Spencer

New York

Copyright © 1997, 1999 by John and Anne Spencer. All rights reserved.
Sci-Fi Channel logo copyright © 1997 USA Networks.

First published in 1997 by The Orion Publishing Group Ltd., London.

No part of this book may be reproduced or transmitted in any form or by
any means, electronic or mechanical, including photocopying, recording,
or by any information storage and retrieval system, without permission in
writing from the publisher.

Publisher's Cataloging-in-Publication Data
Spencer, John, 1954–
    Alien contact / John and Anne Spencer. — 1st ed.
        p. cm. — (True life encounters)
        Includes bibliographical references.
        ISBN: 1–57500–023–7
        1. Human-alien encounters.   2. Alien abductions.   3. Unidentified
    flying objects—Sightings and encounters.   4. Life on other planets.
    I. Spencer, Anne, 1956– II. Title.
        BF 2050.S64 1999   001.942
                                                    QBI98-1774

TV Books, L.L.C.
1619 Broadway, Ninth Floor
New York, NY 10019
www.tvbooks.com

Interior designed by Rachel Reiss
Manufactured in Canada

Contents

Introduction

It seems logical that in an infinite universe of infinite time intelligent alien life must exist, or have existed, or be going to exist, somewhere. It does seem inconceivable that we could be the only intelligence in all the universe. But it is not impossible; we do not know why we exist. If our lives are the product of random evolution then others like us, or not so like us but intelligent none the less, should surely have developed elsewhere. But what if we are a freak accident? Or a one-off design by God? Or some other notion that we cannot even conceive of? We do not know enough about ourselves and the universe to have certainty in the answers.

We have searched for the aliens, scientifically, using listening ears, searching for signs of life. We have been successful in finding planets around stars, but not in finding even a single intelligent communication from elsewhere. Why? Are they not there? Or are we using the wrong ears? Or expecting the wrong kind of "voice"? Our failure to locate "them" does not mean they are not "out there."

And we must consider the widespread phenomenon of reported alien contact embraced within the subject of "UFOs," which contains literally thousands—and suspected millions—of people who believe they have had actual contact with aliens. The variety of claims is wide. Those claims cannot be dismissed as easily as science would like to dismiss them. But neither should they blindly be taken at face value as many proponents of UFOs would like us to do.

There is no doubt that there is a hard, scientific reality within the phenomenon known as UFOs. Multiple witness sightings, radar returns, ground traces and physiological and psychological aftermath give testimony to a world-wide phenomenon. However, it would be naïve to believe that such an influential modern phenomenon would not also bring with it myths and mythologies. A great many of the UFO claims probably do not represent that hard scientific reality but wishful thinking, self-delusion, cultural interpretation, sociological influence and so on. Furthermore there is clear evidence that a mythology is forming around UFOs in the true mythological tradition. Mythology gives a culture a way of identifying itself, its rules, its boundaries, its taboos and so on. It is possible that in the West the failing of traditional religion and the lack of belief in "old mythologies" has created a climate where a belief in the existence, and presence on Earth, of aliens has become the anchor of the building of a modern mythology.

Those who seek the scientific answers to the hard scientific reality must learn where the boundaries are, and they must learn not to ignore the myth and mythological claims but to understand how, where and why they arise.

So, do aliens exist? In this book we set out the scientific searches, the probabilities, and the stories of those who claim to have contacted them. We set out the arguments in support of the claims and the evidence, the contrary problems of belief at face value, and the alternative possibilities.

The question "do aliens exist?" is the most exciting challenge to our modern view of the world. And should the answer turn out to be "yes," then it is surely impossible to disagree with the Report of the Astronomy Survey Committee of the National Academy of Sciences in 1982, which stated: "It is hard to imagine a more exciting astronomical discovery or one that would have greater impact on human perceptions than the detection of extraterrestrial intelligence."

I

Aliens in the Cosmos

1

Listening

It was an alien world of magic and mystery populated by strange and wonderful creatures. It was surrounded by a desert and at its heart lay the City of Emeralds. It was approached down the Yellow Brick Road... In 1900 Lyman Frank Baum published *The Wonderful Wizard of Oz*, the first of 14 books describing adventures in the mystical land of Oz. To the queen of the land he gave the name Ozma. It was this name—Project Ozma—that was adopted by Frank Drake for the first attempt to detect evidence of intelligent life in outer space. This was the first SETI project: the Search for Extra Terrestrial Intelligence.

Hollywood placed Oz "somewhere over the rainbow," but it was not the visible spectrum of light that Drake was concentrating on. He was a radio astronomer then working at the National Radio Astronomy Observatory in Green Bank, West Virginia. Mankind's first attempt to "seek out new life and new civilizations" would scan the invisible spectrum of radio signals from the stars, listening for their signals.

Frank Drake chose two stars as his target for this first examination: Tau Ceti and Epsilon Eridani. Both stars were thought to be approximately the same age as the Sun, increasing the possibility that planetary formation and development of intelligent life might have paralleled the Earth's own development.

The project ran from April to July of 1960. For six hours a day an 85-foot radio telescope listened in to the 21-centimetre band (1420.4 MHz). A 100-Hz channel receiver scanned the 400-kHz bandwidth. What Drake and his colleagues were looking for was a pattern in the pulses which would have indicated a deliberate transmission by an intelligent source. Any repeated pattern might have indicated intelligence; even better would have been a mathematical transmission, perhaps a sequence of prime numbers, the random transmission of which would be almost incalculably against the odds.

During the first day of the search a signal was received when the dish was listening to Epsilon Eridani. They were receiving a constant uniform pulse eight times a second, every second. Ten days later the same thing happened again; but this time Drake held a small antenna to another point in the sky and received the same signal. This was a confirmation that the signal was man-made, and coming from the Earth rather than from the stars. It is thought that Project Ozma's first "hit" was caused by listening to a secret military experiment. Outside of that one false alarm and excitement Project Ozma did not locate any meaningful signals.

The basis of the search lay in the "Drake Equation." This purports to be an estimation of the number of intelligent, communicative civilizations in the universe. In fact it is scientifically dressed-up guesswork which, depending on the user's own estimates, could produce figures anywhere from none to several billions. As the SETI Institute comments: "Although there is no unique solution to this equation, it is a generally accepted tool used by the scientific community to examine these factors." If the equation serves a purpose then it is probably, as the SETI Institute also states, "an effective tool for stimulating intellectual curiosity about the Universe around us."

The Drake Equation is:

$$R^* \times fp \times ne \times fl \times fi \times fc \times L = N$$

To summarize these terms:

- **R***

This represents the number of stars which form per year containing a large enough habitable zone and which have a long enough lifespan to allow for the development of planets that might contain intelligent life.

The habitable zone is the region around the star in which suitable planets can form; it is the distance from the star where the temperature on the planet allows water to be liquid, i.e. it is neither boiled away by too close a proximity to the star, nor turned to ice by too great a distance from it. Exobiologists believe that water is the primary ingredient for the formation of life on Earth and that therefore if we were to encounter an intelligence similar to our own it would have to have arisen in a world containing liquid water. Indeed it is not just the temperature but the atmospheric pressure which dictates these properties, leading to a speculation that intelligent life like our own would have to form on planets not dissimilar to the Earth in both size and proximity to their star. Too small a planet will not be able to hold an atmosphere that could sustain biochemistry similar to that which developed on Earth; too large a planet may have too much pressure in a dense atmosphere. It should also be remembered that even though large planets such as Jupiter may not be suitable for the formation as life as we know it, such planets may have moons that approximate Earth-like temperatures and pressures. Of course, none of this rules out the possibility of life developing on non-Earth-like planets in a way quite different from that on Earth.

· fp

Of the suitable stars in R* the term fp represents the fraction of those stars which *actually* develop planets. It is currently believed that stars form from clouds of gases and dust by a process of coalescence and that in some cases there is leftover debris which forms the planets. The number of stars similar to our sun around which planets are formed is unknown.

This theory of star formation was proposed when the Infrared Astronomy Satellite (IRAS) observed that some stars emitted more infrared radiation than expected, suggesting that the stars were surrounded by dust clouds. Visual observation of such stars confirmed that the dust was indeed present. Recent observations by the Hubble Space Telescope have identified such "protoplanetary discs" around newly formed stars in the area of the Orion nebula.

There have been some recent successes in locating planets. In October 1995 astronomers Michel Mayor and Dider Queloz detected a planet around the star 51 Pegasi. The star is similar in mass, size and temperature to the Sun, but the planet that has been detected is not like any other in the solar system. It is a planet with an orbital period of just four days and is at least half the mass of Jupiter.

Several other planets have been identified around other stars, in some cases many times the mass of Jupiter. It is believed that at least one of the new planets discovered is in the habitable zone of its star, and although the planet may not be suitable for sustaining Earth-like life, it may have a moon which has Earth-like properties. This is similar to conditions in the Earth's solar system, where Jupiter is not conducive to terrestrial-like life but where one of its moons, Europa, may well be.

In June 1996, at the meeting of the American Astronomical Society in Madison, Wisconsin, Dr. George Gatewood gave details of the discovery of a planet orbiting the nearby star Lalande 21185. The planet approximates to the mass of Jupiter. Other data also indicate that the same star may have another planet closer to it, also about the mass of Jupiter.

An Associated Press and Reuters release in April 1997 indicated that a "Jupiter-like" planet had been located around 50 light years away. The planet orbits the star Rho Coronae Borealis, situated in the constellation of the Northern Crown. The new discovery was announced by Robert Noyes of the Harvard-Smithsonian Astrophysical Observatory together with seven other astronomers. The planet orbits its star at a distance of approximately 23 million miles; this is very close and probably makes it far too hot to support life as we know it.

However, more hospitable planets could be orbiting the same star. Noyes confirmed what the discoveries noted in this chapter indicate: "This discovery helps show that giant planets like Jupiter may be reasonably common around ordinary stars. There could well be many smaller planets in these systems that we just can't see by present techniques." It should be remembered that the fact that large planets are currently being identified is a factor of the sensitivity of the equipment being used and that the existence of smaller Earth-sized planets is not ruled out by their lack of discovery to date.

More importantly, perhaps, in May 1997 two Brazilian astronomers, Gustavo Porto de Mello of the Federal University of Rio de Janeiro and Licio da Silva of the National Observatory identified that the star 18 Scorpii, 46 light years from the Earth, is a near twin of the Earth's star, Sol. Its mass, temperature, colour, surface gravity and iron content are all similar to that of Sol, and therefore it becomes a possible nearby location of planets similar to those found in our own solar system, and by implication a possible home for "life as we know it." 18 Scorpii is also a single star, again like our own. The scientists recommended that "it be considered for strong priority in the ongoing planet searching programmes as well as in SETI (Search for Extra Terrestrial Intelligence) surveys."

The overall conclusion of current research is that planetary formation around stars may be normal, increasing the possibility that the Earth is not an isolated case.

· **ne**

This represents a number of *Earth-like* planets in each planetary system. This directly relates to the habitable zone around the star. The Earth-like planets are sought out as being the likeliest to evolve a compatible life form to our own.

· **fl**

This represents the fraction of Earth-like planets where life *actu-*

ally develops. Even given that there are a number of planets where life could develop it is possible that it will not develop in all such cases. At the present time we only know that life has developed on Earth. We have no proof, and only circumstantial evidence, that life has, or could, develop elsewhere. Recent discoveries suggesting life once existed on Mars, evidenced by findings in a meteorite (see Chapter 2), and suggestions of life on one of Jupiter's moons, have greatly increased the possibility that the formation of life is not a unique phenomenon, possibly not even a rare one.

• **fi**

From the fraction of Earth-like planets where life actually develops we then have to move on to examine the fraction of those planets where *intelligent* life develops. The problem with calculating this is that we do not know how tenacious life is. It may be that given the billions of random chemical and other "accidents" which can arise some life will always win through and some intelligence will always win through beyond that. On the other hand it may be that life is very fragile and that to succeed in producing intelligence is a rarity with most life dying off in the early stages, beaten by odd combinations of random events. Although the Earth represents an apparent success story, we cannot be certain even of the factors which allowed intelligent life to develop on this planet, and it is therefore impossible to meaningfully extrapolate the data to other planets. Even if we could do so we would then be faced with the difficulty of understanding the very meaning of intelligence itself. If we consider terrestrial biology we can only observe it from the point of view of our own intelligence, which becomes a benchmark, and a seemingly insurmountable prejudice, against which we examine all other intelligences. In short we cannot even be certain that there are not greater intelligences on Earth than ourselves in the insect world or even the plant world—intelligence which manifests itself in a way we simply cannot understand. If such intelligence were to form on other planets it might be unable to contact us on Earth or even if it did, it might be impossible for us to identify it.

· **fc**

We need, then, to consider not just intelligence but something akin to our own type of intelligence; perhaps measured by technology. Of the planets where intelligence develops we must then examine the number of those planets where technology develops. Again, if we first look at terrestrial biology we are faced with the fact that the dolphin brain appears to be as complex as the human brain while at the same time it is clear that it has not developed a technology. It may be that the dolphin uses its complex brain for philosophical thought, even for complex fun and play, whereas we have turned our minds to technology. It might be arrogant to suppose that ours is the better use of the brain, but certainly in the search for extraterrestrial intelligence we would be looking for that fraction of complex, intelligent brains that have developed a technology and are therefore capable of broadcasting their presence beyond their own planet and solar system so that we can detect them.

· **L**

This represents the length of time in years that intelligent, technological civilizations would exist and transmit their presence to the stars. Again we are faced with unknowns; this time in the question of the tenacity of life. There is the possibility that mankind will destroy itself by misuse of its ecology, of its technology such as atomic power, or of biological experimentation and so on. It may be that self-destruction is the natural fate of technological intelligence and that therefore all technological intelligences have a very short lifespan. If so, then it would be difficult for one civilization to detect another, as they would have to exist for their short lifespans at precisely the right time in relation to each other, reaching their technological peaks at precisely the right times also. If their two stars were far enough apart, then by the time the signals were heard by the receiver the originating race might be extinct. In such a case the information would be sterile, and the receiver would only know that an intelligence had once existed.

On the other hand the human race may be long-lived as an intelligent technology or, even if we are not, some races may reach a peak of intelligence and technological activity lasting millions of years.

Such unknowns make it very difficult to ascertain the likelihood of detecting intelligent signals from the stars.

· N

This therefore represents the number of communicative civilizations within our own galaxy, the Milky Way, who may be transmitting radio signals which can be detected by us. It is this figure which is the "answer" to the Drake Equation.

The problem with the Drake Equation is that we start from a sample of one. We only know of the Earth as a planet which has evolved a communicative technological intelligence. Perhaps it is even more sobering to remember, at a time when science fiction bombards us with images of all kinds of aliens, that we only know for certain of one planet, the Earth, which has evolved any life whatsoever. The Drake Equation begins to look more exciting, however, if the fossil microbes in the meteorite from Mars (see Chapter 2) turn out to be evidence of life that existed on that planet. That would indicate the possibility that life in some form may have developed on two separate planets—doubling the initial sample. There would still be a long way to go, but the odds would be improved.

The equation is more of a thought-experiment than a piece of mathematics. However, it is a thoughtful reminder of the vastness of both space and time, and also of the number of variables that must "break in our favour" before we can establish a contact. Later in the book we shall be describing the multitude of claims of alien contact by "UFO witnesses" and these must be considered alongside the odds suggested by the Drake Equation.

Assuming that we determine there are at least a number of intelligent, technological civilizations that actually form with a chance of making contact with the Earth, the method of contact becomes another problem. If radio transmissions are the method, then they would appear to be limited by the speed of light. So if the nearest star to the Earth, around four light years away, should happen to have developed a compatible technology, correspondence with them would take eight years to send and receive each transmission. But it would be an almost incalculable coincidence that so close a star should happen to be suitable, and reach a peak of technology at the same time as ourselves. If a compatible technology formed just 50 light years away—still only "round the corner" as the universe goes—each correspondence would take 100 years. A compatible technology does not have to be far away before correspondence begins to be very long-duration indeed. (You send a message, wait one thousand years and then receive the answer: "We're sorry, no one is at home right now, please leave your name, number . . .")

We must also consider that we might make contact with a race so different from our own that we would never even know it. As a tongue-in-cheek "mind game," suppose that our signals are received—and even understood—by a totally incompatible alien life form which does not have ears but which receives the signal in a way we cannot even dream of. Suppose that it sends a signal back to the source of the radio signal but not in a way we expect. Would we know it? Perhaps every time your foot itches you are receiving the reply to SETI . . . but what do you do? You scratch your foot and the itch goes away. Another cosmic conversation lost! More seriously, we have to recognize that we are at an undefined stage of technological development, and have no real idea how far our technology will develop. Countless books have pointed out that 100 years ago the modern computer, the music CD, fibre-optics, and a whole lot more, would have been inconceivable. In the future we will probably invent other ways of sending transmissions. Perhaps some other race already has, but we are not equipped to perceive it until we invent the similar technology. Perhaps radio just isn't what is being used by the ETs.

Despite the lack of success thus far, there is scientific support for the general idea of SETI from many quarters. Dr. Melvyn Calvin, then of the Department of Chemistry, University of California at Berkeley, has stated: "There are at least 100 million planets in the visible universe which were, or are, very much like the Earth ... This would mean certainly that we are not alone in the Universe. Since Man's existence on the Earth occupies but an instant of cosmic time surely intelligent life has progressed far beyond our level on some of those 100 million planets."

There was a time when support for SETI was viewed in a rather similar light to support for UFOs—the kiss of death for "serious" scientists. SETI has done much to promote its cause and has, correctly, divorced itself from the UFO phenomenon. In truth, the two do not share a common origin. It has for some years been acceptable to support SETI in most scientific circles.

Dr. Su-Shu Huang, then of Goddard Space Flight Center, Maryland, has stated:

> ... planets are formed around the main-sequence stars of spectral types later than F5. Thus, planets are formed just where life has the highest chance to flourish. Based on this view we can predict that nearly all single stars of the main sequence below F5 and perhaps above K5 have a fair chance of supporting life on their planet. Since they compose a few percent of all stars, life should indeed be a common phenomenon in the universe.

Dr. A. G. W. Cameron, then Professor of Astronomy at Yeshiva University, in New York City, commenting on nearby single stars to the Earth, added:

But there are about 26 other single stars of smaller mass within this distance (5 parsecs), each of these should have a comparable probability of having a life-supporting planet according to the present analysis.

Dr. R. N. Bracewell of The Radio Astronomy Institute, Stanford University, has calculated:

As there are about 1 billion stars in our galaxy, the number of planets would be about 10 billion...Now not all of these would be habitable, some would be too hot and some too cold, depending on their distance from their central star; so that on the whole we need only pay attention to planets situated as our Earth is with respect to the Sun. Let's describe such a situation as being within the habitable zone.

This is not to imply that no life would be found outside the habitable zone. There may very well be living things existing under most arduous physical conditions...After elimination of frozen planets and planets sterilized by heat, we estimate there are about 10,000 million likely planets in the Galaxy [suitable for life]...Of the 10,000 million likely planets, we frankly do not know how many of them support intelligent life. Therefore, we explore all possibilities, beginning with the possibility that intelligent life is abundant and in fact occurs on practically every planet. In this case the average distance from one intelligent community to the next is ten light years.

The good news for the Drake Equation is that there are basic observations about the universe that seem to suggest a possible positive outcome. It appears from observations of stars that planetary formation is the norm rather than the exception. When we consider the formation of life on Earth it seems probable—though not certain—that it formed naturally in a primitive environment and within fairly basic laws of physics, chemistry and biology. Since we can observe that some of those basic laws, particularly of physics and chemistry, are at work elsewhere in the universe, then we can suppose that the mechanisms that caused life here might have caused, or be causing, life elsewhere. For example, planets orbiting stars must have equators and poles, warm and cold climates, probably seasons and both seas and lands; these are probable common environments and strengthen the possibility of something forming akin to life on Earth. We can assume that the present human, technological intelligence on Earth was the product of natural selection and that such evolutionary random forces may be at work elsewhere. Lastly, we can assume that the evolution of intelligence starts from a natural desire to survive; if survival is a natural urge, then intelligence is probable on a widespread basis. The contrary argument is based on the possibility that intelligence is not normal, nor that useful for long-term survival. The debate is not going to be answered quickly.

Modern Seti

But SETI has come a long way since its initial work. It was brought into the purview of NASA for a time though many believe it was even then underfunded. NASA has a remit to "study of the origin and distribution of life in the universe." The principal NASA project was the High Resolution Microwave Survey (HRMS). But after just one year Congress pulled the budget. The project continues as a privately funded operation under the name "Project Phoenix."

The HRMS project was the most far-reaching and comprehensive such project to date. As SETI point out: "in the first minutes of operation, the HRMS accomplished more searching than all previous programs combined."

SETI—and the work of HRMS—is now conducted under the auspices of the SETI Institute, a private, non-profit corporation which receives sponsorship from highly regarded scientific institutions and other private sources. Project Phoenix is expected to run until at least 2001, depending also on any successes that might be achieved.

Wow!

The SETI programme has not been successful to date. It has not detected anything that proves, or even strongly suggests, the existence of extraterrestrial life broadcasting signals. There is only one incident which SETI enthusiasts hold on to, and that occurred 20 years ago. The so-called "Wow!" signal is still the subject of controversy.

At Ohio State Radio Observatory, on 15 August 1977, a signal was detected which seemed to be the proof that a broadcast from an extraterrestrial intelligence had been picked up. The "Wow!" signal received its name simply because SETI volunteer Dr. Jerry Ehman scribbled that exclamation on the computer print-out. "I came across the strangest signal I had ever seen, and immediately scribbled 'Wow!' next to it," said Ehman. "At first, I thought it was an earth signal reflected from space debris, but after I studied it further, I found that couldn't be the case."

It was not, however, a message. It was an unmodulated signal; so strong that it "catapulted the Big Ear's recording device off the chart." Ehman confirmed: "It was the most significant thing we had seen."

But as to it being a communication from an alien intelligence, researchers remain cautious to say the least. Frequent searches in that same area of the sky have failed to receive a duplicate signal. Ehman himself is currently very cautious about the signal now firmly associated with him. "Even if it were intelligent beings sending a signal, they'd do it far more than once," said Ehman. "We should have seen it again when we looked for it 50 times. Something suggests it was an Earth-bound signal that simply got reflected off a piece of space debris."

Perhaps there is a little more support for the exotic possibilities from Dr. H. Paul Shuch, executive director of the SETI

League Inc. He states, in an address prepared for the AMSAT Annual Meeting and Space Symposium of November 1996: "From the 'Wow!' signal's temporal correspondence to the antenna pattern, we know that its source was moving with the background stars. From its Doppler shift signature...we can eliminate terrestrial interference, aircraft or spacecraft from consideration." He went on to add: "If the 'Wow!' signal is typical of the type of evidence which SETI seeks (and we have no reason to assume otherwise), then we can expect valid SETI hits to be extremely strong, highly intermittent signals which appear once (as the transmit beam sweeps path Earth), and never repeat on human time scales. Thus we do not expect to again encounter the 'Wow!' Yet there may be countless other signals, similarly strong and intermittent, falling on our heads even now."

The Declaration Of Principles Concerning Activities Following The Detection Of Extraterrestrial Intelligence

What would happen if we were to detect an intelligent civilization elsewhere in the universe? The problem has been addressed in the "Declaration of Principles concerning Activities Following the Detection of Extraterrestrial Intelligence." This is set out below (provided by the SETI Institute):

> We, the institutions and individuals participating in the search for extraterrestrial intelligence,
>
> Recognizing that the search for extraterrestrial intelligence is an integral part of space exploration and is being undertaken for peaceful purposes and for the common interest of all mankind,
>
> Inspired by the profound significance for mankind of detecting evidence of extraterrestrial intelligence, even though the probability of detection may be low,
>
> Recalling the Treaty on Principles Governing the Activities of States in the Exploration and Use of Outer Space, Including the

Moon and Other Celestial Bodies, which commits States Parties to that Treaty "to inform the Secretary General of the United Nations as well as the public and the international scientific community, to the greatest extent feasible and practicable, of the nature, conduct, locations and results" of their space exploration activities (Article XI),

Recognizing that any initial detection may be incomplete or ambiguous and thus require careful examination as well as confirmation, and that it is essential to maintain the highest standards of scientific responsibility and credibility,

Agree to observe the following principles for disseminating information about the detection of extraterrestrial intelligence:

1. Any individual, public or private research instutition, or governmental agency that believes it has detected a signal from or other evidence of extraterrestrial intelligence (the discoverer) should seek to verify that the most plausible explanation for the evidence is the existence of extraterrestrial intelligence rather than some other natural phenomenon or anthropogenic phenomenon before making any public announcement. If the evidence cannot be confirmed as indicating the existence of extraterrestrial intelligence, the discoverer may disseminate the information as appropriate to the discovery of any unknown phenomenon.

2. Prior to making a public announcement that evidence of extraterrestrial intelligence has been detected, the discoverer should promptly inform all other observers or research organizations that are parties to this declaration, so that those other parties may seek to confirm the discovery by independent observations at other sites and so that a network can be established to enable continuous monitoring of the signal or phenomenon. Parties to this declaration should not make any public announcement of this information until it is determined whether this information is or is not credible evidence of the existence of extraterrestrial intelligence. The discoverer should inform his/her or its relevant national authorities.

3. After concluding that the discovery appears to be credible evi-

dence of extraterrestrial intelligence, and after informing other parties to this declaration, the discoverer should inform observers throughout the world through the Central Bureau for Astronomical Telegrams of the International Astronomical Union, and should inform the Secretary General of the United Nations in accordance with Article XI of the Treaty on Principles Governing the Activities of States in the Exploration and Use of Outer Space, Including the Moon and Other Bodies. Because of their demonstrated interest in and expertise concerning the question of the existence of extraterrestrial intelligence, the discoverer should simultaneously inform the following international institutions of the discovery and should provide them with all pertinent data and recorded information concerning the evidence: the International Telecommunication Union, the Committee on Space Research of the International Council of Scientific Unions, the International Astronautical Federation, the International Academy of Astronautics, the International Institute of Space Law, Commission 51 of the International Astronomical Union and Commission J of the International Radio Science Union.

4. A confirmed detection of extraterrestrial intelligence should be disseminated promptly, openly, and widely through scientific channels and public media, observing the procedures in this declaration. The discoverer should have the privilege of making the first public announcement.

5. All data necessary for confirmation of detection should be made available to the international scientific community through publications, meetings, conferences, and other appropriate means.

6. The discovery should be confirmed and monitored and any data bearing on the evidence of extraterrestrial intelligence should be recorded and stored permanently to the greatest extent feasible and practicable, in a form that will make it available for further analysis and interpretation. These recordings should be made available to the international institutions listed above and to members of the scientific community for further objective analysis and interpretation.

7. If the evidence of detection is in the form of electromagnetic signals, the parties to this declaration should seek international agreement to protect the appropriate frequencies by exercising procedures available through the International Telecommunication Union. Immediate notice should be sent to the Secretary General of the ITU in Geneva, who may include a request to minimize transmissions on the relevant frequencies in the Weekly Circular. The Secretariat, in conjunction with advice of the Union's Administrative Council, should explore the feasibility and utility of convening an Extraordinary Administrative Radio Conference to deal with the matter, subject to the opinions of the member Administrations of the ITU.

8. No response to a signal or other evidence of extraterrestrial intelligence should be sent until appropriate international consultations have taken place. The procedures for such consultations will be the subject of a separate agreement, declaration or arrangement.

9. The SETI Committee of the International Academy of Astronautics, in coordination with Commission 51 of the International Astronomical Union, will conduct a continuing review of procedures for the detection of extraterrestrial intelligence and the subsequent handling of the data.

Should credible evidence of extraterrestrial intelligence be discovered, an international committee of scientists and other experts should be established to serve as a focal point for continuing analysis of all observational evidence collected in the aftermath of the discovery, and also to provide advice on the release of information to the public. This committee should be constituted from representatives of each of the international institutions listed above and such other members as the committee may deem necessary. To facilitate the convocation of such a committee at some unknown time in the future, the SETI Committee of the International Academy of Astronautics should initiate and maintain a current list of willing representatives from each of the international institutions listed above, as well as other individuals with relevant skills, and should make that list continuously available through the Secretariat of the International Academy of Astronautics. The International Academy of Astronautics will act as the Depository for this declaration and will annually provide a current list of parties to all the parties to this declaration.

Public Reaction

A workshop sponsored by NASA and the SETI Institute examined the likely social and cultural effects of an announcement of proof that extraterrestrial intelligence had been located. They concluded that such an announcement would, inevitably, create widespread interest. Cautious about media reaction, their recommendations take into account a need for a systematic release of information to ensure proper public appreciation of the discovery.

They recognized that detection would result in philosophical debate. In particular they were concerned about two public responses: firstly, that there was already a body of fear arising based on "millenniumist" predictions; and, secondly, there were alarmist comparisons being made to situations when cultures suffered at the hands of a technologically superior, "discovering" culture. Being North American they may have been considering their own history and relationships with native Americans, so this perspective was inevitable. The workshop recommended that the widespread population should be educated about beneficial contacts; citing the introduction "of Arab knowledge to medieval Europe, with consequent flowering of European scholarship." Their positive views are not shared by all scientists. Cambridge Professor Stephen Hawking, writing in the *Sunday Times* of 30 March 1997, observed: "Meeting a more advanced civilization might be a bit like the original inhabitants of America meeting Columbus. I don't think they were better off for it."

At the individual level the workshop recognized that it was difficult to predict responses which would range from "indifference through mild positive or negative curiosity, through millennial enthusiasm or catastrophist anxiety, to full-scale pronoia or paranoia." Some reactions might be "irrationally extreme or even violent." The workshop recommended further research into the social implications.

It has often been speculated within UFO interest groups that the entertainment industry has been used to "educate" the population along government-approved lines. One persistent rumour has been that the film *Close Encounters of the Third Kind* was a government propaganda film. Whether that is true or not, the workshop did accept the possibility of such uses. It recommended that "SETI researchers or their designees should make greater use of popular media, including movies, computer games, and popular music, to present SETI and ETI themes. These avenues could greatly increase public interest and exposure." Indeed the workshop recommended that "HRMS researchers should consider encouraging a filmmaker to develop a major feature about SETI and receipt of an ETI signal in a responsible dramatic way." Alongside this they also suggested that "the creation of a panel of expert behavioral scientists as a 'reaction team' should be considered. Such a team should be available for advice and help in situations where information about an ETI signal seems to cause unusual disruption of normal patterns of life."

The recommendations take into account the existence of "vested interest" and "pressure" groups and recognize that people would use the announcements to their own ends, political or otherwise. This is reasonable, indeed to some degree inevitable, but only takes account of individual interests. The workshop does not appear to give weight to the, probably paranoid, suggestion rife within UFO circles that there is a "World Government" which controls each and every act and would be able to suppress or disseminate the news according to global financial, religious or other interests. Indeed, they point out that most governments have no policy in this regard and they recommend that these should be formulated.

Of religions, there is a belief among members of the workshop that the existence of extraterrestrial life can be incorporated into religious dogma. "While some religious groups are expected to reject the idea that we are not alone, most would not, and some would embrace the discovery as reinforcing their own beliefs." Indeed it has already happened. On 16 February 1997, Dr. Christopher Corbally, vice-director of the Vatican Observatory in Arizona (also a Fellow of the Royal Astronomical Society and a member of the American Astronomical Society), in an address to the American Association—the world's largest general science meeting remarked: "While Christ is the first and last word, the alpha and the omega spoken to humanity, it is not necessarily the only word spoken to the entire universe." He believed that the discovery of life beyond the Earth would create a sense of "being an integral part of a cosmic community." A Roman Catholic Church spokesman commented that "We have always believed that God created all things. If He created life elsewhere, then fair enough."

The workshop points out that "efforts to suppress or control information are unlikely to succeed, given the widespread SETI verification and data-sharing network and the likely ability of most nations to 'tune in' an ETI source with modest equipment." The public understanding of the contact will, they point out, be enhanced—or distorted—by available reading material in libraries, bookshops and other places. The workshop was concerned about what they regarded as "a disproportionate availability of materials on UFOs and pseudoscientific aspects of extraterrestrial life" and suggested that libraries need to be educated about what reading material is "suitable." The tabloid media were not thought to be a useful outlet for any material, as they "will certainly misrepresent all stories and cannot be persuaded to do otherwise."

Even responsible media were thought likely to "push" vague possibilities of detection into perceived "certainties," and it is clear that the workshop believed that the release of information should be fairly strictly controlled by the scientific bodies concerned. One important point has been taken into account; there will be no knee-jerk reply to the contact. As the SETI Institute points out: "Under an International SETI Post-detection Protocol now under consideration, the nations of the Earth would decide together whether and how to reply."

That said, we might remember that we have been "leaking" radio, television, and other broadcasts into space, and many of those signals—which would clearly indicate an intelligence—are now over 50 light years distant.

There have been a few attempts to send direct signals, i.e. a broadcast in 1974 from Arecibo Observatory depicting the solar system, the DNA molecule, and the human shape; but these have not elicited responses as far as we know.

2

Looking

SETI presumes a contact by radio with an intelligence living elsewhere in the universe, but this is not the only contact possible. In fact it is almost certain that on Earth we have had contact with extraterrestrials, though perhaps of a kind less exciting than science fiction would usually have us believe. The more certain reality is contact with micro-organisms, through meteorites. It has been speculated that in the many thousands of meteorites that must have hit the Earth in aeons past—and even up to relatively contemporary times—some alien organisms are likely to have been present. Some believe that possibly it was life in a meteorite that triggered the explosion of life on Earth in the first place; that our genetic ancestors were in fact from another world.

Life On Mars

One meteorite in particular has caused recent controversy. After the flurry of interest in the planet Mars created by the Viking Lander probes of the 1970s, the Red Planet came back into the equation in the 1990s. It started with the possibility that there had been, or was, life on Mars yet to be discovered.

In late 1995/early 1996 the NASA Ames Research Center, in Mountain View, near San Francisco, were admitting that in the decades since the Mars Viking missions scientists had been aware that signs of life on Mars could have been missed. They were now contemplating the possibility that primitive life could still exist underground on Mars, in minerals in dry lake beds, and particularly in hot springs.

"After Viking, there was a feeling we had been there, done that, and so much for looking for life," said Jack Farmer, NASA Ames geologist and palaeontologist. But this view has been revised in the years since: "We think there are certain kinds of deposits . . . where we can capture evidence of life." Attention was being paid to the similarities between Martian and terrestrial geology, and the possibility that 3.5 billion years ago there was water on Mars when life was forming on Earth.

In August 1996 this theorizing was given a shot in the arm when scientists believed they had found evidence of Martian life in meteorites located in Alaska. The research was centred on a meteorite known as Allan Hills 84001, one of 12 such meteorites confirmed as having originated from Mars. They were believed to have been "blown away" from the Red Planet during a massive collision, possibly with an asteroid, billions of years ago, and fallen to the Earth around 13,000 years ago. The meteorite was found in 1984.

The findings were of organic molecules called Polycyclic Aromatic Hydrocarbons (PAHs). These can form either by the biological action of micro-organisms, or during planetary formation. Scientists believe the evidence in this case suggests the former. Controversy still abounds at the time of writing; a contrary theory being that the PAHs could be the product of Earth-based bacterial action.

Scientists were being customarily cautious about the findings: "There is not any one finding that leads us to believe that this is evidence of past life on Mars. Rather, it is a combination of many things that we have found," stated Dr. David McKay, joint team leader of the investigation at NASA Johnson Space Center (JSC), Houston. "They include Stanford's detection of an apparently unique pattern of organic molecules, carbon compounds that are the basis of life. We also found several unusual mineral phases that are known products of primitive microscopic organisms on Earth. Structures that could be microscopic fossils seem to support all of this. The relationship of all of these things in terms of location—within a few hundred thousandths of an inch of one another—is the most compelling evidence."

The significance of the possibilities, however, was not under-stated. Doug Millard of the National Science Museum observed: ". . . if these do indeed turn out to be indications of life on another planet, then clearly, the whole question of probability of finding life elsewhere in the universe, is turned on its head." And John Pike, Director of Space Policy, Federation of American Scientists, commented: ". . . even if it stopped with germs or viruses on Mars, it would suggest that the sort of 'alien' people that we've been seeing in *Star Trek* and *Star Wars*, may turn out to be much more plentiful than might have been thought."

In fact evidence of life in outer space detected through meteorites is not new. In 1961 Drs. Bartholomew Nagy, Douglas Hennessy and Warren Meinschein of the Esso Research Company found hydrocarbons in a French meteorite that "resemble in many important aspects the hydrocarbons in the products of living beings and sediments on Earth. Based on these preliminary studies, the composition of the hydrocarbons in the Orgueil meteorite provides evidence of biogenic activity." Nagy also discovered "microscopic size particles, resembling fossil algae, in relatively large quantities within the Orgueil and Ivuna carbonaceous meteorites." He commented of his finds: "This tends to confirm that life exists outside the Earth, but where and how we are not in a position to say."

The scientific community immediately divided on the subject of fossil microbes in the AH 84001 meteorite. Some scientists believed that the case was proven; others dismissed it as unlikely and questioned whether the fossil bacteria, if present at all, could have been terrestrially based.

An article in the journal *Science* of 14 March 1997, by a team led by University of Wisconsin-Madison geochemist John W. Valley, presented the view that the most current research supported the belief that the meteorite does indeed contain evidence of ancient bacterial life from beyond the Earth. New iso-topic analyses of the meteorite suggest a low-temperature origin, supporting the idea that features of the meteorite may have been formed by living organisms. The procedures used by Valley and his team were developed specifically for the Martian meteorite. The results, according to the article, contradict claims that the carbonate globules found in the meteorite were formed at tem-peratures too hot to support life, or were formed on Earth; these had been the two main arguments advanced against the mete-orite as evidence of ancient life on Mars. Early criticisms that the fossils were considerably smaller than anything on Earth were refuted when researchers found examples of terrestrial bacteria comparable in size to the "Martian" markings.

"Everything we see is consistent with biological activity, but I still wouldn't rule out low-temperature inorganic processes as an alternative explanation," said Valley. "We have not proven that this represents life on Mars, but we have disproven the high-temperature hypothesis."

The conclusion is that the carbonates most likely formed at tem-peratures below 200 degrees Fahrenheit—conditions hospitable to some forms of microscopic life. A panel of scientists debated the meteorite on 19 March 1997 at the 28th Lunar and Planetary Sci-ence Conference in Houston. Various scientists found evidence for their own beliefs in the meteorite; ranging from that it proved ancient life on Mars to that it could be proven that the markings were not the product of organic life. The scientists' only conclu-sion was that any conclusion was premature at this stage.

"If life forms ever existed on Mars, either by having been formed in an independent origin or having been transferred there from Earth, it is possible that they have continued to exist up to the present time," stated the US National Research Council in a report entitled *Mars Sample Return: Issues and Recommendations*.

On 6 March 1997, a panel of the US National Research Council announced that measures should be taken to prevent possible con-tamination of the Earth by Martian microbes. This is relevant because of possible future retrieval missions to Mars—see below. (The NRC is the research arm of the National Academy of Sciences, probably the US's most authoritative scientific organization. It is the main advisor to the US government on scientific issues.) Although the council thought it unlikely that Martian microbes could adapt to the Earth's environment and cause harm here, it was nonetheless a possible risk. They recommended that samples "should be isolated physically and biologically and regarded as hazardous until proved otherwise." Suggestions made to protect the terrestrial environment included: (a) to be prepared, if deemed necessary, to sterilize a returning robot probe while still in outer space, before bringing it back to the Earth; and (b) to leave the probe in space where alien microbes could not cause harm. This would presumably allow for remote studies to be undertaken or for astronauts to retrieve the samples to a space station for study there.

The debate is well reflected in science fiction that has examined this dilemma. Michael Crichton's *Andromeda Strain* purports to show the impact of a non-terrestrial organism let loose on the Earth and the film *Alien* is based on the conflict between safety and risk in deciding whether to sterilize a known aggressive alien species or allow it to be brought to the Earth. In both cases the "authority paranoia" theme is prevalent: the authorities seek to take the risk in order to see whether the alien organisms can be turned to biological warfare advantage. Such scenarios are still a long way down the road as far as is known; but the motives of the players in this unfolding drama will no doubt be watched very carefully as the explorations and research continue.

However, the council offers much comfort. It points out that Martian or other non-terrestrial germs will have to compete against "well established" organisms developed within the Earth's own ecosystem; the aliens might not survive. Even if they did, most organisms on Earth are not harmful, so statistically even a surviving alien "bug" might do no harm to any of the Earth's own life forms; including humans. Conversely they could even turn out to be beneficial.

Resurgence of the Space Race

Two NASA spacecraft, Mars Pathfinder and Mars Global Surveyor, were dispatched to Mars. The first arrived in July 1997, the second two months later. Pathfinder successfully deposited a small rover-device on the Martian surface; Global Surveyor is designed to make observations of minerals and rocks from orbit. Neither is intended to return to the Earth, though later "retrieval" missions are planned for the next century. Russia also has Mars missions in the pipeline. Any retrieval missions should consider the advice of the American National Research Council when considering possible contamination.

Ufology and "space mysteries" have been inextricably linked with Mars, and these missions will be closely watched by the advocates of these subjects. The evidence they produce may well be a further boost to such interest groups, and will possibly be a source of further antagonism with conventional science. It is hoped, for example, that as well as finding evidence of life, albeit primitive, the orbital photography will solve the mystery of the Cydonia region—claims of pyramids and a face carved on the Martian surface.

The history of Mars probes has been one of sometimes mysterious failures. Mariner 3 failed during launch on 5 November 1964, though its twin performed well. The Soviet Mars 3 failed after 20 seconds on the surface; Mars 4's braking motors failed and the craft sailed into solar orbit; Mars 6 failed after one second, and Mars 7 missed the planet altogether. At the time of writing the curse seems set to continue; Global Surveyor was on course, but the first Russian probe, launched on 16 November 1996, immediately failed and crashed into the Pacific Ocean.

Europa!

But Mars and the meteorite in Alaska were not the only source of recent hope that science fiction might become science fact.

On 10 April 1997, scientists announced, with what looked like a
little more unanimity and confidence, that there might be life on
Europa, one of the moons of Jupiter. John Delaney of the University of Washington announced that he believed Europa contained all the necessary ingredients to allow for the creation of,
and maintenance of, life. His announcement was based on the
photographic survey by spaceprobe Galileo. It showed a red sea
but with surface crust. Markings on the surface look like wind-
patterns, but since there is no air that cannot be the case. The
only explanation on offer so far is that the movements are
caused by uneven warming from beneath—volcanic activity. Un-
dersea research on Earth has indicated that volcanic activity can
support life without sunlight. The photographs show that the
sea has a crust of ice three feet thick and contains many icebergs
several miles across. Richard Terrile of the Jet Propulsion Laboratory in Pasadena commented that he believed organic material might be present, and said: "On Earth, these same
ingredients . . . gave presence to life."

However, a certain amount of current thinking on the subject is pulling away from the "life as we know it" search and
considering the possibility of life *not* as we know it. This seems
reasonable enough, since the Earth is teeming with life quite
different from humans and in many cases evolving in what for
humans would be hostile environments. The *New York Times* of
6 May 1997 carried an article by William J. Broad which considered that if life on Earth could form in such environments of
different pressures and temperatures then perhaps life could
do so on other worlds. Not all life on Earth seems to have
needed the direct heat of the sun to develop. If so, that would
open up the possibility of life much nearer to home, within the
solar system. As Broad put it: "A quiet revolution is now shaking the foundations of exobiology, the study of the possibility
of life elsewhere in the cosmos." And these speculations were
not limited to micro-organisms which it has long been speculated might develop in a variety of environments. "Large beasts

and beings higher up the extraterrestrial food chain" were being brought into the thinking. Such thinking has of course been triggered by the findings on Europa mentioned above, as well as by terrestrial observation.

Dr. Wesley T. Huntress Jr., Associate Administrator for Space Science at NASA, stated: "Now we've found that life on Earth doesn't need light and can exist under extreme conditions we never expected. Those aren't so different from what exists on other planets. So the probability that life may have arisen somewhere else in this solar system has gone up."

Frank Drake, with whom Chapter 1 begins, has joined in the debate with understandable enthusiasm since the speculation increases the likely positive outcome of his "Drake Equation." "We're in a paradigm shift," he said. "We're realizing that biology is very opportunistic and can adapt to a much greater variety of conditions than we imagined. The number of planets capable of supporting life is probably much greater than we thought in the past."

Further study of the biology of the Earth is now thought to yield additional clues in the hunt for life beyond the Earth. Taking into account the moons and planets, it is now thought possible that there are ten such worlds in the solar system that might be capable of supporting life. It may be that active exploration of the solar system will target these possibilities in the future. The National Science Foundation, which is the main source of funding for basic science projects in the USA, has recently commenced its programme "Life in Extreme Environments" which will look for clues to extraterrestrial life. The plans for probes to Mars, Jupiter and Saturn are expected to be revised to take into account such searching.

One of the possible search-targets is Titan, a prominent moon of Saturn, which is already slated as the destination of the NASA spacecraft Cassini, due to be launched in late 1997. It is expected to launch a parachute-held probe into the dense atmosphere.

Alien Intelligence on the Move

If we show that alien life is common, then we must now look at the possibility of direct alien contact; of visitation.

The principal division in the "travel" argument is the debate on the speed of light. Many astronomers and scientists in related fields believe that the speed of light is an absolute which cannot be broken. (But then so-called experts used to say that of the sound barrier. Chuck Yeager, the first man to fly faster than sound, argued he could do it because he didn't understand the objections!) The maths suggests that at the speed of light matter becomes "two dimensional," and energy only, so any life within a spaceship would cease to exist. But it is possible that such maths is potentially accurate only within the *known* laws of physics, and that in, say, a thousand years' time there may be a great deal more known about the universe. Scientists of that time will understand why we were wrong in the present day.

If we assume that faster-than-light travel is possible, then we have no way of calculating any further upper limits to the speed, if there are such limitations. Races could cross galaxies in an afternoon. But this is well beyond our ability to understand at the present time.

If we assume that faster-than-light travel is not possible, then we must consider the ways of crossing vast distances more slowly. And the possibilities are rich and plentiful, though each of the summaries set out briefly below has been the subject of scientific debate, sometimes hotly contested.

Black Holes/White Holes/Wormholes

Even within a universe where the speed of light is absolute it is theorized that sufficient gravitational "distortions" may arise which would provide for shortcuts across "normal" space. The classical analogy used is to put two dots on the same piece of paper; the shortest distance between the dots is a straight line. But if the paper is folded the two dots can be brought closer together, even to touch. The shortest distance between the dots is then much reduced. Gravitational distortions may offer such "folds in space."

Black holes are gravity "wells" thought to be formed when a star collapses. The extreme gravity beyond the "event horizon"— the "edge" of the black hole—prevents any leakage from the black hole. Even light cannot escape; hence the "blackness." Anything, particularly living matter, entering the black hole would presumably be crushed to death very quickly. However, if some way of maintaining life could be developed by a future or more advanced science, then it is also speculated that black holes may have "white hole" counterparts where matter comes out. Travelling across these "bridges" may be one way of "bringing the two dots closer together."

Long Lifespan

Another very simple way of crossing vast distances of space is just to take a very long time about it. It is possible that there are races that have a quite different appreciation of time from ours. If their lifespan was measured in billions upon billions of years, then perhaps they could spend a few hundred thousand years sitting in an armchair in a spaceship coming to the Earth with no greater danger than that of slight boredom. We cannot really appreciate this, as our whole comprehension of life is geared around a measureable, finite life of around 100 years. To turn the analogy on its head; consider that some mayflies live their adult lifespan in 24 hours. If a mayfly could appreciate human life at all, how would it view our longevity by its own standards? Could there be races that would see the human lifespan as equivalent to the mayfly's 24 hours?

Cryogenics

If "slow" travel at no more than the speed of light is necessary, then it may be possible to use "suspended animation" to "freeze" the travellers and then reactivate them when the spaceship reaches its target world. There are many objections to this; total suspension is thought impossible as the biology of the life form would deteriorate during such inactivity (but both the idea and the objections are still highly theoretical). Even suspension down to a level of "close to death" may involve such degradation, so that the distance that could be travelled would be limited by the normal lifespan of the race attempting such travel, even multiplied hugely by the effects of suspension.

An Artificial World

If we consider that plodding slowly through the universe is the only way to travel vast distances, then perhaps that is possible even for a race with a lifespan similar to our own. It has been speculated that huge artificial worlds could be constructed where the "astronauts" who eventually found themselves within, say, our solar system, were the many-millions-of-years-on descendants of the original astronauts who left their home world. A planet is just a huge spaceship in essence (in fact, to get the logic right, a spaceship is a small planet), and if a spaceship could be developed with a recyclable biosphere (plants, breathable air, food etc.) and a sufficient population to allow for breeding and population maintenance, then such a concept is possible. Something similar was suggested by the Arthur C. Clarke novel *Rendezvous with Rama*.

Templates

Clarke's *Rendezvous with Rama* also came up with an interesting addition to the "suspended animation" debate. He suggested that spaceships could carry biological "building blocks" and templates across vast distances. No food or air would be needed. Then, when the spaceship reached its target, something (perhaps a computer) would activate the biology aboard. In effect, it would use basic hydrogen, carbon, and other building blocks to form "humans" using a genetic template of a human.

Machines

All of the above speculations have centred around sending life forms across the vast distances of space. The main problems relate to sustaining that life in some form for the duration as well as keeping it intellectually stimulated or in an environment where mental development was possible. But all of those problems are removed if machines instead of biological forms are sent. They could be deactivated and reactivated as needed. They may be able to "while away" a few billion years without boredom. Furthermore, if the technology that created them was sufficiently advanced, then these artificial life forms may—at least to primitives like us—be indistinguishable from "real" life. There are studies of cyborg technology theorized today (one project was called OPTIMAN) to create a mixture of life and machinery. An extension of the theory: perhaps, even if it is never possible to produce a truly thinking, intelligent machine, it may be possible to house a mind in a machine with virtual immortality.

Science will almost certainly find a way to cross the vastness of space one day; it is mankind's proven history to conquer obstacles. It may require sciences, and recognition of natural laws, as yet undreamed of. But if there are other intelligences out there somewhere, one or more might have already developed that science. The question addressed in the next chapter is: will we be able to understand them when we meet them?

3

The Barriers Between Species

Even if there are races "out there" that have developed an intelligence, there are a number of challenges to be considered before we could expect to enter into meaningful communication with them.

How Do We Define Intelligence?

Human thinking is essentially anthropomorphic. We measure intelligence against our own scale. We have developed technology and no other animal on Earth has done so on a comparable scale. We have manipulated our environment to a degree no other Earth creature has achieved. But these may not be the best scales—or even measures of intelligence at all. We might set aside our own human thinking and try some thought experiments. We might consider that if intelligence is a factor of survival—and develops for that purpose—then we could be very low on the scale indeed. The dinosaurs lived for millions of years; clams are thought to be largely unchanged over millions more. Humans may not survive more than a few million years precisely because of technology and environmental adaptation; on that basis perhaps we have very little absolute intelligence at all.

If intelligence, however, is designed to make our lives freer, more artistic and less dependent on toil and risk, then again we might be failures on the absolute scale. It is possible that dolphins have achieved a life composed largely of play and leisure and that their whole lifestyle is one of constant artistic expression through movement. A romantic notion, perhaps, but not one to be dismissed too easily and certainly not just because it does not seem to equate to our own achievements as land mammals.

Different Developments?

We must also remember that other creatures may not use their brains in the way we do. The traditional view of the applications of the brain is in the separate hemispheres, left and right. The left brain represents the "scientific" side; logical and sequential. It is unable to process information satisfactorily unless it can see cause and effect. It is this side of the brain that deals with reading, writing, numeracy and analysis. The right brain is the artistic, creative, intuitive, holistic brain. It perceives illogically, not requiring sequence, but uses images, colour, music, spatial relationships, to comprehend the world. It is the side of the brain which is the seat of emotion. While the left brain would understand the word "square," for example, the right brain would appreciate the image of the square.

Business training today is largely centred on teaching people to use their right brain more than they do at present. It is clear that large numbers of figures can be more easily understood if presented in charts and bar-graphs, and is even more understandable if strong colours are used to emphasise points. But getting people to "follow their instincts and intuitions," to find out how to "be lucky," to guess the right course of action rather than demand a sequential action plan—these are often more frightening changes for people. Yet down that road might lie a more efficient use of the brain.

The evidence of some paranormal studies is that our scientific learning may have limited our ways of retrieving stored knowledge. The subject of "channelling" may be the clue that there are faster and more efficient ways to access the brain's databanks. Witnesses have reported "automatic writing" at high speed. Yet this is an intuitive thing that cannot be learned or handled rationally. Perhaps the dolphins have mastered this. Their lack of apparent science or technology may suggest that the left side is less used, but the fact that they may have an enviable and more evolutionarily sustainable lifestyle based on play and fun may mean that they have developed their intuitions and creativity.

If this is true, then we may never be able to appreciate dolphin concepts. If aliens too have developed their brains differently from humans, there may be a chasm between our thinking that we cannot bridge. Bear in mind also that we may share more with a dolphin—the same planet anyway—than we do with an alien.

And we must remember that we have not yet achieved even one genuine communication with any other creature on Earth.

How Do We Identify Intelligence?

Of course, one reason why we have not achieved a meaningful communication with another Earth species might simply be that we are the only intelligent species present. It is risky to be dependent on such anthropomorphic reasoning, but it is still a possibility. The notion of, say, dolphins being equally intelligent but in a different way may simply be a romantic idea.

A few background points on the quest for the seat of intelligence may be useful here. The cetaceans—dolphins, whales and porpoises—have seemingly large and complex brains, which is why they are favoured as the likeliest seat of intelligence on Earth apart from ourselves. John Lilly, in his book *Mind in the Waters*, published in 1967, considered the size of the cetacean brain and generated a great deal of interest in the possible intelligence of those creatures.

At the turn of the century absolute brain size was thought to be a factor in intelligence. This was largely rejected and replaced with a scale measuring brain size as a percentage of total body weight. Large brains may only be a factor of large bodies, it was argued, perhaps no more than a factor of blood supply to the body. Whereas cetacean brains were often bigger than human brains, on this scale the humans came out on top, though some argued that the cetaceans were comparable. Jerison, in 1978, for example, used a scale he called the encephalization quotient (EQ) to compare brain and body weight relationships. This indicated that some cetaceans have comparable brains to humans.

More recently, intelligence has been thought be to a factor of a combination of the development of the neocortex and the degree of "folding" of the brain material. Dolphins have brains as complex and convoluted as humans, though their neocortex is less developed.

Ridgway, in 1986, showed that bottlenose dolphins have brains with a much higher index of folding than the human brain. But he also discovered that the neocortex of cetaceans is relatively thin—half that of humans. Furthermore, cetacean neocortical design is basically much simpler than that of land mammals, although that may be a factor of environment more than intelligence.

Holloway, in 1979, argued that brain weight does not reflect the internal structural complexity of the brain, which he held to be the most important component in the development and measurement of intelligence. Some studies have shown that the internal structure of dolphin brains reveals that they have not developed final stages of complexity as have land mammals. (See, for example, Kesarev, Malofeyeva and Trykova, 1977; Morgane, Jacobs and Galaburda, 1986; Garey and Revishchin, 1990; Glazer, Morgane and Leranth, 1990.)

The neocortex is the area of the brain which most clearly differentiates mammals and non-mammals, and many believe that it is the neocortex which is responsible for the development of intelligence. If so, then cetaceans are less intelligent than many land mammals, but this is by no means certain. Macphail, in 1982, for example, dismissed the argument for the neocortex and intelligence being linked in this way.

F. Crick and G. Mitchison, in "The Function of Dream Sleep" (*Nature* 304: 111–14), suggest an interesting reason for brain size. They argue that all animals need to clear out their thinking periodically—for humans possibly this happens when sleeping, during REM sleep. Biologically, what may be happening is the removal of undesirable interactions in networks of cells in the cerebral cortex. Creating desirable networks is the process of learning, and Crick and Mitchison refer to this "dumping" as "reverse learning." They argue that creatures unable to use sleep as a method of "reverse learning" must have an alternative to take the strain away from the neural networks; perhaps a bigger brain simply allows for this process more easily. In short, some animals perhaps have bigger brains because they do not dream.

All of this—and a host of other attempts at measurement—demonstrates that we have no real certainty as to the relative intelligences of other animals with which we share the planet. We may have similar problems in identifying intelligence in aliens. As a way of circumventing the measurement and moving on to demonstration, many studies have concentrated on behaviour, starting with language itself.

Language Barriers

All creatures seem to have developed ways to communicate with each other using body language, various sounds and tones, touch, and so on. But as far as we know only very rudimentary communication—almost instinct—is expressed in these ways. Territoriality is determined and challenged, food supplies are communicated, mating rituals are established. There is no evidence that any non-human species has developed a language in the sense of the word used by humans. Furthermore, attempts to teach the human language to non-humans have not been particularly successful.

E. M. Macphail, in *Brain and Intelligence in Vertebrates*, sets out the history of such attempts with such animals as chimpanzees, gorillas, bottlenose dolphins, California sea lions and pigeons,incalculably against the odds.

During the first day of the searlated to reward-based behaviour rather than true understanding of language. Returning to dolphins, although there are some arguments for their intelligence, there is little in the way of interactive communication that we can point to. They learn tricks, but these could be simply reward-based. The fact that many people report a sense of communication with dolphins, even trainers who believe they get genuine enjoyment from their tricks, does not confirm anything other than primitive rapport, or even projection of human feelings by the human counterpart.

In the same book Macphail makes a point that is particularly relevant for our discussion of communication between humans and aliens. He suggests that human superiority in problem-solving is so dependent on language that it may only be a factor of language. This could be independent of intelligence in its purest form. In that way, language could mask intelligence rather than be its product. When we meet aliens, we might not recognize their intelligence simply because they do not communicate as we do.

But even if we meet a humanoid race that has developed a language as we understand it, and assuming that one or both of us can learn the other's language so that we can communicate, what will we talk about? We shall be able to communicate in the strict sense of the word, of course, but will it be very meaningful?

Even communication between humans is not always very effective, so between two races that evolved in different biospheres, with different environmental advantages and challenges, the probability is that what is a meaningful concept to one race is unlikely to be meaningful to the other.

In short, it would take an incredible degree of fortune for the people of the Earth to meet a race that was so compatible that we could exchange something of value. Yet we must now ex-

amine just that challenge in the next section of the book, because according to thousands of witnesses around the world
there have been contacts a-plenty with races of all different
types, and most of them apparently meaningful. If so, then either our basic assumptions about random forces and chance
are wrong, or those witnesses are not having the experiences
they think they are having.

II

Aliens On Earth

4

Ancient Astronauts

No account of alien visitation can ignore the highly popular belief that the historical records of early civilizations are telling us in the language of the time that they were visited by aliens from space. This is augmented by the archaeological and artifactual evidence brought to the public attention most famously by books such as Erich von Däniken's 1968 *Chariots of the Gods?* and its successors. But how reliable is the evidence?

In 1958 George Hunt Williamson wrote *Secret Places of the Lions*, which is probably the earliest formal presentation of the so-called ancient astronaut theory, though there are traces of discussion of this in earlier articles. Williamson set out his suggestion that the Earth had been visited by aliens 18 million years ago; these visitors then brought about the evolution of the human race. Just two years later parallel thinking had led to the same broad suggestion in *Morning of the Magicians* by Louis Pauwels and Jacques Bergier. In fact in the early 1960s this was a popular theme among devotees but one that did not receive very wide public attention. Robert Sharroux wrote *100,000 Years of Man's Unknown History*, which looked at the ancient astronaut theme; other writers on the subject included Yusuke J. Matsumora in 1964, Alexander Kazantsev, W. Raymond Drake and Paul Misraki.

The theme was picked up within the UFO literature, as for example in *Strangers from the Skies* by Brad Steiger, published in 1966. Steiger writes: "Other scientists are suggesting that not only are we not alone, but we may have been 'planted' here a bil-

lion or so years ago by an extraterrestrial expedition. Periodically, the celestial gardeners come back to see how their
'seedbeds' have been progressing." Steiger quotes Dr. Thomas
Gold, Professor of Astronomy at Cornell University as saying:
"Life may have been initiated and spread by space travellers
who visited Earth a billion years ago. From their abandoned
micro-biological garbage, forms of life proliferated into intelligent beings." Steiger was not the first to suggest that the search
for the so-called "missing link" between apes and man could not
be found because in essence it never existed. The bridge between
the two, having been deliberately generated by extraterrestrials,
would have passed by too quickly to have produced evidence for
historians and archaeologists in modern times to locate. Steiger
was not the first, and certainly not the last, to interpret as technology the imagery of earlier writing. For example, he quotes the
story of Ezekiel: "Over the heads of the living creatures there
was the likeness of a firmament, shining like crystal," of which
he comments: "One thinks instantly of a non-oxygen breathing
alien in his clear helmet." Steiger refers to the Mayan legend of a
giant eagle that came out of the sky "with the roar of a lion" and
hints that we might consider the myth as "an alien-reality" when
the account continues: "From her beak came four creatures,
strange to our tribe, who did not breathe the air we breathe."

In *Fate* magazine in December 1964 W. Raymond Drake
commented:

> Our theologians dismiss the ancient gods as anthropomorphisms
> of natural forces, as if entire races for hundreds of years would
> base their daily lives on lightning and thunderbolts! Yet logic sug-
> gests that the old Gods of Egypt, Greece, Rome, Scandinavia, and
> Mexico were not disembodied spirits or anthropomorphic sym-
> bolisms but actual spacemen from the sky. It seems that after the
> great catastrophes remembered in the legends, the "Gods" with-
> drew and henceforth have been content merely to survey the
> Earth, except for an occasional intervention in human affairs.

Another UFO writer to take up the theme with great enthusiasm was Brinsley le Poer Trench, otherwise known as Lord Clancarty. Le Poer Trench had been an editor of *Flying Saucer Review*, certainly the earliest and for many years the most authoritative magazine on the subject, and was president of Contact International and vice-president of the British UFO Research Association. (In 1979 he instigated a debate in the House of Lords which produced a record interest in the published proceedings and created the, now defunct, House of Lords All Party UFO Study Group.) In 1960 le Poer Trench published *The Sky People*, which set out the basic theme, largely examining the Christian Bible. Le Poer Trench wrote:

> This is the story of the Sky People who have been coming to Earth for millions of years. Countless legends and myths in the folklore, mythologies and sacred books of races everywhere refer to a period—a golden age—when the Gods came down and mingled with mortals. The myths themselves are but the fairy story coverings these true happenings of a bygone age were wrapt up in to preserve them for posterity . . . While on Earth, some of the Sky People were elected rulers. For instance, Osiris became one of the earlier divine pharaohs of Egypt. Subsequently, after their withdrawal, and Osiris is a case in point, they were worshipped as gods.

Le Poer Trench sets out his belief that the Bible accurately describes a visitation by extraterrestrials in ancient times during which they conducted genetic study programmes on the humans they found on Earth and indeed created an evolving man from what they found. Le Poer Trench linked these ancient sightings with modern-day sightings in his conclusion, where he states:

> All through the ages . . . the Sky People have been visiting Planet Earth and showing the way for hu-manity to realise its Manhood and potential Galactic status. Ever since hu-man beings were

manufactured by the Jehovah to guard and till their Garden of
Eden, the Sky or Serpent People have had compassion on them
and have been coming here to help Earth Man know himself . . .
Today, these extraterrestrial visitors are to be seen again our skies
in their traditional space ships.

This was a theme that le Poer Trench maintained through
many books, including *Men among Mankind*, published in 1962
(later republished as *Temple of the Stars*), *Operation Earth* and
Mysterious Visitors. The latter contains a number of illustrations
depicting events in the Bible in "flying saucer" terms: Moses
leading the Israelites, Ezekiel, the ascension of Elijah, the dream
of Jacob, the transfiguration, the angels at the tomb of Christ and
the ascension of Christ.

Erich Von Däniken

Although these accounts were of interest to those with a fascination for flying saucer-type mysteries, they did not receive wide
public attention or acclaim. That changed in 1968 when one
writer, Erich von Däniken, published *Chariots of the Gods?*,
which basically brought together the same themes with a good
deal of original thinking on von Däniken's part, most of which
has been criticized since. Von Däniken's books sold around the
world in many languages in their millions, instantly bringing
this theme to very wide public attention. (And they are still selling: his latest, *Return of the Gods*, was published in 1997.) The
reason why von Däniken succeeded so publicly while his predecessors did not was not that the message was particularly different—it wasn't—nor even that the package was presented in a
particularly different way. Von Däniken's advantage was that he
happened to be very much in tune with the spirit of the late
1960s, which represented the emergence of a New Age, a search
for new spiritual meanings, and a surge of interest in astronauts
generated by the Apollo astronauts who in 1968 orbited the

moon and the following year landed and walked on it. He also latched on to a growing trend within "the young" which was disaffected with the Church. For many teenagers and young people the rejection of the cultural values which were upheld by their parents almost inevitably required the rejection of the established Church, which in England in those days was often referred to as "the Tory party at prayer." The Beatles had declared themselves devotees of the Mahareshi Mahesh Yogi and had introduced the concept of alternative religions, and particularly Indian mysticism, as an alternative to standard Christian worship. Von Däniken's publicity was in no way harmed by the almost simultaneous release of the film *2001—A Space Odyssey*, which contained much the same theme: that an alien presence visited the Earth many millions of years ago and artificially generated the modern human race out of primitive ape beings roaming about on the African plains.

In fact von Däniken was not the only researcher at that time working on the theme. T. C. Lethbridge, perhaps best known for his work on dowsing and ghost phenomena, published *The Legend of the Sons of God*, based on his own independent research, in which he stated: "As it happened, I had been interested in the problem of who were the 'Sons of God' for many years and had sought enlightenment from archaeologists, anthropologists and theologians at Cambridge and elsewhere without getting the slightest satisfaction." Stringing together the same clues that so many other people had happened upon, Lethbridge concluded that "perhaps 5,000 or more years ago" aliens had visited the Earth and prompted the evolution of Man. As Colin Wilson writes: "Because Lethbridge was such a loner, he was unaware that he had simply tuned in to the 'spirit of the age,' and was raising questions that had occurred to other speculative thinkers. Lethbridge was, in fact, devastated to discover just before his death that his 'space men' idea had been suggested by the Swiss writer Erich von Däniken."

Von Däniken's writings provoked a predictable series of responses. Firstly he was lauded as a visionary who had seen what

others had not seen—mainly because not many had read the
work of the others—and, as his books were well written and well
presented in a simple easy-to-read style and serialized in "popularist" newspapers, a great many people immediately felt that he
probably had the right answers. His success as a writer, in terms
of books sold, was overwhelming, and even 30 years later his
popularity on the lecture circuit is virtually undiminished. That
said, the second stage of response to his writings was equally inevitable; a great many people leapt on him and tried to tear him
to pieces. That doesn't seem to have been as hard as it might
have looked. The assumptions that von Däniken had made in
Chariots of the Gods? may have been rather bold and his jumps to
conclusions rather athletic, but there he stuck to the more solid-
looking and thought-provoking evidence. The pressure of success was on him, though, and the book was followed up by a
number of subsequent, similar books on the same theme, including *Return to the Stars, Gold of the Gods, In Search of Ancient
Gods, Miracles of the Gods, According to the Evidence*, and more. Almost inevitably his arguments sought out evidence that needed
a little more "stretching." His analysis was more tentative, his
leaps to conclusions were even more athletic, and many in the
end accused him of actual deceit.

Peter James, writing in *The Unexplained*, comments: "Hardly
a single thought contained in his books is original. Every link in
the von Däniken argument can be found in the work of earlier,
often far sounder, exponents of the 'ancient astronaut' theme."
James goes on to comment: "Most of his evidence is a mish-
mash of half truths, cooked up with insinuations made in the
form of questions."

Von Däniken got himself locked into highly publicized arguments. He gave an interview to *Playboy* magazine which
seemed to admit many of the things he was being accused of,
and got into a fairly furious debate with Colin Wilson from
which he did not emerge very well. For example, James sets out
the debate relating to the lines at Nazca in Peru. In the debate

with Colin Wilson, von Däniken commented: "I have not claimed that extraterrestrials had built the lines at Nazca" and challenged Wilson to prove otherwise. James writes: "On Wilson's behalf, here is an extract from von Däniken's *Return to the Stars*: 'At some time in the past, unknown intelligences landed on the inhabited plain near the present day town of Nazca and built an improvised airfield for their spacecraft.'"

Both James and Wilson were particularly indignant at von Däniken's claim, in his book *Gold of the Gods*, to have visited and explored an underground cave system in Ecuador, finding there writings in unknown hieroglyphics on strange metal sheets. The person who he claimed helped him explore this cave system started legal proceedings against von Däniken, stating that he had shown him a blocked-up entrance, that he was not aware that von Däniken had ever gone into the cave system, and that the photographs that von Däniken had taken were shot in a local museum. Von Däniken, however, insisted: "What I have said in *Gold of the Gods* about these underground caves is all true."

Probably the most devastating single destruction of von Däniken's work was by Ronald Story in *The Space Gods Revealed*, which a *Northern Echo* review (highlighted on the cover of the paperback edition) described as "The chariot of the Gods turned into a pumpkin." Story systematically took the main themes of von Däniken's argument chapter by chapter and waded through them with a scythe, leaving a bloody trail of wounded and dead in his wake. He reviewed the claims for: the Piri Re'is map (claimed to have been inspired by aerial photography in the distant past); the Nazca Plain (a landing field for aliens); Easter Island (statue carvings inspired by and assisted by alien "gods"); the Egyptian pyramids (beyond the technology of the times); the Palenque astronaut (a figure von Däniken believes represents an ancient in a space suit); caves filled with gold, and so on. Story showed that von Däniken had been very selective in his evidence, or had made presumptions without sound knowledge of authoritative research into the areas on which he was commenting.

Whatever the nature of von Däniken's research, the main points he seems to have missed are twofold:

1. The archaeological evidence from around the world indicates that it is possible our ancestors had a much better working knowledge of metals, architecture and so on than is often credited. Rather than having to attribute this to the intervention of the gods, a growing body of evidence over time is successfully showing the logical step-by-step progression of this knowledge rather than the sudden influx which the von Däniken theories would demand. Carl Sagan has commented: "Essentially, von Däniken's argument is that our ancestors were too stupid to create the most impressive surviving ancient architectural and artistic works."

2. Secondly, the literal interpretation of ancient writings and carvings ignores the context in which these images can be very clearly seen to represent mythology, story telling, folklore and so on. The technique of all of these writers, culminating in von Däniken, has been to select the evidence that suits the argument and ignore the rest. Stripped of context, the arguments look very persuasive. Reset into context, it becomes increasingly unlikely that modern scientific interpretation is appropriate.

Whatever the pros and cons of the arguments of von Däniken and those like him, the belief in ancient astronauts is still very strong. Books continue to be written on that basic theme, most recently by Zecharia Sitchin, and continue to produce some remarkable interpretation. Perhaps the most scientific interpretation of Biblical stories is J. F. Blumrich's *The Spaceships of Ezekiel*. Blumrich is described as "Chief of the systems layout branch of NASA." He has worked on spaceship construction and was a co-builder of the Saturn 5 rocket. Blumrich has basically taken the story of Ezekiel and turned it into a scientific blueprint, largely concluding that the Biblical account can be seen as referring to a physical flying machine.

All of this argument aside, the fact that the evidence has been rather "over-trawled" does not mean that the basic premise is impossible. Ancient astronauts might have visited the Earth in ancient times, and there might be some evidence—a good deal less than is possibly speculated nowadays, but some evidence nonetheless—of those visitations.

We will need to know far more about the history of the human race and its "natural" achievements before we can be sure of the validity of any evidence produced or certain of what interventions might have taken place. Any look in detail at evidence therefore must be somewhat inconclusive.

Nonetheless many researchers, for example Colin Wilson, agree that the best *potential* evidence seems to lie in the knowledge of an African tribe known as the Dogon. Even this evidence has been challenged but, such as it is, it is set out in the following chapter.

5

Dogon Knowledge

In 1931 two French anthropologists, Marcel Griaule and Germaine Dieterlen, began a long-term study of the Dogon people of Mali in West Africa. They lived with the tribe and were eventually allowed access to their secret beliefs and histories. Indeed, Griaule was so honoured by the Dogon that when he died his funeral was attended by 250,000 tribesmen.

In 1950, in a scholary essay, "A Sundanese Sirius System," published in the *Journal de la Société des Africainistes*, they set out some of their findings related to the Dogon's knowledge of the star system of Sirius. In 1965 Dieterlen, then Secretary General of the Société des Africainistes at the Musée de l'Homme, wrote up their studies of the Dogon.

What was very clear from their findings was that the Dogon possessed an extraordinary knowledge of astronomy which many believed was far ahead of its time, and was certainly far beyond the tribe's technological capabilities.

They recorded a "heavy star" orbiting Sirius A; an accurate description of Sirius B, which is a "white dwarf"—a collapsed star made of super-condensed matter. Their account of it moving in a 50-year elliptical orbit is also true (actually 50.04 plus or minus .09 years). "All earthly beings combined cannot lift it," they claim, in their symbolisms. They refer to it as "sagala," meaning "strong." They also, perhaps strangely without modern knowledge, described it as the smallest object; they used a tiny grain to depict it in the sand-drawings with which they explained their beliefs. Sirius B is quite invisible to the naked eye. It was first seen in 1862 using the largest telescope then in existence, and is estimated as 100,000 times less bright than Sirius A. It was not photographed until 1970.

The "official" discovery of the companion star to Sirius A began in 1862, when the American astronomer Alvan Graham Clark saw the companion star while testing a new telescope; he named it Sirius B. Even then it took half a century more for the mathematics to catch up with this observation. Arthur Eddington, in the 1920s, speculated on the existence of "white dwarfs," which explained how such a small object could exert such a massive force on nearby objects. Eddington published his findings in 1928. But the Dogon appeared to have this knowledge—which they claimed was part of their long tradition—in 1931 when Griaule and Dieterlen arrived. They commented: "The problem of knowing how, with no instruments at their disposal, men could know of the movements and certain characteristics of virtually invisible stars has not been settled."

Their work and writings came to the attention of American researcher Robert K. Temple. He was a scholar of Sanskrit and Oriental Studies. Temple discovered, and conversed with Dieterlen on the subject of, the Dogon's extensive astronomical knowledge. Apart from their knowledge of a far-distant star, their knowledge of other astronomical matters was considerable. They described the moon as "dry and dead like dry dead blood," and the planet Saturn as having a ring around it. They accepted that the Earth and other planets revolved around the sun—though a great deal of "tribal" lore places the Earth at the centre, as was believed "conventionally" in earlier centuries. They referred to Jupiter as having four moons, which, while much understating the number currently discovered, possibly reflects the four major moons of Jupiter. Indeed, it has been argued that the four major moons are the only "true" moons, with the others being captured asteroids that will "come and go" over time. They also accepted that the Milky Way was a spiral collection of stars.

However, the claim of the Dogon as to how they acquired their knowledge, while fascinating to their Western biographers, simultaneously earned the whole subject a measure of scepticism and rejection. They claimed that a race of beings from a planet within the Sirius system visited the Earth in the distant past and gave the knowledge to their ancestors. They called the planet "nyan tolo" or "emme-girin," orbiting Sirius B. They refer to the aliens as Nommo, describing them reverently as "monitors of the universe, the fathers of mankind, guardians of its spiritual principles, dispensers of rain and masters of the water." The Nommo are depicted by the Dogon as fish or dolphin-like water creatures.

The Dogon sand-drawings in which they explained their beliefs—also verbally reinforced in non-ambiguous terms—depicted the Nommo landing in a spacecraft. In Temple's words:

> The descriptions of the landing of the ark are extremely precise. The ark is said to have landed on the Earth to the north-east of Dogon country, which is where the Dogon claim to have come from (originally . . .). The Dogon describe the sound of the landing of the ark. They say the "word" of Nommo was cast down by him in the four directions as he descended, and it sounded like the echoing of the four large stone blocks being struck with stones by the children, according to special rhythms, in a very small cave near Lake Debo. Presumably a thunderous vibrating sound is what the Dogon are trying to convey. One can imagine standing in the cave and holding one's ears at the noise. The descent of the ark must have sounded like a jet runway at close range.

They also referred to "spurting blood" from the ark, which some have interpreted as a description of the exhaust flames of a rocket. The Dogon also seem to understand that the ark might have descended from a "star-like" object in the sky which has been interpreted as a "mother ship" remaining in orbit.

Temple published his findings in a book, *The Sirius Mystery*, in

1976. It was well received—Colin Wilson describes it as "an impeccably scholarly book" containing "far more convincing evidence" of ancient extraterrestrial visitation than the works of Erich von Däniken—but it naturally created great controversy. Von Däniken himself seized on the book at the time as support for his own basic premise, and stated it represented "conclusive proof . . . of ancient astronauts." Despite arguments that the white missionaries brought the knowledge with them and fed it to the Dogon (though they maintain it is a part of their ancient tradition), or claims by such as Carl Sagan that the mythology of the Dogon has been misinterpreted (though they seem to have been remarkably unambiguous in their descriptions of "orbits" etc.), Temple ultimately became convinced that something truly extraordinary had arisen. Asked if he believed the claims, he stated, "Yes, I do. I have become convinced by my own research. In the beginning I was just investigating. I was sceptical. I was looking for hoaxes, thinking it couldn't be true. But then I began to discover more and more pieces which fit. And the answer is: Yes, I believe it."

The question of contamination is not ruled out; the knowledge the Dogon possess could have been known to Marcel Griaule and Germaine Dieterlen when they lived with them. Sirius B had been discovered in 1862, and had even been suspected since 1844. F. W. Bessel had discovered that the movements of Sirius A, which he had been studying since 1834, suggested an influence that might have been a companion star. C. H. F. Peters had calculated the orbit of "Sirius B" in theory in 1851. In 1915 a spectral analysis of Sirius B was obtained by W. Adams at the Mount Wilson observatory though it was not identified at that time as a white dwarf. The rings of Saturn the primary moon of Jupiter had been long discovered. (Having said that, there is no evidence that this knowledge was thus imparted—and the tribe itself denies it.)

If not contamination and not extraterrestrial visitation, then it would seem that their knowledge could only be explained by involving even more extraordinary areas of the paranormal. Did they channel the information from some distant race? Did they use remote viewing to "see" the distant and faint star—and presumably the rings of Saturn and the moons of Jupiter? There is little doubt that the question deserves its general title of "the Sirius Mystery."

Temple attempted to trace the origins of their belief; given that the Dogon say that the information was given to their own ancestors. He discovered parallels between the Dogon belief in the Nommo as "water creatures" and Oannes, an amphibious god of the Babylonians. Oannes and his colleagues apparently taught the Sumerians their advanced sciences: astronomy, mathematics, language and agriculture. The Greek priest Berossus described Oannes:

> The whole body of the animal was like that of a fish; and it had under a fish's head another head, and also feet below, similar to those of a man, subjoined to the fish's tail. His voice, too, and language, were articulate and human; and a representation of him is preserved even to this day . . . When the sun set, it was the custom of this Being to plunge again into the sea, and abide all night in the deep; for he was amphibious.

Temple learned that ". . . the ancient Egyptians had the same Sirius tradition which we have encountered from the Dogon tribe in Mali." He states: "We know that the Dogon are cultural, and probably also physical, descendants of Lemnian Greeks who claimed descent 'from the Argonauts,' went to Libya, migrated westwards as Garamantians (who were described by Herodotus), were driven south, and after many, many centuries reached the River Niger in Mali and intermarried with local Negroes." According to Temple, "The Dogon preserve as their most sacred tradition one which was brought from pre-dynastic Egypt by 'Danaos' [king of Argos] to the Greeks who took it to Libya and thence eventually to Mali, and which concerns 'the Sirius mystery.' We have thus traced back to pre-dynastic Egypt well before 3000 B.C. the extraordinary knowledge of the system of the stars Sirius A [i.e. Sirius, the Dog Star], Sirius B, and possibly 'Sirius C' possessed by the Dogon."

So Temple begins to track the source of the stories into one of the richest areas of "secret knowledge" tradition: the ancient Egyptians and Greeks. "The earliest Egyptians believed Sirius was the home of departed souls, which the Dogons also believe," Temple states in *The Sirius Mystery*. He also sets out his belief that the Egyptian calendar was based around the "movements" of Sirius. The year started with the "dog days" when Sirius started to rise.

The writings of others confirm the connection between Sirius and the Egyptians. "In the astronomical science of the Egyptians, the most conspicuous solar system near our own, represented in the heavens by the brilliant Sirius, was of supreme interest. Cycles of immense importance were determined by it, and it entered into the highest mysticism of Egyptian initiation," stated G. R. S. Mead in *Thrice Greatest Hermes*.

In *Cosmic Trigger*, Robert Anton Wilson wrote:

According to Philip Vandenberg, [in] *The Curse of the Pharaohs*, an archaeologist named Duncan MacNaughton discovered in 1932 that the long dark tunnels in the Greater Pyramid of Cheops function as telescopes, making the stars visible even in the daytime. The Greater Pyramid is oriented, according to MacNaughton, to give a view, from the King's Chamber, of the area of the southern sky in which Sirius moves throughout the year.

In Lucy Lamie's book, *Egyptian Mysteries*, the orientation of the pyramid is explored in detail:

A north/south section of the Pyramid of Cheops shows that the two so-called "air-shafts" leading out from the King's Chamber are, within one degree of accuracy, inclined so that the northern one is centered on the celestial Pole and the southern one on the three stars of Orion's Belt. Virginia Trimble pointed out that, in the light of the ancients' mystic sense, it is obvious that these openings were meant to be guide ways for the soul, aiming either towards the Circumpolars in the northern sky or to the constellation of Orion in the southern sky.

In the north the approximate time of the pyramid's construction in 2700 B.C., the Pole was occupied by Alpha Draconis, the star around which turned the Circumpolars—called the "Indestructibles" since they never disappear below the horizon. Thus they were the symbol of immortality. The King then, triumphant over the trials of terrestrial life, will ascend imperishable in the northern sky.

From the southern sky, the ancients had chosen 36 stars or constellations, the decans, whose consecutive helical risings occurred approximately every ten days. The rising of each decan occurred after it had passed 70 days of invisibility, a period corresponding to that of mummification. Among these stars are Osiris (Orion) and Isis-Sothis (Sirius), symbols of yearly renewal, of the regeneration of the Nile, of cyclic death and rebirth.

The alignment of the shafts became a central theme in a book that could well re-write some of our modern knowledge of the Egyptians: *The Orion Mystery* by Robert Bauval and Adrian Gilbert.

Sirius "C"

So we have, in Sirius, an apparent connection between the Dogon and the Egyptians, and perhaps a more direct connection somewhere in history. But we also have the possibility of "contamination" of data regarding the Dogon beliefs by modern missionaries. To move the argument further the search is on for something that would support the Dogon beliefs and that the missionaries could not have exported to them. This quest most commonly centres on the issue of "Sirius C."

The Dogon beliefs include a reference to another star, larger and four times brighter than Sirius B, which, they believe, orbits Sirius at right angles to Sirius B. Their belief is that it follows a near-circular orbit rather than an elliptical one. This star has not been identified with certainty by modern astronomers. It was speculated to exist in the 1920s and therefore could still have been part of the "contamination," should that have happened. R. T. Innes in South Africa and van den Bos, for example, reported seeing the third star. (However, in 1973 a study by the US Naval Observatory concluded that there is no astrometric evidence for a third star.)

Such a star, should it exist, would probably be a "red dwarf," that is, a star that flares up and brightens periodically. Several writers have pointed out that if the star flared up in the 1920s, or in earlier periods, then it might have been seen then but not since after it died down again. Quite how the Dogon would know of this is uncertain, however; this quality of red dwarfs was not known until the 1970s.

The whole subject was given a boost in 1978 when two astronomers from London University, Richard Donnison and Ivan Williams, published a paper speculating on the likely orbit of a Sirius C, if such a star existed. They believed that the orbit would be near-circular—exactly as the Dogon believe.

6

Walk-Ins and Star People

The basic theme of the "ancient astronaut" beliefs—that aliens visited the Earth in the distant past and began a process which artificially "evolved," or accelerated the evolution of, the human race—comes forward into the present day as part of the phenomenon of alien contact.

There are those who believe that some humans are in fact "seeded" from the stars, where lies their spiritual home, and that they are here for a purpose yet to be revealed. Rather like "sleeper" spies who lie dormant in enemy territory, living and working normally as citizens of that country until given a coded message to undertake the act they were sent there for, these aliens live and work as humans—even believe that they are humans—but gradually realize that they are "different"; that they have a mission in life connected with "the stars." They discover that they are extraterrestrial at heart.

These Star People often identify their origins through dreams which they believe to be memories. They tend to work in the professions and caring vocations, and advocates believe this is so that they are in a position to play key roles "when the times comes." They identify themselves, and recognize others, by a series of physical characteristics. Author Brad Steiger lists "the essential pattern profile of the Star People" including:

- Compelling eyes
- Personal charisma

- Lower than normal body temperature
- Hypersensitivity to electro-magnetics
- Lower than normal blood pressure
- Requiring of little sleep
- Born unexpectedly to his or her parents
- Had unseen companions as a child
- Express alien environments in artwork, dreams or fantasies
- Children or animals are attracted to them

In addition they often have a mental sense of their special origins:

- A yearning for their real home beyond the stars
- A sense of urgency and of a special mission to be completed

Star People are most characterized by contactee-type encounters with UFOs and often attribute a spiritual dimension to them. Several reports refer to alien entities in religious terms. For example "At age 5 or 6, I saw an angelic bearded figure in my front yard."

Star People also seem to have a pattern in their lives which commonly recurs. Many have "unusual" births, perhaps trauma or complications, and they go on to a troubled babyhood.

At the age of five or six they have a first "awakening." For example, Barbara May: "At the age of five, I was sitting alone in a field of flowers in California, when the entire field became a brilliant light. I was looking at my hands, and a feeling of not belonging came over me. I was frightened, and I thought to myself, 'What am I doing here?'"

At around the age of 11 or 12 they have a key event in their lives; often a serious illness, but sometimes something more positive. Betty B, at age 11, contracted scarlet fever. She was unconscious for periods and reported leaving her body and going to other realities and dimensions.

Later in life, from their teenage years onwards, they may develop, or believe they develop, psychic talents. They commonly associate themselves with UFOs, though often without passion. They simply *believe*; they are not on a crusade to convince others. Any such crusade is usually personal—to explain their own situation or beliefs.

The assumption is that the Star People are there to be "activated" when a time of crisis for the Earth or the human race arises. However, the alternative possibility that the Star People are fantasizing and playing out a personal game to meet their own psychological needs cannot be ignored. Perhaps this is suggested by a detail in Brad and Francie Steiger's book *The Star People*, when they admit that they achieved a good deal of public exposure through an article in the tabloid *National Enquirer* in 1979. Francie revealed in the magazine that she believed she was one of the Star People and explained her own inner drives, and the fact that she had interviewed around 60 people of similar belief. The result was that they were flooded by calls and letters from people who had come to realize that they too were Star People. "After the article appeared, our telephone began non-stop ringing, and we received nearly a thousand letters testifying to the writers' beliefs that they were Star People. Some of them claimed to have been activated by the very appearance of Francie's photograph . . ."

To be activated in times of cataclysmic upheaval is one thing; to be activated by an article in a tabloid magazine at least suggests the possibility that the respondents found in the idea of being a Star Person something satisfying and attractive. One characteristic of Star People is a sense of detachment from the rest of the human race, a sense of belonging elsewhere. On the basis that everyone needs someone, lonely people could find it an attractive proposition to belong to so special a group. Take for example one of the respondents the Steigers heard from: Bonnie Davis, a nurse. "My hair stood on end when I read the *Enquirer* story. I have always thought I was alone. I knew right then it was time to come out. The Golden Age is coming. When it arrives there will be no sickness, poverty or illness. People will live long, happy lives free of trouble and worry." Another, Joyce Burnett, commented, "I've never felt I belonged in my family...." "Soren," included in Scott Mandelker's book *From Elsewhere— Being ET in America*, saw an illustration of a crystal city and was "seized by an achingly painful sensation of homesickness."

But many argue that our world does face crisis in many areas. They might argue that the time is ripe for "awakening"; that the tabloid article was part of the cosmic plan . . . The contactee-type arguments rely a great deal on such belief and faith. Let us then look further into some of the claims of the Star People.

One common characteristic is the "awakening" itself. During dreams which often include UFO-related scenes, the Star Person is told, "Now is the time"; which they almost universally take to be an instruction to "come out" and admit their special heritage. Meanwhile the reference to "the time" also tends to make them feel that their work is needed urgently.

So when did the Star People come to Earth? For the most part the claims are a continuation of the "ancient astronaut" theories made so popular by writers such as Erich von Däniken, discussed earlier in this book. According to a channelled message received by Francie Steiger, thousands of years ago the aliens came to Earth and created the Starseeds. The Star People are humans who carry the genetic characteristics of their alien ancestors. In addition, in the modern day, are the Star Helpers. These are the human descendants of earlier humans who served the genetically altered Starseeds. They may not have any of the physical attributes of Starseeds, but they are highly evolved humans with race memories of their special ancestors. One author, referred to anonymously in the Steigers' book, had a "memory" of coming to Earth in a disabled spaceship. He carried with him special DNA memory so that he would not forget his true origins nor lose contact with his home world. He referred to this as "phylogenic memory"; the dormant memories that could be activated at certain times or by certain needs.

Dr. Scott Mandelker has recently been writing up and lecturing on his work with Star People. He believes that he is a Star

Person. "I ended up reading a wide selection of ET-related texts, Eastern and theosophical metaphysics, doing my own channelling (for a short time), and piecing together the many paranormal experiences and clues scattered throughout my life. From this it became abundantly clear that I am a Wanderer, an ET soul, and that this issue would be a fine subject for my dissertation." Mandelker believes that there could be as many as 100 million Star People living among us on Earth.

Mandelker is cautious of all claimants. "I was also quite aware that some people who might say they are ETs were in truth quite glamored and unreliable." But he goes on: "I also wanted to help the millions of Wanderers, or Star People, around the world wake more clearly to their own identity." He believes the Star People are alien souls "on short loan to Planet Earth" and that "in the long-run I am certain that ideas of soul-transfer and interplanetary origins will become widely accepted."

Walk-Ins

Another type of Star Person is a Walk-In; a fully physical human into whom an extraterrestrial intelligence places itself. The Walk-In is the product of a voluntary agreement the human engages in of his or her own free will, it is not an invasion or possession. Many describe such "revelations" as a rebirth; the human component remains but is augmented by the alien presence. One such Walk-In known as "Bob" in Mandelker's book states: "Bob is still here, the memory is here, but it doesn't feel like Bob ... I am Bob ... and I am not Bob."

It is interesting that many Walk-Ins, the majority it would seem, realize their alien counterpart at times of life crisis. "Bob" was "not a nice person" when at the age of 37 he was prompted to change. Another, "Soren," was of a mind to end his life. "Peter," another of Mandelker's subjects, also had a revelation-like experience at a time when he sought to end his life. At a crucial time Peter was visited by an intelligent ball of light that came into his room and gradually nurtured his spiritual side. (Such awakenings are not always traumatic. Mandelker refers to "Vicky," who had "the most gradual, gentle awakening..." and who described it herself as "no big deal.")

The recognition of the "change" at times of life crisis has close similarities to claims of religious experiences. Mandelker relates the story of Christin, who heard "inner voices" that directed him to uplifting experiences. The voice would tell him to drive to a particularly beautiful location and meditate. On one occasion he heard a voice say, "Remember this moment...," but it was a moment of pain and paralysis. He thought he was going to die. Then, in hospital, he heard the voice say, "Just go home now!" and finally it said, "I have given you a new spirit." He felt he had died and been reborn. The tone of the story is very similar to the turning-point, the moment of revelation, of one woman we interviewed who saw her experiences as religious. She was a "stigmatic"—that is she displayed, on her body, the crucifixion wounds of Christ. She had had a troubled and painful life, and was despairing. Then she heard a voice from a white mist say, "You are not alone any more." After that her life began to change, mostly in a spiritual way, for the better.

The Star People have only their own intuitive feelings to guide them, and that is the only evidence that is available to others. There is nothing to prove their claims; but in fact there is not much more to support the statements of contactees and abductees either. It is worth noting that the "Star People" syndrome is a "hybrid" motif: the reader is directed towards the discussion of hybrids in Chapter 14.

Overlap

What is fascinating is that the various claims of the UFO witnesses are overlapping. In Chapter 7 we shall examine the claims of the contactees, and in Chapter 10 it will be seen that these claims, which for many years fell into disrepute, are now surfacing again within the reports of alien abductions. They can be found, principally, in the work of John E. Mack, Professor of Psychiatry at Harvard Medical School, in his book *Abduction—Human Encounters With Aliens*. Mack, it is clear, is more open to a "spiritual" side to these events than some of his fellow UFO researchers.

One of Mack's clients, Scott, seems to have elements of "Star Person" thinking. He was apparently encouraged to see himself as "part of their family" and comments: "I want to be one of them, I want to be one of me, but I can't be both." When Mack asked him why not, he commented that it would mean he would never be home either way. When Mack discovered that Scott seemed to be denying part of his experience, Scott surprised him by replying that he was "denying that I am one of them." Mack in fact states that Scott always knew he was different and not from "around here." He always wanted to run away but could never work out where to run away to. He clearly sees himself as a hybrid, referring to his human side and "the other side."

Scott appears to have found peace, but only, it seems, by embracing his "alien side." In a letter to Mack he clearly takes an "alien" perspective with phrases such as "our intellectual abilities and the scope of our view is too much for humans to understand . . .," "I have reached the turning point where my power of uncontrol has overcome that of my human side . . .," and "I fear humans more than anything else . . . we have tried to change you many times. Many members of our species . . ."

Joe is another of Mack's abductees whose memories were triggered not by a UFO or by conscious recollection involving a UFO but by more oblique circumstances. In this case he was lying on a massage table and the therapist was working on his neck when "Joe suddenly had an image of lying on a table, surrounded by small beings with large heads, one of whom was putting a needle in his neck." Joe is also one of those abductees who has explored the personal development aspect of the encounters. Mack comments: "Joe, like other abductees, has felt that his relationship with what he calls 'the ETs' has provided emotional nourishment, support, and love . . ." Joe was no stranger to such personal exploration. Even as a teenager he had apparently explored spiritual understanding and personal growth activities including "mind/body healing workshops, psycho-synthesis, different forms of meditation, and membership in a Spiritualist Church." Joe's own spiritual counsellors had apparently told him that one day he would be "working with people from other planets."

Mack used regression hypnosis to explore Joe's memories. During the first hypnotic session, Joe recalled the image of an alien-like being with triangular face, large forehead, narrow chin and the large black elliptical eyes so commonly reported. He was at the time around 14 or 15 according to his recollections and had gone outdoors and walked behind a barn to the rear of the house, "as if 'drawn' there by a 'real subtle' force." A ship came down which looked like a "standing up egg" (perhaps not unlike that reported by Maurice Masse or Lonnie Zamora at Socorro) and stood on some kind of feet or landing pads.

Joe has a recollection of an implant and the same recall of the power of the alien's eyes that many other abductees have reported. The alien—unusually he offered Joe a name, Tanoun—told Joe to look "inside his eyes," and Joe had the feeling that he could "disappear" and "not come back." Although scared, eventually Joe reported feeling "like I'm inside him—inside his head, inside his eyes." At that point some kind of needle penetrated his neck and Joe believed that they were "taking a little bit of something out, and they are putting something in." Joe clearly believed it was a tracking device, something which would enable them to follow him.

The degree of connection between Joe and the alien is uncertain, but it appears that Joe believes himself to have an alien identity of his own—either that he can see as if inside the alien or that he is in some way part alien himself. Several accounts, and particularly more recent ones, have included the suggestion that the aliens can take any form they want to and adopt these forms for the sake of abductees. Joe makes a similar claim, but in this case with himself as the chameleon-like alien. He claims his own form kept changing, and that he felt "more comfortable in the shape like them . . . somewhat translucent." He continues his description: "A large gray head and big elliptical eyes, long and thin in the torso, light grayish in color, the hands a little webbed with long arms and fingers—three and a thumb." He states: "I feel like I'm inside me."

Joe and his partner Maria have a son named Mark. Joe believes that Mark "himself was once a gray ET." Of his own "ET self" he comments that it was "like another manifestation of my soul."

Joe states that he was brought up in an Irish Catholic family where emotion was suppressed, and believes that the abduction experiences, to quote Mack, "had become a 'conduit,' opening him to a wide range of strong feelings." Mack comments: "Joe felt that for himself his abduction experiences, especially as revealed in this session, were 'like a rite of passage,' a 'single step of growth' toward becoming 'more human.'" Mack, discussing the regression hypnosis, states that "Joe spoke of the aliens again as 'midwives' helping him stay connected with his divinity."

At one point Joe recalls being flooded by images, as if "a full circular tray of 60 to 70 slides containing 60 to 70 separate experiences" were being fed to him. This is very similar to the claim of Ed Walters, who believes that several times the aliens interrupted his thinking by making him look through what were like flashing pictures of animals and of pornographic material. Presumably this corresponds to the belief that the aliens occasionally create images simply to see or feel what the response of the human is and thereby to learn from that experience, as examined in Chapter 10.

In his commentary Mack states: "The aliens are also agents of Joe's own integration and reensoulment. In the second regression he discovered he possessed both the human and alien identity, which many abductees are discovering about themselves, and that he is a kind of double agent, functioning as a bridge between the Earth and the realms from which the beings derive." Whether this is true in actuality or whether it is a way

in which the humans learned to expand their own consciousness is probably the primary debate on abduction yet to be resolved or even to be properly explored.

John Mack writes of his client Sara: "Sara is one of an increasing group of abductees who bring a degree of spiritual interest to
the understanding of their experiences." Like so many she is
committed to ecological problems and has a feeling of "mission"
based on her experiences.

The creatures Sara reported during her regression sessions
are somewhat different from the conventional Grays. For example: "I see a lot of things that look a little bit like skeletons, but a
cross between a skeleton and a walking insect ... He has some
sort of a bubble thing on his head." And on another occasion she
saw a creature with penetratingly dark eyes, insect-like with an
oval-shaped head and a shrunken body, but she feels that this is
"a being that looked like Miguel" or "a disguise of Miguel."
Miguel is a friend of hers whom she believes she has a natural
affinity with and who she refers to as her "extraterrestrial
friend." Sara has had a history of involvement in the paranormal, Mack reports that "apparently from an early age [she] has
exhibited certain paranormal powers, such as the ability at least
to create the impression of levitating another child."

Another of Mack's regression clients, Eva, has a wide range of
paranormal experiences which she connects to UFO-related
phenomena. For example on one occasion she saw a white figure
flying in the room which she describes as a ghost; it wanted to
take her but "I didn't want to go." She told Mack that her daughter saw the white ghost figure too. Eva also saw alien-like figures
walking through walls approaching her in the bedroom and
touching her and has several memories of what seem to be flying
saucers. On another occasion during a slow night shift on Air
Traffic Control she appears to have had an out-of-body experience coming close to a near-death experience. "I knew at that
point I had a choice of living or dying ... I wasn't interested in
dying." (A choice many times reported in near-death experi-

ences.) She also reported seeing a violet rectangle which she felt was "like a doorway into/out of somewhere not visible, maybe another dimension." She has fairly "classical" memories of abductions and medical examinations with some sexual overtones.

Eva, like many of Mack's abductees, appears to speak sometimes as if she is the alien and houses a dual identity, and also as if she has a mission, which is perhaps "to be a healer...enabling people to break away from the unhealthy effects of institutional systems." It appears in one dialogue that Eva is being used by the aliens. Speaking in her "cosmic voice" she states that the beings must "adjust our communication from high vibratory levels to those of Earthly (verbal) vibration...We are using Eva's body with her consent full-time now. Earthly Eva has not left, but she has defused with us so that her Earthly powers have been greatly enhanced..." But relating an experience which she was certain happened in the year 1652 she comments: "It's like I was brought to Earth—I don't know why I was brought for five or six years, or however old I was at the time, and then I was taken out to another dimension that has no space or time as we know it." Eva in fact has many recollections of past lives—during the 1930s or around the Second World War; in Morocco many years before that; as a merchant named Onrishi in the early thirteenth century, and so on.

Mack comments: "Her lifelong abduction experiences are a powerful vehicle for the evolution of her consciousness and they bring her in touch with the depths of her purpose." He further comments that her descriptions of her abduction experiences give "a consistent picture of the evolutionary purpose of the alien–human relationship, at least as it affects our consciousness." He believes that her past life memories are "part of the process of the expansion of her consciousness beyond a purely physicalist or materialist perception of reality." Perhaps mirroring the claims of the power animal by shamanic leaders, Mack comments: "The alien beings function as spirit energies or guides, serving the evolution of consciousness and identity."

Like many of Mack's regression clients, Paul also believes that he has a dual identity, both human and alien, and a mission to help humans. Paul seems to think like one of the Star People. "All my life to my mother I always said I was adopted. I'm not from here." Under hypnosis he recalled a lifetime series of abductions starting around the age of two or three. Mack does point out, however, that Paul lived for much of his life with a fear that his father was not his real father, and finally his mother broke down and confessed that that was indeed the case and that Paul was the product of a long-standing affair she had had with another man. This may well have contributed to his feeling of disconnection from his family.

Paul's sense of dual identity is not restricted to his human side and his alien side. On one occasion he describes a UFO sighting, viewing it simultaneously as an adult and as a child, or, as Mack puts it, with "the adult Paul observing the actions of the little boy from 'right behind his eyes.'" In the subsequent description of the UFO sighting it seems that Paul the child and Paul the adult can describe their own different feelings almost within the same narrative.

During one encounter Paul describes one of the aliens as "a friend" who explains that Paul is also from the ship. Indeed he is shown his quarters on the ship which he uses "when we go on these trips." Paul believes the quarters felt familiar and thinks he may have been there 70 times. In one description he thinks that he was on the ship when he first came to Earth.

Paul's view is that he is rather like a spy placed on Earth for a purpose—a common claim of the Star People, who believe that they are rather like a secret column, to be activated when the time is right. The alien told Paul, "Your spirit is from here," by which he meant the ship rather than the Earth. For much of his time Paul speaks as an alien, describing how "we've been hurt here before," and so on. Paul's view of the human race is that it is too violent, too hostile and needs to be helped. Maintaining a dual identity is stressful, Paul claims, perhaps best illustrated by the fact that during questioning by Mack, Paul "found himself 'bouncing' or 'jumping' back and forth between his alien and human identity or perspective, which he found difficult."

Paul became particularly fascinated with the age of reptiles, the dinosaur period. The aliens were able to make contact with the reptiles, who were highly intelligent, he claims. Paul believes that we have misinterpreted the aliens. "You've got some bones, you know . . . You don't know anything about them."

Perhaps uniquely among abductees, or contactees, Paul seems to have memories of being at the Roswell Incident in 1947. Quite whether he is there as a human or an alien is not entirely clear. At one point he describes himself as human but also says: "I don't want to be human. I'm sorry for being human. I didn't mean to hurt them." He then also describes himself as having been in another ship that went to rescue the dead aliens and "felt anguish that several of his dead 'friends' could not be 'collected' and had to be left behind in the desert." Paul believes that the aliens came to Roswell "with open arms" but were shocked to discover that they were being attacked. Mack points out that Paul was not born until 19 years after the Roswell Incident, but Paul has no explanation; he is simply relating his feelings, which he believes are memories. In conclusion Mack believes that "Paul experiences himself as a bridge between two worlds. He feels deeply that he has both a human and an alien identity. The task of integrating these two basic dimensions of himself—a challenge that many abductees who experience double life must face—is formidable . . ."

Contactees

Before the identification of the alien abduction phenomenon within UFO experiences—now a phenomenon written about at length in books and articles around the world—and setting aside the "mere" sightings of aliens by witnesses who experienced little interaction with them, the first people to claim contact reported a respectful, mutual and generally beneficial experience. They became known as the "contactees." Their claims dominated the image of the UFO phenomenon throughout the 1950s.

A Variety Of Contacts

The first UFO contactee was George Adamski (George the First, as writer and researcher Frank Edwards called him), who reported a meeting with an alien in 1952. He published his account the following year. An enduring image of "contact" as a physical meeting, usually in remote locations, derived from this. But in fact over time the forms of contact have varied. These include channelled messages, telepathically received or given through mechanisms such as "automatic writing." Although such reports are relatively new within the UFO frame of reference—which itself is only 50 years old as a recognized, discrete phenomenon—they are comparable to claims from earlier centuries which were usually religious or spiritual in nature. Messages from the dead, or from God, have been reported throughout history; for example Joan of Arc claimed that she received a divine message which impelled her to lead the French armies into battle against the English. Consider also the beginnings of Spiritualism, when the Fox sisters in Hydesville heard what seemed to be intelligent "rappings" which they believed were from deceased people communicating across the "veil of death." As early as 1866 the Denton family of Massachusetts were claiming to receive messages from outer space through psychic means. Sherman Denton was the most successful; he claimed he could project his own "essence" into space and reported "trips" to Mars and other planets. Denton reported that the Martians lived in a "Utopia" and looked "very much like everyone here on Earth. In a crowd, a Martian could remain undetected if he was dressed in our type of clothing." The Martians were also apparently coming to the Earth to study us, he stated. "They started arriving in the late nineteenth century—their first trip taking place around 1860." The Martians used flying machines made of metal.

These claims are close to those of the UFO contactees whose stories are set out below. Few consider that the events the contactees reported happened objectively in the physical world, but there is the possibility that they (ignoring the obvious hoaxers) were undergoing some mental experience which was interpreted in the light of the new "flying saucer" fad of the time.

If so, then perhaps Denton, Adamski and others were really trying to describe something perceived in an "altered state"; a shamanic experience, an out-of-body experience, or some sort of remote viewing sensation.

George the First

Adamski's story is well known. On 9 October 1946, while watching a meteor shower, he saw his first flying saucer: "a gigantic spacecraft hovering high above the mountain ridge to the south of Mount Palomar, towards San Diego." Adamski reported that at the time he was unprepared for the sighting. "For the greater part of my life I have believed that other planets are inhabited. And I have pictured them as 'class rooms' for our experience and development ... however, I had never given too much thought to the idea of inter-planetary travel in man-made ships ... I, too, believed the distances between planets to be too great for spanning by mechanical constructions." After the meteor shower was over, Adamski saw another object in the sky, "a large black object, similar in shape to a gigantic dirigible ..." Shortly afterwards it raised its nose and shot off upwards, leaving a trail of fire.

The following year, his interest now alerted, he saw a chain of many lights moving "in squadrons of 32." Adamski claims that later that year the military asked for his help to photograph flying saucers because his telescopes were more manoeuvrable than the main observatory telescopes. He succeeded in getting two good pictures and many more in the two years that followed. During this time Adamski gave a number of lectures on the subject, feeling "that the people must be told about these space craft that were moving through our atmosphere in ever increasing numbers."

Adamski states that he made a number of trips to chosen spots, "hoping to make personal contact and to learn just what these space people looked like and what their purpose was in coming Earthwards." Adamski was rewarded with success on 20 November 1952, when he became the first person to report mutual, lengthy contact with an alien.

Having earlier been contacted by two couples, the Baileys and the Williamsons, Adamski had promised to include them in his next attempt to make contact. Thus, these four people accompanied Adamski to the 20 November meeting. They saw a cigar-shaped object high in the sky. Adamski went to, and remained alone at, what he felt might be "the contact point"; the other four stayed behind, watching from around a half mile to a mile away.

A few minutes later a small flying saucer descended and hovered near Adamski, who photographed it. He believed that at least part of the object was visible to the couples watching from a distance. Then Adamski noticed a man standing about a quarter of a mile away. "I was sure he had not been there before," Adamski stated. The man looked normal, human, and was approximately 5 ft 6 in., average weight and young-looking. He had perfect white teeth, peaceful green eyes, long blond hair and a suntan. He was dressed in a one-piece brown overall and wore what looked like sandals. Adamski later stated: "Now, for the first time I fully realized that I was in the presence of a man from space—A HUMAN BEING FROM ANOTHER WORLD!...The beauty of his form surpassed anything I had ever seen...I felt like a little child in the presence of one with great wisdom...."

Adamski tried to speak to the alien, but apparently he was not understood. He tried a new tack: "I am a firm believer that people who desire to convey messages to one another can do so, even though they neither speak nor understand the other's language...above all, by means of telepathy." Adamski formed the picture of a planet in his mind, and pointed at the sun. Gradually a communication formed involving sign language, spoken word and telepathy, and the alien managed to indicate that he came from Venus. Adamski learned that the alien believed in God, that there were visitors to Earth from other planets within the solar system and from beyond, and that these races were concerned about atomic radiations being emitted from the Earth.

After the Venusian re-entered his craft and it took off, Adamski marked the footprints that the alien had left in the sand and showed them to the rest of the group. The group had, fortunately, thought to bring plaster of Paris with them, and with this they were able to make casts of the prints.

The saucer made a return visit the following month. During the initial meeting Adamski had given the alien a photographic plate which the alien had promised to return. When Adamski next saw the saucer the plate was dropped out of the window near him. The original image had been removed; the plate was now covered in "hieroglyphics."

In later contacts Adamski travelled aboard the spaceships to other planets, meeting Martians, Saturnians and Jovians. Desmond Leslie, who co-authored *Flying Saucers Have Landed*, Adamski's story of contact, comments of one of these trips:

> Now this brings us to Adamski's later claims to have visited the planet Saturn in a large mother ship, at a time when some of his staunchest followers believed him to be in bed and on Earth... He informed me that to reach the UFO he was drawn up in a beam of energy at incredible speed, and that on return to earth he felt his whole being had radically changed, and that it was very difficult to accept earth-like conditions again. This account has all the marks of a spiritual, out of the body experience.

Adamski's claims have been largely discarded by "mainstream" UFO research as either profiteering, wishful thinking, or just plain fantasy. Yet a great deal of support and belief has recently been extended to the work of abduction researchers Budd Hopkins, David Jacobs and John Mack. When reading the accounts of their work in this book consider the detail in the above paragraph of Leslie's: "drawn up... at incredible speed"; "radically changed"; "the marks of a spiritual, out of body experience." It is remarkable how similar these details are to the hypnotically retrieved memories now surfacing from abductees.

In *Flying Saucers Have Landed* Adamski concludes his story of first contact with the words "Surface thinkers might like to conclude that I had had a very original dream. Or that I may be out to make money for myself in the field of science fiction. I can assure such persons that nothing is farther from the truth." It is difficult to credit Adamski with any real probability that he genuinely, objectively experienced all of the incidents he claimed, yet it is possible that he was doing his best to explain in relatively prosaic terms the same sorts of inner feelings and mental impressions, out-of-body and shamanic-like experiences, perhaps, that modern abductees are claiming. Those claims are being taken seriously by qualified individuals such as John Mack, and perhaps if the contactee claims were viewed in this light they would not be rejected so easily.

Second, Third, Fourth And Fifth ...

Adamski created an image of "flying saucers" that was unacceptable not just to the majority of the public but to many in UFO research—who instantly tried to distance themselves from such claims and to some extent suppressed the reports they had been receiving of "little men" sightings, for fear that they would be discredited along with Adamski.

But he had hit a "hot button" for the times. His claims that the aliens were concerned about our development and use of atomic power were absolutely in tune with the thinking of the early 1950s. The atomic bomb had been developed in the mid-1940s and used to end the Second World War in Japan. In November 1952 the first hydrogen bomb was exploded in the Pacific, and people were becoming wary of this awesome power. Within a few years the worldwide "ban the bomb" movement was well under way. Adamski's claims offered the hope of salvation, or at least a watchful eye, from superior beings. They suggested that a greater brotherhood rather than just the people of the Earth existed "out there." Many people were searching for a new meaning to life in the years following the Second World War, Adamski offered such meaning for those who sought his type of belief. Whatever the truth, or level of truth, of Adamski's claims, the books he wrote were hugely successful (1955 saw the publication of *Inside the Space Ships*). He embarked on lecture tours around the world and became a celebrity.

It is therefore no surprise that copy-cat claims followed. Even though some might equally have been true—whether they represented people travelling to other worlds or people exploring areas of their own inner mental processes—the odds are high that some were just money-making stories designed primarily to sell books.

Publishers, not having Adamski on their books, would have cast around for one of their own. Their criteria would have been simple—and no different from the pressures put on authors today: the next story must be bigger and better! And so they were.

Even before Adamski had his second book out, Truman Bethurum and Daniel Fry both published their own accounts in 1954. Bethurum's *Aboard a Flying Saucer* told of his invitation by a group of small aliens from the planet Clarion to join them on a huge flying saucer. There he met Aura Rhanes, the female captain, who was "tops in shapeliness and beauty." She explained that Clarion was in our solar system but positioned "behind our sun" where it cannot be seen from the Earth. The aliens from Clarion had apparently been visiting the Earth for some years with a mission to reaffirm the values of marriage, religion and loyalty. Bethurum explained: "They're very humble, kind, religious, people with great understanding. They're concerned about a dreadful Paganism that's at work on Earth." Like Adamski's contact, the people from Clarion were concerned because "they believe that the Earth may be headed towards an atomic war. They hope to prevent our planet from being destroyed during such a war. If that should occur, it would create a widespread catastrophe and considerable confusion in space."

Daniel Fry's *The White Sands Incident* took up the "atomic horrors" theme. "The entire population of your planet is now in constant danger of total destruction by an agency which you yourselves have created, with great labor and diligence, and at great expense in time and money. Why should a race be threatened by its own creations? The answer, of course, is simply that the race has not progressed far enough in the foundation sciences to enable its people to control their own creations, and so their creations control them." Fry was asked by his alien contact to write a book to warn the world of its nuclear follies, and *The White Sands Incident* was the result. In his presentations he often stated his concerns about what would happen when humans ventured into space. "The human ego is the greatest obstacle to human learning. Up to now we've stayed in our own backyard, and we've been able to beat ourselves on the chests and think how important we are. But now we are getting ready to go out into other people's backyards, and we had better prepare for it."

In 1955 Orfeo Angelucci produced *Secret of the Saucers*, which further promoted the human race's failings. In this case it was our materialism which was causing our downfall. Angelucci's claims were much more spiritual in nature than his predecessors', and eventually Angelucci met Jesus himself. The aliens' mission was to study "the spiritual evolution of man."

In 1959 Howard Menger published *From Outer Space To You*, which told of his many previous encounters, some pre-dating Adamski's. (He later also produced a second book, *The Carpenter Returns*.) His first contact was in 1932, when he met a beautiful blonde girl in a translucent tight-fitting suit displaying the "curves of her lovely body." "The space people are watching over you," she told him. In the 1940s Menger had sightings of flying saucers, and reported other encounters with aliens, including one looking the same as the one he had met in 1932, and later still he met the original who, he was shocked to discover, looked no older than when he had first encountered her. She was apparently over five hundred years old. He took trips on the spaceships, including one trip which he is certain was to the Moon, where he also took photographs. Menger believed that breathing on the Moon was as easy as on Earth, and reported seeing structures there. Even more recently he confirmed his sightings despite the evidence of the lunar landing missions: "This was in 1956. We landed in a section where it was dark and light . . . and we did see things that they claim are not there now. So I can't prove anything. We saw dome-shaped buildings, we saw people working there; Chinese, Russians, Americans, all working together in a common interest in these dome-shaped buildings. It was just amazing." Unlike many of the contactees, Menger did not claim to be overly exceptional; in his flight to the Moon he was apparently accompanied by several other Americans. Menger was rewarded for his efforts by being given a part of the working mechanism of the saucers to display to the world. Menger's messages were also spiritual in nature: "The people on this planet are barbarians compared to these aliens," he said. "These aliens are angelic; they gave up wars thousands of years ago. The scriptures came from them, a lot of the scriptures came because of their help."

These five—Adamski, Bethurum, Fry, Angelucci and Menger—have been called the five leading contactees; but they were not alone. A good many other claimants came forward.

And Others Still . . .

Ms. Hayden was one. She explained: "In this particular solar system we do not rank very highly, in fact we're rather an ordinary speck of dust as a planet, but we are progressing . . . for that reason we must have this outside help, this additional education." She rather enigmatically denied one suggestion that she was a Venusian, but admitted, "I rather like the planet Venus." Speaking of the aliens she confirmed the Adamski impression: "I understand that they can mingle quite freely with human beings on this planet and not be recognized . . . they are human beings, they just happen to come from a different background, so to speak." In the early 1950s Ms. Hayden passed on one prediction: "I understand from many sources that in 1956 there will be great mass landings and then the question of flying saucers can no longer be denied." Not the most reliable of sources, it turned out.

There are also contactee groups, such as Unarius, which claims that it is a "vast brotherhood of advanced human beings" who are concerned for man's spiritual evolution. It was created by Dr. Ernest and Ruth E. Norman in 1954 and was still promoting itself into the 1990s with incredible razzmatazz and almost garish video promotions. Ruth was known as Uriel, "the director and founder of this organization, Unarius. Our mission is to teach people that whatever man has done in the past good, bad or indifferent he will repeat it in the present." She was, they say, "the

embodiment of the force that holds the planets in their orbits."
They display the "Cosmic Generator," a symbolic representation
showing "that the infinite mind, that has incarnated as Uriel
through her energy and understanding is able to, and does, sustain the planets . . . The little lights [on the display] that go from
one planet to another are symbolic of the electromagnetic fields
of energy that are part of an infinite mind that sustains these
planets in their orbits." Uriel herself explained: "The world at
large is fascinated with so-called flying saucers. However, they
do not fly, they oscillate in between dimensions." She went on to
add, "I have piloted many spaceships, starships we call them."

In 1997 the Unarius Academy made headlines when it announced a certain empathy with the suicides of the Heaven's Gate
cult (see Chaper 17), though they stressed that suicide was not
their own requirement. Carol Robinson of the Academy announced that in 2001 they would travel to the Caribbean to meet a
spacecraft from the planet Myton. The Academy believes that one
thousand people from that planet will come to Earth to build a
"power tower" which alone will suffice to generate the Earth's energy needs. The spacecraft will also help to resurrect the lost con-
tinents of Lemuria and Atlantis. "The human beings onboard are
called Muons," Carol Robinson stated. "They'll be coming to
stay." They will apparently bring with them a spaceship which will
be used by Earth people to travel in space. Robinson explained:
"At first they'll just bring one ship, but then they'll bring others."

Frank Stranges is a contactee, and now also a minister of the
Christian religion. "There is a beautiful harmony between
space and science and religion. And for many years many cler-
gymen have missed the mark by insisting that there is a clash,
but there is not a clash, there is harmony between space and
science and religion. This is reflected in all holy books including the Holy Bible. If a person would examine it in the light of
what is happening today whereby space people have come to
this planet not to preach another gospel, because there is no
other gospel than the truth that was preached by Christ . . .

some of these space people could fall into the category of angelic beings . . . here to help mankind." Stranges' contact was known as Valiant Thor; he came from the inside of the planet Venus. According to Stranges, "Commander" Thor worked for three years inside the Pentagon and was given an audience with President Dwight Eisenhower and Richard Nixon. Thor "offered to give them information on how the American people could successfully live without sickness, without poverty, without disease and without death." Stranges says that Thor was rejected because the information he was offering would ruin the American economy. Thor left the Earth in 1960.

In 1958 there was a "contactee" conference at Giant Rock Airport in the California desert; around five thousand people turned up to listen to a variety of claims by contactees who had met or flown with aliens in their flying saucers. These annual conferences had been arranged, starting in 1954, by contactee George W. van Tassel. Frank Stranges spoke at the conferences there even before he had his own contact. Van Tassel had become interested in the subject of space flight after the Second World War while working for Howard Hughes in his aircraft companies. In 1951 van Tassel made contact with "The Council of the Seven Lights" which was based in a spacecraft in Earth orbit. In 1952 he published his story in the book *I Rode a Flying Saucer*. He founded the "College of Universal Wisdom" to study rejuvenation, and, in the late 1950s, began construction of a dome-shaped building known as "The Integritron"—"under guidance of the space beings." It is designed to "create a unique time field" which can restore missing limbs, slow down the ageing process, and create a "unique vibration that raises the consciousness of all the people within the interior of the dome and oftentimes sends them into an altered state of consciousness."

A First-Hand Account

The contactee beliefs continue to the present day, with consistent themes still arising. In May 1997 we interviewed Helga Douglas. She had had several UFO sightings in Yorkshire and Essex, where she now lives, but her contactee experiences arise from a different stimulus; visions experienced with her former husband. The following is her account, in her own words, of the visions they shared:

We started having the same dreams, which apparently is not unusual between a husband and wife. We were very close and we worked together [as musicians on a ship] and ate together and so forth. The dreams became so vivid. We were later told this was "the third eye" opening...

This experience started in 1978. We were on a ship. We were lying in bunks; he had the top bunk and I had the bottom bunk. It was broad daylight, we both had our eyes open looking at the ceiling. I had the bottom bunk, so I couldn't see any ceiling. We were having a chat about the evening, very general. And I started seeing visions on the bunk. Eyes wide open. And he started seeing things. When I say "visions," we were seeing either faces that were sort of coming towards us or lines and lines of humanoids. They were not, I would say, of this earth. They were more like what I call a Gray but not exactly like that. They had a short, broad nose, like a parrot beak. In other words just people, but different. And they appeared to be poverty stricken, like you would see in African famines. My husband also started seeing the same things. We were wide awake; not asleep. We hadn't drunk. We had taken no drugs. We'd just had tea or coffee and a good meal and we were wide awake. He called to me: "Can you see what I can see?" And I described what I was seeing. He said, "Yes I can see that but slightly different."

Then we started seeing the sky; pink and grey, with cloud formations of yellow. These are the nearest colours I can give you, but they are not the real colours. Someone later suggested that perhaps we were seeing a planet with a sulphurous atmosphere.

We'd ask: "Can you show us something different?" We didn't know where any of this was coming from.

And we started seeing colours that I cannot describe, because how can I tell you of a colour that you have never seen? Like brown but not brown; not black, not red, it's not even like a mixture of the three. It's something different.

After a period of time my husband started hearing noises in his head. I want you to bear in mind that we didn't concentrate on this. We weren't getting paranoid about anything and it didn't happen every night. It was occasionally. One night he said, "Can you hear that noise?" I said "No." He said, "I have been having these noises in my head for a long time—like a twittering." I suggested he see a doctor in case there was something wrong with his ears. Being musicians, maybe he'd been too near speakers or amplifiers, or whatever. But he said it wasn't like that; it wasn't in his ears, it was in the centre of his head. He started talking to the ceiling and I thought, "He's going loopy-loo now." Then he said, "I've got a communication, a communication is coming through to me but I don't know where it's coming from."

Maybe a week later I suddenly started getting a vision and I said, "Look, if this is an alien being or something supernatural, I'm not frightened of you. Please tell me what it is." We didn't hear voices but it came into our minds, almost like a picture. They were saying that they were trying to communicate with us and they came in peace. We said, "Who are you?" This wasn't immediately answered; eventually they called themselves the watchers, the carers. We said, "Who are the watchers and the carers?" This took days. I said, "Right, if you really are aliens, if you really are spaceships, if you really are whatever you are, we need proof. People will never believe us if we want to tell anybody about you. Please can you give us some proof." So they told us to be on the deck at midnight. The way they described it was: "When the two fingers on your clock are completely together." We should have been playing music then but we took a break and went up on the deck. And we looked in the sky but we could see nothing. It was a beautiful night, clear stars—at sea you've got no land and light pollution. All of a sudden we saw this object in the sky right above our heads. And we looked up and I said, "That's an aeroplane moving." My husband said, "No, it's too high up." I asked him if he thought it was a spaceship we were looking at. Then another object appeared at the same height as that one. And it looked as if they were going to collide. We looked at our watches. It was exactly midnight. At the same time both these objects sent a huge beam which was neither silver nor gold; it's like a mixture, if you can imagine it, of those two colours. Two beams coming straight down. And we could see aeroplanes underneath. There were two aeroplanes flying underneath. And I said, "Well, that looks like we've seen our spaceships. What's going to happen now? Are they going to just disappear or what?" Then one went one way and one circled twice and went in the opposite direction and just disappeared; it went straight up vertically.

Going a little further forward in time now, to 1983, my husband was still getting this twittering in his head. So we said, "We'd like to go in one of your spaceships." Maybe we can see something more close up. My husband then started drawing and the spaceships we actually saw were shaped like his drawings; the shapes of a grand piano and a harp. I said I'd like to go on one of these spaceships. They said it was possible. But they explained that they couldn't take our bodies, only our minds, our thoughts. We didn't lie down, we just sat like I'm talking to you now. We didn't have to concentrate. The next thing I know is I am on this spaceship.

Everything was warm to touch. And there was a smell on the ship, but I've only recently found something that smells like it: perm solution, the stuff you use to do your hair. I was in a circular type corridor; a bit like you see on *Star Trek*. There were no doors, but this section sort of opened and I was in another corridor. There were computers in there; we were told they were computers but they were, like, organic. There were no aliens on this ship by the way. Just these biological computers. They could move. They were warm to touch. When you touched them, they had skin. They didn't look humanoid. They looked like—I can't even describe what they looked like. Sort of a big square rounded off, rectangles rounded off, quite huge. I don't know how they moved; they just seemed to move and come with you. They were warm, blood warm. And they communicated. And they told us that they were a scout ship. Their job was to collate information, and to try and communicate if possible. But they had certain rules. They weren't allowed to alter any of our lives or do anything to us. They said that they had found a communication through me, a psychic link. They felt it was easier for people who had any psychic channels to receive them.

They said they were taking samples of earth, water samples, and so on. I asked if they were taking samples of human beings. They said no.

They were very upset with what was happening on this planet; they told us that. And one of their purposes was to see if we would tell other people to stop chopping down trees and all the ecological things that we have now come to realize. They told us about three disasters which were going to happen which did happen. One was an oil spillage, with wildlife deaths. One was a volcano; I assume it was that one that went off a couple of years back. The third was an earthquake.

They talked about AIDS. They said that we were going to have a disease which if it was not controlled would stop reproduction on this planet completely and utterly. At least I assumed that they were talking about AIDS, but maybe the real disease is yet to come.

We were being given warnings. When I asked about the visions of the lines of humanoids, they told me that is what had happened to other life forms. They were warning us: "Don't let this happen to your planet."

They were horrified at what we were doing with this planet. Absolutely. When I say horrified that's only a word. You could actually feel a sort of shuddering with these computers that we were talking to.

Contactee Groupings

There can be no more profound a realization when studying

claims of alien intervention on Earth than to recognize that a significant percentage of the world's population has changed, in that it now believes in the reality of aliens, even though there is no proof of their existence, and less still of their visitation to the Earth. There may be some culture-shocks yet to come if undeniable proof of alien visitation were ever found, but many of the changes that such revelation would bring about have in fact already happened. People accept the existence of aliens as part of the background of existence within a vast universe. Before 1961—before the first man in space—such a concept was regarded as the purview of science fiction only; now it is accepted as probable, only awaiting proof. People respond to what they believe. And perhaps there are no stronger belief systems than those found in the cults that have developed on the back of UFO belief.

Cults have been defined as "religion without political power." Certainly the cults that have arisen within UFO circles have an element of the religious about them, and indeed some are registered religions.

In some ways the cult is just an extension of the contactee belief; it is to do with belief and not to do with extraterrestrials. But that is not, of course, the perception of the members of the cult, for whom the reality behind the belief is presumably paramount.

A number of cults have formed based on a belief in contact with extraterrestrials. The "One World Family" started by Allen-Michael Noonan was triggered by Noonan's belief that while at work he was suddenly interrupted by a voice that asked: "Will you agree to be the saviour of the world?" "Light Affiliates" was the result of channelled communication between Robin McPherson and an entity known as "Ox-Ho"; the "Space Brothers" were selecting certain worthy people and would save them after a major cataclysm.

Rael

The Raelian movement is a world-wide organization believed

to have representation in over 80 countries, with 35,000 members. It is based on UFO/alien beliefs. The central figure in this is Claude Vorilhon, a former racing driver and sports journalist. According to the Raelian movement's own literature his mother was inseminated aboard a UFO on Christmas Day 1945 and he was the product. Her memory of this event was erased "so as not to psychologically unbalance her." On 13 December 1973 Vorilhon was contacted by an alien who "entrusted him with a message for humanity which clarifies our origin and our potential future." Rael—the name Vorilhon has adopted—spreads this message by addressing conferences around the world and by teaching "sensual meditation," which apparently helps develop human potential.

Rael was chosen by the space beings known as the Elohim because he lived in France ("a country where new ideas are welcomed..."), because his father (the Earth-based one presumably) was Jewish and his mother Catholic, which suggested that he would be a free thinker without being anti-religious, and because he was born in the post-Hiroshima age.

The movement's purpose is to make people aware of the messages of the Elohim, and to build an embassy on Earth in internationally recognized neutral territory where the Elohim and Earth's political and scientific leaders can meet. "Without the neutrality of an embassy, free air space and an official welcome, an unannounced and undesired landing would have enormous political, economic and social repercussions with disastrous consequences world-wide," they believe.

The Raelian movement places great emphasis on the further development of humanity, even by artificial means. They believe that humanity was created artificially by the Elohim. According to Rael, "One day, without a doubt we will be able to synthesize a human being... bringing us one step closer to what the ELOHIM scientists did a long time ago."

In 1997 the Raelian movement achieved exposure by associating its publicity with the successful cloning of a sheep, an event which made headlines around the world. The United States Raelian movement announced, on 28 February, that the cloning of the sheep by Dr. Ian Wilmut was a confirmation of the messages of the Elohim. It was, they said, "a first step toward eternity for humans... When Rael, 23 years ago, brought a message from the Elohim, these extraterrestrials, who created all life on Earth scientifically in laboratories thanks to a perfect mastering of DNA, stated, among other things, that the mystery of the resurrection of Jesus was in fact a cloning performed at that time by the Elohim. Many were those who thought it was impossible." Rael announced, on 11 March 1997, in Las Vegas, the formation of a company, Valient Ventures Ltd, which it is said will offer, "Clonaid," to assist infertile parents to clone a child from one of them. "Clonaid will charge as low as $200,000 for its cloning service," Rael said.

The Master Aetherius

The most enduring, and perhaps most famous organization to flourish from the contactee claims is the Aetherius Society. Early in 1954, George King received a contact from an Interplanetary Master. King called this "The Command." While doing relatively routine household chores in his London home King heard a voice which stated: "Prepare yourself. You are to become the Voice of Interplanetary Parliament." King believed that the reason he was able to receive this message was that he had spent the years since the Second World War studying yoga and meditation. Richard Lawrence, a long-standing member of the Aetherius Society, wrote in *Contact with the Gods from Space– Pathway to the New Millennium*: "He was not chosen for this task because Interplanetary Beings particularly favoured or liked him, but because he was in the right position to receive these communications." Lawrence adds, "He had gone beyond psychic development and was capable of raising his consciousness to a very high level, which made it possible for Interplanetary Beings to communicate with him telepathically."

King spent time trying to understand the message, and was later visited by an Indian spiritual leader of the time, whom he recognized instantly, and who walked *through* his closed door and sat before King in his rooms. The visitor explained to him: "You are one of the many called upon to prepare yourself for the coming conflict between the materialist scientist . . . and the occult 'scientist.'"

The basis of the Aetherius Society is to reconcile science and religion. "Gradually through the centuries, science has become separated from religion . . . A time of change is now upon us," Lawrence writes. "The barriers between different religions will gradually be broken down and there will be a return to oneness which is the very essence of Spiritual expression. More than this, the barriers between religion and science will be broken down and they will be seen again as two essential aspects of the one search for Truth."

The Aetherius Society was created as a vehicle to deliver the messages King received from the "Masters." It is named after the "Master Aetherius," the orginator of the first, "Command" contact. They are a religious organization but at great pains to distance themselves from the word "cult." In the sense that a cult is a religion without political representation they probably are a cult, but the word now carries the very unwelcome meaning of an oppressive, family-breaking sect and it is hardly surprising that the term is avoided. "The Aetherius Society is not a 'converting' organization," Lawrence writes. "We certainly do not use persuasive methods to recruit anyone." And in an interview with us he pointed out: "We do not ask people to give up their possessions to join us. We do not worship our leader."

King receives messages by telepathy, sometimes while in a trance, King's contacts have set out a history of mankind as, it would seem, something of a warning to the Earth to mend its ways. The history offered to King starts with a planet called Maldek, which was destroyed and now forms the asteroid belt. Mankind started there, destroyed it and was reincarnated on

Earth; it created the civilizations on Atlantis and Lemuria and destroyed both of them as well. The Cosmic Masters would like to stop the Earth people from repeating this yet again.

In practical terms there are a number of activities which are the essential work of the Society. One relates to the "Spiritual Push." The Cosmic Intelligences have placed in orbit around the Earth what is known as Satellite Number Three, which is under the command of a Master known as Mars Sector Six. Periodically the satellite is in a position where "colossal amounts of Spiritual Energy are beamed down to anyone on Earth who is ready to use it. Aetherius Society members use these special times to 'send out as much Spiritual Energy as possible through Prayer and Mantra.' The purpose of this energy is to potentize all selfless actions, no matter who is performing them, by a factor of 3,000 times." King visited the satellite during an "out of body" voyage and described "a huge room, housing a tremendous amount of beautifully designed apparatus. The whole place was filled with a soft, exquisite radiance, more beautiful than that found in any place on Earth."

Another well-known activity of the Aetherius Society is called "Operation Prayer Power." Instead of directly sending spiritual energy around the world the energy is generated by mantra and prayer but stored in "batteries," which can then be directed at specific places as and when needed. The Society claims some success with the use of its "batteries." These are examples, quoted from *Contact with the Gods from Space–Pathway to the New Millennium*:

> April 23rd, 1981. Three hundred and sixty-three Prayer Hours from an Aetherius Society Prayer Battery, and 1,046 Prayer Hours from a Battery of the Great White Brotherhood, were released to Poland. After this discharge, against all the predictions of political experts, the Soviet Union decided not to invade Poland... Poland was later to become the catalyst for the downfall of communism throughout eastern Europe.

January 6th–8th, 1993. Two separate discharges of over 550 Prayer Hours each were made following the oil spill of the *Braer* tanker in the Shetlands, Scotland. Despite dire warnings of eco-logical disaster, the final death toll reported in the press on June 16th, 1993, was only 1,542 birds, six otters and no whales. This was in contrast to the *Exxon Valdez* spill in Alaska during 1989 when 300,000 black guillemots alone died, and this spill was only half the amount of oil released by the *Braer* tanker. Some reports described the ecological recovery in the Shetlands as miraculous.

Other claimed successes relate to the Turkish-Greek war on Cyprus in 1974, limitation of earthquake casualties and tornado prevention. Lawrence summarizes: "The work of the Aetherius Society is to bring as much positive change to our world as pos-sible before the coming of the Next Master, so that when that does take place, as many people as possible are prepared to re-spond to it."

Romantic Interlude

But not all the contactees were concerned with mankind's future and the wider sense of a brotherhood among the stars. Elizabeth Klarer's contact, as told in her own book *Beyond the Light Barrier*, was of a much more personal nature.

On 27 December 1954 Klarer heard a commotion among the farmhands on her farm in the foothills of the Drakensberg mountains in South Africa. She saw a flash of light in the sky, ran to "her hill," where years before she had had a UFO sighting, and there saw a large saucer-shaped craft descending towards her. It hovered near her, and although afraid, she was determined not to run away. Through a porthole in the side she could see a hu-manoid looking out at her. The craft then took off again.

In April 1956 she felt compelled to go out to her "flying saucer hill" and, on arriving, found a landed flying saucer waiting for her. Standing outside the craft was a tall, good-looking man in a one-piece cream-coloured suit. He had clear grey eyes and white hair. He asked her if she was afraid this time, referring to her hesitance at the earlier encounter. She was not, and allowed herself to be taken aboard the craft. Inside, after it took off, she was treated to views of the Earth from aloft. The ship made rendezvous with its mother ship, where Klarer met many others like Akon, as she had discovered her acquaintance was called. On board she was shown pictures of his home world, Meton. The race was vegetarian, non-political, free of dispute and war, and free of illness. Elizabeth fell in love with Akon, became pregnant and spent the last four months of her pregnancy on Meton, where her child now lives with his father.

For those with an interest in the overlap of science fiction and UFO claimants, this story has remarkable similarities with the film *This Island Earth*, not least Klarer's drawing of Akon from Meton, so similar to the alien called Exeter from Metaluna in the film.

Image Problem

The contactees presented UFO research in the 1950s with a huge problem. The researchers were convinced that they faced a scientific problem. UFOs were returning on radar, they were being seen by thousands of reliable and authoritative witnesses, and they were being photographed. The Air Force and others government agencies were taking them seriously, even when they went to great pains to say they were not. As such, UFO researchers sought to attract serious scientific effort to apply itself to the problem. But the contactees were almost made for the media. The media couldn't get enough of the stories of flights to the planets, encounters with gorgeous alien women and nights whiled away with them. The language of the contactees was far removed from critical, searching scientific questioning; it was the language of certainty (they *knew* the saucers were real—they'd been on them after all), it was the language of religion, it was the language of the prophets of doom or deliverance. And the media lapped it up, made documentaries and included the sillier bits on news broadcasts. The subject was clearly fit for humour as it was being presented, and it was affecting people in strange ways. In October 1954 a man in Sinceny in France shot at his neighbour while he was fixing his car on the assumption (logical, apparently, to him) that he had caught a Martian trying to fix his flying saucer.

The public image of the flying saucer in the 1950s was the image of the contactees. Reasonably enough, scientists avoided the subject by a margin measured in light years. But even the UFO researchers had a problem they found hard to deal with: although they presented the subject as an analytical survey of objects in the skies, they too were receiving claims of entity sightings and contacts. These were not the bringers of religious and prophetic messages; the "other" reports were of astronaut-type beings plodding around outside landed saucers, collecting samples. They wore breathing apparatus, carried technology and beat a hasty retreat when spotted. Some of the cases are mentioned in Chapter 8. They seemed worthy of scientific study, but how could researchers ask the media to ignore the "crazy" claims of aliens from the contactees but listen to *their* alien stories instead? So UFO research censored itself: for years such claims were deemed "unacceptable," and although several researchers collected the reports they only discussed them privately. Eventually they released the information to the media, partly as an attempt to stem the contactee tide. But for a subject largely driven—in the public's perception at least—by the media, the image created by the contactees persisted, indeed has persisted to some degree to the present day. It would be the abduction phonomenon that would eventually "take over" as primary contact-claim material, but not until the 1980s in any major way.

Reconciliation of the Claims?

David Jacobs, whose work with abductees we shall examine

shortly, believes that at least some of the contactees were being "tested" by the aliens and should not have believed the literal truth of the images they were presented with. He believes the aliens test emotional responses to situations, and that perhaps the "atomic war" scenarios, for example, which the contactees were presented with, were just images to test reaction, and not to be taken as prophetic, or as messages to be handed down. In the light of recent abduction research this is one fascinating explanation for the contactees; that in effect they were the first abductees but just did not know it.

John Keel, in his 1971 book *Operation Trojan Horse*, alluded to something similar, though—as usual for Keel—he was years ahead of his thinking.

> A complex and frightening hoax is involved in all this. But it is not the product of run-of-the-mill practical jokers, liars and lunatics . . . No, the real truth lies in another direction. The contactees . . . have been telling us what they were told by the UFOnauts. The UFO-nauts are the liars, not the contactees. And they are lying deliberately as part of a bewildering smoke-screen which they have established to cover their real origin, purpose and motivation.

8

Early Sightings

The UFO field of study has become so familiar with the description of "Gray" aliens—large domed heads, huge wraparound dark eyes, reduced facial features, small stature and build—that it is sometimes forgotten just how diverse and strange the entities seen in the early days were. Something like the Grays was, even in those early days, being reported, though they seem of late to have become somewhat "more alien," and there is still some diversity even in the modern day. But we shall have to consider as we go through this book why there should have been such diversity, and then why such diversity should turn into conformity.

These claims were arising at the same time, and even before, the contactee claims, but they were also largely suppressed, even by UFO researchers of the time. The contactee claims had become for many a convenient peg on which to hang their ridicule of the UFO subject, and for many years serious researchers, while prepared to discuss objects seen, returns on radar, and so on, were not prepared to face the ridicule of reporting aliens. In fact the qualities of these "non-contactee" alien reports was quite different, not at all the "religious" experiences that the contactees were reporting, but it is probably true that the media would not have appreciated the difference.

Many of the following cases are from South America which, at least in the early days, had the greatest diversity of reports.

· On 23 July 1947, José Higgins and several workers watched a large, Saturn-shaped flying saucer land at Bauru in Brazil. The others ran away, leaving Higgins to confront three seven-foot-tall entities wearing transparent suits. The entities seemed to be wearing coloured clothing under the suits. They had large round bald heads and large eyes; Higgins described them as "beautiful." What was to follow was even more strange. He hid in some bushes and watched the three engage in "play activities"—leaping about and throwing large stones around. Then they boarded the saucer and flew off.

· On 18 March 1950, an Argentine rancher, Wilfredo Arevalo, watched the landing of a flying saucer, and saw another hovering overhead. He approached the landed craft, and saw that in a transparent glass cabin there were four tall entities which he described as dressed in something like Cellophane.

· In August 1953, at Cuidad, Mexico, Salvador Villanueya was working underneath his broken-down taxicab, trying to effect repairs, when he saw two pairs of legs near him. He got out from under the vehicle to see two figures in front of him, each around 4½ feet tall. They were dressed in one-piece clothing, with wide perforated belts, metal collars and shiny black boxes on their backs. They carried helmets under their arms. They talked for some time—one of the strangers could speak Spanish—and eventually Villanueya offered them shelter in his car when it started to rain. During the course of their continuing conversation one said to Villanueya: "We are not of this planet. We come from one far distant, but we know much about your world." In the morning they offered evidence when they took him to see their 40-foot-wide saucer parked in a clearing a few hundred yards off the road. He noticed that as they walked "mud sprang away [from their boots] as if repelled by some invisible force." They boarded the craft, Villanueya declined an offer to join them, and it took off.

- Late at night on 4 November 1954, José Alves, at Pontal, in Brazil, was out fishing. In his book *The Great Flying Saucer Hoax*, Coral Lorenzen tells how Alves watched as a flying saucer landed "so near to him that he could have touched it." Scared, he watched as three figures in white clothing and skull caps got out. They ignored him, and spent their time collecting samples of vegetation and river water. Then they reboarded and the craft took off. Not being familiar with the claims of flying saucers, Alves assumed he had seen "devils."

- In the early morning of 28 November 1954, Gustavo Gonzalez and José Ponce, driving through Caracas, in Venezuela, saw a glowing globe hovering over the road. It was the start of a strange encounter by any standards. Gonzalez ended up fighting with a powerful creature described as hairy, dwarf-like, with glowing eyes and wearing a loin-cloth. At one point Gonzalez struck the creature with a knife, but it bounced off as if hitting steel. Another creature from inside the globe fired a beam of light at Gonzalez which temporarily blinded him. Ponce watched two more of the creatures emerge from bushes carrying soil and rocks which they loaded into the sphere.

- In December 1954, in Venezuela, two young men, Lorenzo Flores and Jesus Gomez, watched a flying saucer land and four small figures emerge. They were strong, and had "abundant" hair all over their bodies. They tried to pull the youths into the saucer. During the fight Flores hit one with an unloaded shotgun; Flores stated that it was "like striking rock" and the gun broke in two. When examined later by police and doctors, the boys were bruised and hysterical and their clothing was torn.

- Early one evening in October 1958, Señor Angelu, motorcycling near Figueras, in Spain, saw what he thought was an object crash into some woods. When he went to assist he saw a landed flying saucer there. Angelu watched two dwarf-like entities with large heads collecting samples while a third similar figure remained in the saucer. After about 15 minutes the craft carrying the three took off.

· In November 1958, at Braemar, in Scotland, two soldiers from a Territorial Army unit on a weekend exercise had a frightening experience. During the early hours of the morning, while they were on guard duty at a small hilltop, they heard a "gurgling" sound from behind some trees a few hundred yards away. As they approached the trees to investigate, two seven-foot-tall creatures came towards them. The gurgling, they considered, might have been their "talking" to each other. The two soldiers ran away, and shortly afterwards saw a silver disc chasing them along the road, just a foot or so above the surface. It took off over their heads, leaving the two in a state of shock.

· On 28 August 1963, three boys, aged about 12, were playing in their garden in Belo Horizonte, in Brazil. They watched as a UFO floated down towards them, a large transparent, glowing ball. Inside they could see four figures, one of which they thought was female. The figures were around seven feet tall, and wearing what the children described as "divers' suits." They had round, bald heads inside transparent helmets. Their skin was red, and they had one large eye, but no nose or mouth. One of the figures descended into the garden, apparently travelling on beams of light, and, when one child tried to throw a brick at it, paralysed the boy's arm with a beam from its chest. The other boys were unharmed, and watched the sphere float back into the sky, taking the entities with it.

The 1954 Wave of Sightings

In 1954 there was a huge wave of sightings across Europe, arguably one of the busiest periods in the 50 years of UFO sightings. Many of the reports involved entities, though this was, as stated previously, largely suppressed from the public at the time because of the climate of ridicule towards entity reports created by the claims of the contactees. A subsequent analysis has shown that there were literally hundreds of reports of landings, as well as thousands of sightings in the skies, and of these a great many included entity reports. Here are some typical examples:

· On 23 August 1954, near Thonon, in France, a witness saw an object looking like an "aluminium trailer," beside which were two small figures in silver dress, grunting like pigs.

· On 1 October 1954, two witnesses near Jussey, in France, saw a disc approach the ground and two figures emerge, described as very tall and dressed in white.

· On 5 October 1954 at Loctudy, in France, a man taking water from a well in the middle of the night saw an object some ten feet away, from which a figure emerged. The figure was dwarf-sized, with an oval face covered in hair, and eyes "as large as the eggs of a raven." The visitor touched the witness and spoke to him in a language he could not understand. When the young man called for assistance the figure got back into the craft and flew away.

· On 9 October 1954, four children at Pournoy-La-Chétive, in France, were playing when they saw a light near the cemetery. When they investigated it they found a round object standing on three legs, from which a figure emerged. The figure was holding a torch in his hand which temporarily "blinded" the witnesses. He was approximately four feet tall, had large eyes and a hairy face and was dressed in something like a black sack, rather like a cassock. The children ran away when the figure spoke to them in a language they could not understand.

- On 9 October 1954, at Münster, in Germany, a witness saw four figures near an object giving off a cigar-shaped light. The beings, who seemed to be working underneath the object, were wearing rubber overalls. They were approximately four feet high, with a large chest, large head and small thin legs.

- On 12 October 1954, a witness in Monluçon, in France, saw a cigar-shaped craft on the ground. Nearby he could see a figure, covered in hair, emitting sounds that he could not interpret or understand. (On the same day in the Mamora Forest, in Morocco, a witness saw a small figure approximately four feet high wearing a silver suit board an object which took off. And at Tehran, in Iran, a witness saw an unusual craft driven by a small figure dressed in black.)

- On 13 October 1954, several witnesses at Bourrasole, near Toulouse, in France, saw a small figure standing near a 12-foot-wide reddish disc. The figure was described as around four feet in height and wearing what looked like a diving suit. The witness stated: "His head was large in relation to the rest of the body, and he had two enormous eyes. The suit was bright and shiny like glass."

- On 13 October 1954, at Castelibranco, in Portugal, two witnesses saw two figures in shiny clothing who seemed to be gathering fauna samples. They boarded a nearby craft which then took off.

- On 14 October 1954, at Lewarde, in France, a witness saw an alien described as short and bulky with large slanted eyes and a fur-covered body.

- On 15 October 1954, at Perpignan, in France, an elderly man saw a luminous red sphere land approximately 30 yards away. The witness watched a figure, which seemed to be wearing something like a diving suit, walking around the craft, which it then boarded. The object afterwards flew away silently.

- On 18 October 1954, several witnesses at Royan, in France, saw two orange and red discs in the sky linked by a luminous "bridge." The two objects landed, a little figure emerged from each, crossed to the other craft and boarded it, after which both machines took off.

- On 18 October 1954, many witnesses at different locations watched the passage of a cigar-shaped light near Fontenay-Torcy, in France. One man and his wife watched as the light dived towards them and landed near the road. The witnesses approached the site of the landing and were confronted by a bulky human-looking figure approximately 3–3½ feet high. The figure wore a helmet through which the witnesses could see his eyes glowing orange.

- On 20 October 1954, near Como, in Italy, a witness saw a strange figure approximately 4½ feet tall dressed in a luminous suit. The witness described the lower half of the figure as being encased in a funnel. The alien fired a beam at the witness, paralysing him momentarily. On recovering the ability to move, the witness attacked the figure, which then "rose from the ground and fled."

- On 24 October 1954, at Sainte-Catherine, Rhône, France, a young child watched a man emerge from a stationary craft. He was described as dressed in red with clothes like iron. He had large eyes, a hairy face and long hair. As he walked his legs remained stiff.

- On 1 November 1954, a witness reported a dome-shaped object near Arezzo, in Italy. Nearby were two dwarf figures with human faces and small teeth, speaking in an unknown language.

- On 5 November 1954, several witnesses saw a craft giving off an orange light, parked in a field near La Roche-en-Brenil, in France. Near it were three men in dark overalls, one holding a box "which emitted a beam of light three metres long."

- On 14 November 1954, at Isola, in northern Italy, a farmer, described as reliable and sober, saw three dwarf-like creatures wearing metallic suits emerge from a cigar-shaped object that had landed near him. They were paying an undue interest in his caged rabbits, so the farmer got his rifle and aimed at the entities. The rifle wouldn't fire, it seemed to become so heavy that he was forced to drop it, and he himself felt paralysed. The visitors took the rabbits and flew off.

The above list shows some of the diversity of reported alien entities in the early years of the UFO phenomenon. In addition there were many reports of beings of human size and appearance, and all manner of descriptions of their craft. Many reports were associated, rightly or wrongly with the UFO wave, even though no objects were seen.

The collection also shows that there are a number of similarities in the claims—too many similarities, in fact, by different witnesses in different locations, who could not have picked up the minutiae of detail from other claims, sometimes only days apart. These similarities indicate there must have been something genuine happening. That said, however, the diversity of detail is such that either one race or source of aliens has a very great diversity of forms or, alternatively, the Earth was being visited by a huge number of different species. Neither of these suggestions seems likely, at least on the basis of relatively random visits by alien astronauts. Two cases, set out below in detail, one from Kelly-Hopkinsville, in America, and another from Finland, both have sufficient numbers of witnesses or witness after-effects to demonstrate something real happening, and yet the two are so different in character that they hardly seem to be coming from the same source. It is worth comparing and contrasting these to understand the enormous diversity. The Kelly-Hopkinsville case is also set out with details of other cases that arose around the same time.

The Kelly-Hopkinsville "Monkeys"

On the night of 21–22 August 1955, eleven people were besieged in a farmhouse by entities with extraordinary characteristics. At Kelly, a settlement near Hopkinsville in Kentucky, the Sutton farm was that night occupied by Elmer ("Lucky") and Vera Sutton, members of their family and friends. At around seven o'clock in the evening one of the friends, Billy Ray Taylor, saw a UFO in the sky, "real bright, with an exhaust all the colours of the rainbow," lowering itself towards a dried-up river bed near the farm. The other occupants of the farm did not believe his story, and no further investigation of the sighting was carried out.

But around an hour later Lucky and Billy Ray, concerned about the wild yapping their dog was putting up, went into the yard to investigate. Across the fields they could see a distant, strange glow which was growing larger as it came towards them. Gradually they made out the shape of a small creature walking towards them. As it got closer they could see that it was around one metre tall, and glowed as if with an inner, silvery light. It had huge yellow glowing eyes towards the side of the face, a bald head, a wide mouth stretching from ear to ear and massive pendulous ears. The long arms, extended up over the head, ended in claws. The creature appeared to be without clothes, but there was no indication of gender. The two men—obviously alarmed at the sight of the creature and now "sheltering" in their own doorway—opened fire with a shotgun and .22 rifle. The sound of the impact was like shooting into a metal bucket, and the creature somersaulted backwards and disappeared into the darkness, scampering as if on all fours.

The families then heard something on the roof and ran out to investigate, to find the same or a similar creature clambering about up there, and another in a nearby tree. Lucky shot at the one on the roof, knocking it over the roof; then they both fired at the one in the tree, following which it floated gently to the ground and then ran off. They noticed that when the creatures were shot at, or shouted at, their glow increased, suggesting a strange relationship between sound and light.

The family locked itself in and waited for the nightmare to end. By eleven o'clock, three hours into the experience, the frustration and probably fear became too much for them. They all ran from the farmhouse to two cars and drove to the police station ten miles away. They returned with the Hopkinsville Chief of Police, Russell Greenwell, his deputy George Batts, four other officers and the photographer from a local news-paper. Examination of the farm found no UFO in the river bed, no bodies and no entities, though the bullet holes and damage the shooting had caused were evident for all to see. Greenwell stated: "Something frightened these people, something be-yond their comprehension." He related an incident which showed the degree of tension that was present during the search. A cat's tail was trodden on accidentally, and the cat shrieked. "You never saw so many pistols unholstered so fast in your life," said the sheriff.

Unable to do anything further, the police left, promising to re-turn in the morning. But in the early, and still dark, hours of the morning Lucky's mother, Glennie Lankford, spotted one of the entities looking in through her bedroom window. Lucky ran in, ignored his mother's suggestion of peaceful contact, and shot at the creature. For the rest of that night the family watched the creatures moving around outside the farmhouse.

A neighbour, who had seen the lights on at the farm during the night and thought that the families were rounding up ani-mals, stated when he heard the story: "I am glad I didn't go out there—I might have been shot."

The following day, the local publicity resulted in a fiasco by any definition. The hordes of people that besieged the farmhouse must have seemed as frightening as the little glowing men. Researcher Isabel Davis reported:

> As the news spread, the crowds grew thicker. Their cars jammed the Old Madisonville Road. They stared and pointed. They stopped their cars, got out, walked around the house, opened the doors and walked in, asked questions, told the family to pose for pictures, laughed and made jokes. The little men had been terrifying, but at least they had stayed outside ... The human horde grew every minute, swarming more and more as the day wore on ...

The family suffered greatly from the notoriety that the report gave them locally. They were accused of religious hysteria. Lucky's brother, John, lost several jobs because of his association with the experience.

Had the family modified or retracted their claims, they would possibly have suffered less ridicule in the long run. But they refused to do so and insisted on their truth throughout. To our knowledge none of them has retracted their story in the 40-odd years since. Perhaps the most impressive in her testimony was Mrs. Glennie Lankford. She was interviewed by researcher Isabel Davis some ten months after the incident; Ms. Davis noted that Glennie Lankford "made a deep impression on me. I understood what Chief Greenwell meant when he said, 'She was the most impressive witness. She's the type of person who wouldn't tell a lie if her life depended on it.'"

No sensible explanation of the experience has ever been offered. The suggestion that it was a bunch of escaped monkeys (!) offered by Hynek—presumably in desperation—falls down on the grounds that monkeys do not glow or float in the air, are not impervious to bullets, and no monkeys had been reported missing! Whether the UFO seen earlier had anything to do with the experience is uncertain; there was no definite connection between the two events. Without the UFO, the story has more in common with trolls and demons than the perceived high-tech of flying saucers. The entities displayed little intelligence, and seemed to be acting on reflex and instinct. Their milling around indicates curiosity without purpose, and their responses seem to have been self-protective rather than purposeful.

Associated Cases

The 1955 Kelly-Hopkinsville entity case was not the only such case in the United States, though the others were not well publicized at the time. These two following cases occurred around the same time.

In July 1955 a case arose that is generally known as the Loveland Bridge Case. The first witness, known as C. F. aged 19, was serving as an auxiliary policeman with the Civil Defence. He was driving a Civil Defence vehicle across a bridge in the Loveland area when he saw four small figures standing beneath the bridge, on the bank of the river. He noticed a foul smell in the air. He described them as "four more or less human looking little men about three feet high" that had been "moving about oddly." At around the same time, at Loveland Heights, a Mrs. Emily Magnone and her husband were woken up in the night by the frenzied barking of their dog outside. When they went to the window to check, they could see nothing but smelt an extremely pungent odour described as "like a swamp." When Mrs. Magnone spoke to her next-door neighbour she discovered that she had also been woken up by the Magnones' dog, but when she had gone to the back porch she had seen a "little man" of strange appearance. She turned away to put on the porch light but when she turned back the "little man" had vanished. Curiously, every time she turned the light on the figure disappeared; every time she turned the light off (and she did so several times) the little man reappeared in the same place. Mrs. Magnone's neighbour described the figure as approximately three feet high and covered in foliage. During neither of the sightings at Loveland were any UFOs seen, but coming as they did among a minor wave of sightings, the reported figures were associated with the UFO phenomenon.

After a sighting at nearby Branch Hill, two months earlier, in May 1955, Robert Hunnicutt ran to the police, and banged on the door of Chief John Fritz at around four in the morning. Hunnicutt had been driving near Branch Hill on the Madeira-Loveland Pike and had seen several strange figures by the side of the road. He noticed what seemed to be "fire coming out of their hands" and a terrible smell around the area. One of the figures was holding a rod above his head from which blue-and-white sparks were seen jumping. Hunnicutt described them as fairly ugly, with a large straight mouth splitting the lower part of their face and reminding him of a frog. The eyes were normal, the head bald but "corrugated." The chest, the witness reported, was lopsided, with a large bulge on the right side, and the arms were, he thought, of uneven length, perhaps as a result of the asymmetrical chest. The figures looked grey, with their skin or possibly tight-fitting clothing the same colour as the face. After a few minutes Hunnicutt left the scene to seek further witnesses, but was aware of the frightening potential of what he had encountered. Fritz knew Hunnicutt and commented that he was "scared to death . . . The man had seen something, and there is no argument to that." Hunnicutt did not report seeing a UFO, but there had been earlier sightings the same night.

Imjarvi—One of the Few "Little Green Men"

In Finland a case of some significance arose in 1970. On 7 January, two skiers, Aarno Heinonen and Esko Viljo, had stopped in a small clearing to rest. After a short time they heard a buzzing and saw a light in the sky moving towards them. At tree-top height they saw it as a red-grey mist which seemed to contain a solid, saucer-shaped object, metallic and around nine feet wide.

The description of the object seemed reminiscent of the Adamski saucers; the entities within, however, were not the angelic types described by Adamski. A beam of light extended from the base of the craft to the ground. As Heinonen stated,

> I was standing completely still. Suddenly I felt as if somebody has seized my waist from behind and pulled me backwards. I think I took a step backwards, and in the same second I caught sight of the creature. It was standing in the middle of the light beam with a black box in its hands. Out of around the opening in the box there came a yellow light, pulsating. The creature was about 90 centimetres tall, with very thin arms and legs. Its face was pale like wax. *I didn't notice the eyes* [our emphasis] but the nose was very strange. It was a hook rather than a nose. The ears were very small and narrow towards the head. The creature wore some kind of overall in a light green material. On its feet were boots of a darker green colour, which stretched above the knee. There were also white gauntlets going up to the elbows, and the fingers were bent like claws around the black box.

Viljo added that the creature was "luminous like phosphorous," and described it wearing a conical helmet. Heinonen was hit by a light from the box the creature was holding. The craft then appeared to send the mist down to cover the creature and the light beam was drawn up into the craft, apparently taking the entity with it. Then the craft itself was gone. (It is interesting that Heinonen states that he did not notice the entity's eyes. In Chapter 10, in the motifs of abduction, we make the point that the eyes of the entities are probably the most prominently remembered feature of the Grays.)

Heinonen found himself paralysed on his right side, and Viljo had virtually to carry him three kilometres home. "I felt ill," reported Heinonen. "My back was aching and all my joints were painful. My head ached and after a while I had to vomit. When I went to pee the urine was nearly black, it was like pouring black coffee on to the snow. This continued for a couple of months."

The pair were examined at a local clinic; the doctor believed that the men's aching joints and headache would disappear within ten days. But Heinonen suffered from them for over five months, also experiencing balance and short-term memory problems. Viljo also suffered, among other symptoms, from absent-mindedness. Their doctor confirmed: "Both men seem sincere, I don't think they had made the thing up. I am sure they were in a state of shock when they came to me; something must have frightened them."

By August 1972 Heinonen had claimed 23 other UFO contacts, including meetings with "Adamski-type" entities (see Chapter 7) and a beautiful space woman. For many this diminished if not destroyed the value of the earlier report. Whether Heinonen was caught up in something more complex, or whether he fantasized following this first encounter may never be clear.

What can we make of this diversity? The answer in fact is an oblique one, because the problem of analysis of so-called visiting aliens is not that they remained diverse but that *they did not*. If diversity was "the name of the game" we would have to learn to accept that, but in fact in the years since the 1970s, and especially in the 1980s and 1990s, UFO researchers have broadly identified one common type of alien, the Gray, which now arises in the majority of all cases, particularly in those of claimed abductions, and most particularly those abductions investigated by the use of regression hypnosis.

Why then should the diversity which was so apparent in the early years have given way to a commonality? Either something has changed in respect of the visiting aliens, or there is some human interpretation or overlay which is affecting our appreciation of the reports. One possibility is that investigator-contamination is "standardizing" the reports. Some investigators are actually rejecting as non-valid claims which do not involve "Grays" because they believe this to be the "true" shape of the alien-form; indeed some rejected as hoaxes the reports from Russia of "giant" entities on this basis. Other investigators appear to be carrying details of one case to another investigation and, using a "standard" as a benchmark, may even be suggesting detail to witnesses.

In Chapters 10 and 11 the effect of these contemporary claims of alien visits, and the detail derived from their investigation, is set out.

9

MIBs—Alien Agents?

The Men in Black, or MIBs, are a branch of the UFO subject that it is difficult to categorize. Are they government agents suppressing belief in UFOs? Are they pranksters? For the purposes of this book we are forced to consider them because of the belief by many witnesses and investigators alike that they are themselves alien. There is fascinating evidence towards this end, or towards the alien-ness of the mystery they represent.

In *Operation Trojan Horse* American UFO writer and journalist John Keel describes a fairly "classical" MIB encounter. Two women, in November 1966, had seen a UFO near Owatonna, Minnesota, and apparently entered into some sort of telepathic communication with it. In May 1967 a man calling himself Major Richard French visited one of the women, Mrs. Butler, expressing his interest in UFOs. She described him as five feet nine inches tall, with a pointed face and olive complexion. He had long dark hair—"too long for an Air Force officer," she stated. He seemed well educated and spoke "perfect English." He was well dressed in a grey suit, white shirt and black tie, but Mrs. Butler noted that "everything he was wearing was *brand-new*." He drove a white Mustang—it is rare to find white cars in MIB cases, but it is not unheard of.

The following day the "strangeness" of the experience became apparent. On his first visit French had mentioned that he had a stomach-ache, and Mrs. Butler had advised Jello as a cure. On his visit the following day he still had the pain, so Mrs. Butler gave him a bowl of Jello. But he seemed not to know what to do with it. "Did you ever hear of anyone trying to drink Jello?" Mrs. Butler asked. "Well, that's what he did. He acted like he had never seen any before . . . I had to show him how to eat it with a spoon." Keel comments that the pattern is very common, particularly the lack of familarity with everyday objects and the newness of clothing and so on. "Even the soles of their shoes appear to be unwalked on," he comments.

John Keel published in *Saucer Scoop* an "Open Letter to all UFO Researchers," which effectively set out his personal mission to track down the MIBs. He called the MIBs professional terrorists whose job it was to harass UFO researchers who got too close to the truth. He believes that some witnesses have been kidnapped and brainwashed, even physically abused.

"We have checked a number of these cases and these men are not connected with the Air Force in any way," stated Colonel George Freeman of Project Blue Book. When Keel confronted the Air Force he was told: "We would like to catch one. Unfortunately, the trail is always too cold by the time we hear about these cases."

The United States Air Force disassociated itself from MIBs with a document issued on 1 March 1967, signed by Lt. General Hewitt T. Wheless, the Assistant Vice Chief of Staff, which states:

> Information, not verifiable, has reached HQ USAF that persons claiming to represent the Air Force or other Defense establishments have contacted citizens who have sighted unidentified flying objects. In one reported case an individual in civilian clothes, who represented himself as a member of NORAD, demanded and received photographs belonging to a private citizen. In another, a person in an Air Force uniform approached local police and other citizens who had sighted a UFO, assembled them in a school room and told them that they did not see what they thought they saw and that they should not talk to anyone about the sighting. All military and civilian personnel and particularly Information Officers and UFO Investigating Officers who hear of such reports should immediately notify their local OSI offices.

Not the least of the mysteries is that the MIBs sometimes appear ahead of the UFO experiences of the witnesses. One such case is hinted at with the encounter of Connie Carpenter, related in Keel's *Strange Creatures from Time and Space*. Like many cases it also promised fearful things, though they came to nothing.

On 22 February 1967 she was walking down the street when a large black 1949 Buick which looked brand new pulled up alongside her. She was called over by the occupant of the car, who was a young man, clean-cut, wearing a colourful shirt. As she got near the car the driver lunged at her and tried to pull her in. She struggled, and got away, running back to her house. The following day a note was pushed under her door that said, "Be careful girl. I can get you yet." The Carpenters reported the incident to the police, but nothing of the car or the man was ever seen again. They shortly afterwards moved in with Connie's mother, who had previously had a UFO sighting. Whether the two are connected or not is impossible to determine, although Keel certainly implies a connection.

If the attacker was a "normal person" trying to abduct Mrs. Carpenter–all too possible, of course–then it was a fairly reckless decision to use so striking a car, tracing of which would probably not have been all that difficult for the police. This–and the extraordinary newness of the car–make the case a fascinating one in the MIB histories.

Early Accounts

Nor are the MIBs a product only of the modern era of flying saucers which starts "officially" with the Arnold sighting of 1947.

When John Cole joined a party of men in the 1920s to investigate a possible "airplane crash" in West Virginia, he must have realized that something was already strange. The farmer who had seen the object come down reported that it "didn't seem to have any wings, didn't make any noise, and seemed unusually large." One description of it was "as big as a battleship." (Cole later found, on seeing it close up, that it was about 75 feet across, with windows but with no wings, tail or propellers.) They found the wreck in a clearing but were astonished to see other people had already reached the crash site.

> Some of them were dressed in business suits, neckties and all, and that seemed damned silly in that neck of the woods. Others were dressed in coveralls of a funny color—some kind of very shiny material. They were talking about themselves in a rapid-fire foreign language when we found them. They got real excited when they saw us. The men in coveralls ran into the wreck—like they were trying to hide... the strangers were small, just a little over five feet tall, and they all looked like Orientals... high cheekbones, slant eyes, dark skin.

Cole also reported that while he was there he picked up a small object that he found lying on the ground, and put it in his pocket, then he and his companions left. At around three o'clock that morning someone pounded on his door at home; when Cole opened it he was confronted by a US Army uniform worn by one of "those foreigners" from the aircraft. He was told that he had picked up something and they wanted it back. When Cole showed it to him it was snatched out of his hand and taken away without a further word. No explanation was offered as to how he had been traced, or how they knew he had taken anything. A few days later Cole visited the crash site again; there was no trace of the object there—only the flattened trees and bushes to mark the incident.

These next few cases demonstrate further "typical" encounters with MIBs:

- In April 1967 C. N. Crowder spotted a UFO which left trace evidence. Driving home late in the evening he saw an object on the road—grey and featureless, 15 or 16 feet high and about 12 feet wide. As his light hit it the object suddenly flew up in the air, leaving the road on fire. Other witnesses were traced who had seen the illumination at the time. Crowder notified the police, who returned to the scene with him. They found marks on the road, and possible indentations where the object's feet had rested. The following day Crowder received a visit from the military. A Cadillac arrived at his house containing an Air Force lieutenant-colonel, a sergeant *and the colonel's wife* (!) and Crowder was questioned by the men about his sighting. The Air Force later denied that they had sent anyone to talk to Crowder.

· Two men warned off UFO witness Deputy Robert Goode. Just before midnight Goode was driving south of Houston, Texas, with Sheriff William McCoy. Goode had a sore and swollen finger which had been injured by his son's pet alligator. While driving they saw a purple glowing UFO around 50 feet above the ground. Goode felt heat on his hand— including the injured finger—as the object passed over. The two "high-tailed" it out of the area, watching behind them as the object took off higher into the air. When Goode checked his finger later that night he found that it was virtually healed—one of many possible claimants to spontaneous healings that are associated with the near approach of UFOs. Shortly afterwards two strangers sought out Goode at the sheriff's office, found him in a local restaurant and then discussed the UFO sighting with him. They described what he had seen even before he told them of it. He was warned that if he saw anything similar in future he should co-operate with the occupants and keep the details of any interaction with them to himself. The two men were not identified.

· Howard Menger, a contactee, claimed an MIB encounter. He stated: "When I was living in High Bridge, New Jersey, in 1957, two men in dark business suits came to call on me. They flashed authentic-looking credentials and claimed to be agents from a government bureau. They looked like ordinary people. One wore glasses. They wanted me to quit talking about flying saucers and to drop my research ... they claimed to have considerable power. Whether this was power of influence or of strange powers beyond those of ordinary people, I don't know."

· These cases are not restricted to America. Men in Black of a typically British kind were associated with the Templeton photographic case of 26 May 1964. Fireman James Templeton took photographs of his daughter and found, on developing the pictures, that behind her was a human-like person wearing a helmet. Neither Templeton, nor anyone else, remembered seeing anyone around at the time. Curiously, the figure looks rather as if it is wearing a radiation suit, and the location was near an atomic energy facility. Two gentlemen in bowler hats visited the Templetons a few days later, questioning James Templeton. They did not refer to each other by names but by numbers (Keel points out: "Any self-respecting secret agents could invent phoney cover names ..."). They were never identified. Presumably the bowler hats are the equivalent of the MIB "uniform" in America—a badge of officialdom.

Flying Saucers and the Three Men

We can trace the origins of the MIBs—as associated with UFOs—back to the claims of Albert K. Bender in 1952. His story, which is well known, is summarized here to emphasize one or two aspects that are particularly fascinating in the light of modern-day abductions, as recounted in Chapter 10.

Bender created the small, civilian group known as the International Flying Saucer Bureau. Believing himself to have worked out a theory to account for UFOs, he wrote to another researcher. Shortly afterwards Bender was visited by three men wearing black suits and hats, one of them apparently carrying the very letter which Bender had sent to his correspondent. Bender describes the encounter in his book *Flying Saucers and The Three Men*. Lying down in his bedroom, Bender became aware of three shadowy figures.

> All of them were dressed in black clothes, they looked like clergymen, but wore hats similar to Homburg style. The faces were not discernible, for the hats partly hid and shaded them . . . The eyes of all three figures suddenly lit up like flash bulbs, and all these were focused upon me. They seemed to burn into my very soul as the pains above my eyes became almost unbearble. It was then I sensed that they were conveying a message to me by telepathy.

Bender was threatened, and told not to discuss his theory any further. "If I hear another word from your office, you are in trouble," one told him. Shortly afterwards Bender telephoned a friend and mentioned his visit and the discussion. As soon as he hung up, the telephone rang and a voice told Bender that he had made a "bad slip" and warned him not to make another one. From that point on Bender withdrew from discussing his UFO theory and disbanded his organization.

Researcher Dominick Lucchesi kept in close contact with Bender, believing that the MIBs had effectively silenced him: "It was as if he had been lobotomized. He was scared and he later suffered from tremendous headaches which he said were controlled by 'them'! Whenever he would think of breaking his silence, one of these terrific headaches would just about knock him out." Researchers August Roberts further commented "The three men in black shut him up and he's stayed shut up." (Lucchesi has an interesting perspective on the MIBs and their relationship to UFOs. "In my opinion the men in black are representatives of an organization on this planet, but they are not from any known bureau in our government. I believe both these men and the UFOs come from some civilization which has flourished in a remote area of Earth, such as the Amazon, the North

Gobi Desert, or the Himalaya Mountains. It is possible that these are underground civilizations." Lucchesi is not alone in connecting the MIBs and the UFOs, even though more "conventional wisdom" suggests they are both extraterrestrial in nature.)

Some of the motifs that arise frequently in this book are to be found here in this early account by Bender. One of the compelling facets of his encounter with the three men was their eyes—"The eyes of all three figures suddenly lit up like flash bulbs, and all these were focused upon me"—and we will see how important the eyes of the "Grays" appear to be to abductees. Furthermore the MIBs perhaps controlled Bender through headaches; modern abductees often describe the eyes of the "Grays" as having a controlling or other powerful effect.

But the image of the MIBs in UFO-lore was born. Gray Barker, in *They Knew Too Much About Flying Saucers*, comments: "I have a feeling that some day there will come a slow knocking at my door. They will be at your door, too, unless we all get wise and find out who the three men really are."

In the Bender case we see many commonly reported characteristics: dark clothes, a non-human quality, oppression. But we also see another common aspect of such cases: incompetence. Or at least apparently so. By visiting Bender and putting pressure on him to stop talking about his theory they turned what was proposed to be an article in his flying saucer club's magazine *Space Review* into a full-length book with themselves in the title! John Keel refers to this as the "press-agent game" (see below).

Something rather similar resulted from MIB intervention in the case of Robert Richardson. While driving late at night, Richardson saw a light in the road ahead of him, braked, but believed he hit an object. He and his companion, Gerry Quay, searched around the location but could find nothing. However, later Richardson revisited the site and found a piece of metal. Richardson contacted Jim and Coral Lorenzen of APRO by telegram, telling them he had struck a UFO, and in a later telephone conversation told them he had a piece of metal which he believed was from it. The Lorenzens gave Richardson the name and address of their local investigator. As the Lorenzens observed, "One of the most interesting aspects of this case was the series of visitors received by Mr. Richardson in the days following the incident." The first of these visits took place the day after the Lorenzens had received the telegram. Two young men arrived at Richardson's home and talked to him about the incident. They did not identify themselves. Richardson noticed, as they left, that they were driving a 1953 Cadillac with, as it turned out, a licence plate number that had not yet been issued. A week later two other men in black suits—in Richardson's description, "foreigners"— arrived at his home. They tried to convince Richardson he had not hit anything on the road—and then demanded he hand over the physical material he had retrieved! When Richardson told them the metal had been sent to APRO, one of the men told him: "If you want your wife to stay as pretty as she is, then you had better get the metal back." As the Lorenzens point out: "In view of the fact that the piece of metal was discussed only on the telephone between Mrs. Lorenzen and Mr. Richardson, and later in private between Richardson and Paquette (APRO's local investigator), those concerned are wondering how the information got out . . . it would seem that the telephone call from Mrs. Lorenzen to Richardson was somehow monitored." (We know now that APRO was under CIA investigation, which probably explains the telephone "tap," and even perhaps this particular set of MIBs.)

If an agency had wanted to draw attention to an otherwise minor incident, then ensure it a place in the UFO literature, they could hardly have done better than send these MIBs to Richardson.

The Press-Agent Game

John Keel refers to a "branch" of the MIB story as "the press-agent game" in his 1971 book *Operation Trojan Horse*. "Small, dark-skinned, dark-eyed gentlemen appear in an area immediately before or immediately after a flying saucer flap." Keel goes on to put the attention-drawing phenomenon into a historical perspective: "Striking examples of the press-agent game can be found in the religious and occult lore, going back thousands of years," he states. He refers to three dark-skinned men with Oriental features who appeared in Herod's court weeks before the birth of Christ. They "predicted" the birth of Christ and, in doing so, as Keel points out, "made certain that the impending birth would be recorded in the court records and preserved for the ages." Keel seems to doubt that the men were mortal:

> If these men had come from India or even farther away, it would have taken them many months or even years to travel by sea and land to Jerusalem. This would have taken considerable planning and expense and would have demanded that they have advance knowledge of the event. If they had been mortal men, they would almost certainly have created a similar stir when they arrived home . . . there seems to be no such record.

In short, far from seeking to suppress accounts of extraordinary events, these MIBs seem to run about doing their best to ensure them maximum publicity. Rather like pop stars who make sure the press get invited to their "secret and private" weddings and other functions, the MIBs act as if they are a PR agency. In *The Cosmic Question* Keel describes the early-twentieth-century manifestations of the MIBs.

> The Illuminati, the International Bankers, the Freemasons, the Jesuits, and the CIA have all been blamed for the antics of the MIB during different periods in history. In the eighteenth and nineteenth centuries secret societies were popular, not so much to join as to blame. By the turn of the century a new mythical group seized the public imagination—the sinister International Bankers— a loathsome cartel of munitions makers, money manipulators, and archfiends. Like the Illuminati and other phantom orders before them, they were accused of running the world from behind

the scenes. The mischievous men in black suits were tagged as agents for the International Bankers in the 1920s, 30s and 40s.

With regard to the folklore or legendary qualities of Men in Black, it is worth remembering that the imagery is one that comes from many periods of history. Consider the image of Dracula-like vampires from Central Europe; always dark figures swathed in black and moving around in the night. For the black sabbath rite a sixteenth-century manuscript indicates that the designated high priest should wear a simple black cloak with a black magic pentagram on the back, and indeed the prayers to Satan are read from a black book; the black imagery is very strong. However, there is much about UFO-related Men in Black which indicates a modern and fairly discrete set of facts.

The image of "black" is itself a strong one which has permeated our thinking. The Hollywood cowboys of the early films were easy to understand; the good guys wore white hats and the bad guys wore black. We speak of "blackmail," "blackening someone's name," "blacklegs" and so on, all detrimental terms.

Of the violence often threatened, Brad Steiger and Joan Whritenour, in *The New UFO Breakthrough*, comment: "Ever since organized flying saucer research began in the early 1950s, a disturbing number of serious UFO investigators have suffered personal harassment, unusual accidents, and even mysterious deaths...Recently an increasing number of civilian ufologists have been visited by ominous strangers who have made it physically and painfully clear that their orders to discontinue all UFO investigation would be violently enforced." It is worth pointing out, however, that despite a multitude of threats there appear to have been few cases of actual violence. Ignore them and they literally seem to go away! Perhaps Keel is right; they simply want to be memorable!

And memorable they became, although the fear of what they might have done was possibly more alarming than the reality. Frank Edwards was a prominent writer on the UFO subject, and famous in particular for his book *Flying Saucers–Serious Business*.

After raising the subject frequently on a radio show he was warned, apparently by government officials, to leave the subject alone. When he did not, his radio show was cancelled. It was stated that the Defense Department had been irritated by his obsession and had put pressure on the radio show's sponsors—the American Federation of Labor—to stop him. He later "got the bit between his teeth" and got a new radio show, virtually dedicating it to the subject. (Do we see here a subtle version of Keel's "press agent" theory?) But when he died of a heart attack, a debate arose, perhaps inevitably, as to whether his death had "meaning." When his death was announced at the Congress of Scientific Ufologists in New York in June 1967, one delegate suggested that Edwards "had been visited by the same three men in black that shut up Albert K. Bender." Others argued that Edwards was overweight and overworked and that his heart attack was not overly surprising. Still others argued that Edwards was in good health. And so the argument ran . . .

So are the MIBs government agents working on a strange campaign of publicizing UFOs by pretending to suppress them? It makes a certain sense: if they can encourage people to recount "silly" stories, then they can deflect attention from true details which are for some reason embarrassing to their governments. Or are they something mysterious in their own right, as Keel presumably believes—a mystery that needs no context other than the strange world we live in? Any extraordinary event and these curious figures turn up. Or are they pranksters? The next case suggests they had some sort of official backing.

Although famous for their travelling in brand-new looking cars, the "press agents" occasionally use helicopters. Roy Hawks saw a UFO near Boulder, Colorado, in 1960. When he returned to the spot a few days later he found a helicopter and three men in military uniform. They asked him to announce to the newspapers that the UFO would be back "on August 20." Hawks spotted the catch straight away. "I can't do that," he said. "The whole town would come out here on the twentieth, and when the thing didn't show up, everybody would think I was some kind of nut!" This may well have been the purpose of their request. Pranksters who might be able to afford, or even steal, a pristine-condition Cadillac surely could not have got hold of a helicopter; this suggests an authority behind them.

Dr. Herbert Hopkins—The Strangest Case of All

Inevitably, since they have integrated themselves so deeply into UFO lore, we must consider the belief that the MIBs are themselves alien. Quite why they should want to draw attention to themselves is unclear, but the options have been widely discussed. Perhaps to deflect attention from what they're really doing. Perhaps to acclimatize people gradually to accepting their presence by getting the subject talked about. Perhaps because they do not understand how our society works. If they are alien—to humanity or to the Earth—then the very famous case of Dr. Herbert Hopkins is probably the strongest evidence.

Hopkins was drawn into the UFO subject somewhat reluctantly. He used hypnosis to explore the memories of an abductee, David Stephens. On 11 September 1976, the rest of his family having gone to an outdoor movie, Hopkins was alone at home. He received a telephone call from a man claiming to be from the New Jersey UFO Research Organization (no such organization existed). The man wanted to visit Hopkins to talk with him about the abduction case. Hopkins agreed, but could not understand why he did not ask the caller's identity. What's more, he later reminded himself that there had been break-ins at both his home and office, there was illicit drug activity which made doctors vulnerable targets, and there had even been the murder of a pharmacist. Presumably he also had to consider the question of the confidentiality of the witness's account. Perhaps we see here the first sign of "control" of Hopkins, comparable to the state abductees themselves often report finding themselves in—almost manipulated into the abduction.

Just seconds later a man was coming up the outside stairs; Hopkins was certain there was no way he could have made it so quickly to the house from any telephone box. Since we are dealing with the era prior to the portable, cellular telephone, we either have to consider that the caller and the visitor were not the same man—and that therefore an extraordinary coincidence was at work (which seems scarcely credible)—or, given that we are speculating that the MIBs are agents of the abductors themselves, that Hopkins suffered missing time between the call and the visit. Of course, if the visitor was alien perhaps they had invented the cellular telephone!

Hopkins invited the man in, still surprised at his own acceptance of the situation. The man was wearing a black suit, virtually black shirt, black tie, black hat and grey gloves, "like an undertaker," Hopkins said. This image was further strengthened by the immaculate appearance of the man's clothing—not a wrinkle, and perfectly pressed—"like a clothing store dummy," he thought. When the man removed his hat Hopkins saw that he was completely bald, lacking even eyebrows or eyelashes. His skin was dead-white, and like plastic. He had a small nose, bright red lips and slit-like eyes with dark pupils. In fact Hopkins shortly noticed that his "lips" seemed to be purely the product of lipstick painted on! Throughout the visit the man acted like a robot; he hardly moved his head and sat upright and still, almost like a mannequin. His speech was also robot-like: no vocal tones, no accent, no contractions. In the conversation that ensued it became clear to Hopkins that his visitor knew as much about the Stephens case as Hopkins did himself.

But if Hopkins thought his unease at the visit was passing, what was to follow seriously shook him. The visitor told Hopkins what coins Hopkins had in his pocket, and was correct! He asked Hopkins to hold a penny in his hand and told him to watch it carefully. Hopkins watched the penny turn from silver to blue, "and then it began to become blurred to my vision. My hand was in sharp focus, but try as I might I could not seem to focus on the silver-blue penny. It became more blurred, became round like a little blue fuzzy ball, and then became vaporous and gradually faded away." Hopkins could actually feel the weight of the penny disappearing as it faded away.

"Neither you nor anyone else on this plane [sic] will ever see that coin again," the visitor told Hopkins. Then, threateningly, the man referred to the Betty and Barney Hill abduction case of 1961. Barney was by then dead. The man told Hopkins that Barney had died because he knew too much. Hopkins said that the visitor told him Barney had died "because he had no heart, just as I no longer have a coin." Hopkins admitted, "This frightened me." Now in the state of mind that the visitor presumably had wanted to create, Hopkins was told to destroy his tapes and papers relating to his work with Stephens. Furthermore he should destroy any other UFO-related literature he had.

But more "high strangeness" was yet to follow: the visitor's speech slowed down somewhat in the manner of a record player slowly grinding to a halt. The man claimed that his energy was running low and he must go. Slowly the visitor descended the steps from the apartment and walked away. Hopkins watched him go, seemingly to a vehicle with bright blue-white lights. He also thought the man cast no shadow when the lights were on him. When Hopkins looked out to investigate, however, he never saw the car and was not able to understand how the man had disappeared. Later that night, with his son, Hopkins found what seemed to be tracks on the driveway "that looked like a small caterpillar tractor tread . . . No automobile could have possibly made them because the driveway is too narrow for a car to get over far enough so that its wheels would be in the middle of the driveway . . . also they did not continue for any length . . ."

Hopkins spent the rest of the night with the lights on and a gun nearby. He then destroyed his regression tapes. He also asked the *National Enquirer*—who were going to write an article on the case—to drop the story.

Hopkins might have hoped it was all over. But an encounter

that Hopkins' son and daughter-in-law had two weeks later added further strangeness to a case that had hardly lacked for it so far! Hopkins' daughter-in-law, Maureen, received a phone call from a man calling himself Bill Post. It resulted in her and Hopkins' son, John, meeting a couple. The couple, who were wearing old-fashioned clothes, sat together on a sofa, ignoring the drinks in front of them. They made it clear that they knew of John's father, Dr. Hopkins. Throughout the interview the man fondled the woman, asking John if he was doing it correctly. While John was absent the man asked Maureen if she had any nude photographs of herself. When they were leaving, the man stood up but apparently could not move; the woman had to ask John to help move him. Before he could do so the man left, followed by the woman, walking strangely in dead straight lines.

Any resolution of this case is probably impossible at this late stage. It is possible that the strangeness of the experience made Hopkins associate otherwise innocent events with it unnecessarily, for example the marks on the drive. Nonetheless we have what would seem to be a very reliable report of the disappearing coin by a reliable person. If the visitors were government agents they certainly had a curious sense of humour; and if they were, as has been speculated, extraterrestrials or extra-dimensional beings, then whoever sent them certainly used a more defective bunch than are usually reported in UFO encounters.

It is tempting to suggest that they were pranksters associated with the UFO phenomenon, but then we have the incident with the coin to explain. One magician, a former member of the Magic Circle, has desribed how such illusions can be created by "displacement" of the percipient's attention, but for that to be the case we would have to assume that Hopkins' later recollection of how the coin had disappeared was perhaps coloured by his fears. If he genuinely saw and felt it lose weight and *slowly* disappear before his eyes, that would need some other explanation.

10

Abductions

No area of alleged contact with aliens is currently as popular with the general public as that of alien abductions. These stories have been featured in almost every national newspaper in recent times, and have formed the basis of the more dramatic film documentaries. They are sensational in their content, which makes it all the more surprising that these media-forms over-sensationalize them, and distort the reality. They do not need the extra manipulation.

Abductions are the main area of work for most independent UFO researchers, with an increasing number of reportees coming forward continuously. The principal abduction research which affects the world view of the subject is being driven from the United States, and the leaders in the field are Budd Hopkins, Dr. David Jacobs and Dr. John Mack.

The three are linked. Both Mack and Jacobs give credit to Hopkins for inspiring them and "teaching" them their approach. All three have found relatively similar motifs running through the subject. That said, Mack seems to be much more open to the "wider," more spiritual qualities of the claims he hears, which reflects his own beliefs and interests. This is one example of the differences that arise when comparing the work of one researcher with any others; and it leads to the possibility that whatever the reality underlying this phenomenon there is an input from the researcher which is "colouring" an outside appreciation. Mack himself comments: "It may be wrong to expect that a phenomenon whose very nature is subtle, and one of whose purposes may be to stretch and expand our ways of knowing beyond the purely materialist approaches of Western science, will yield its secrets to an epistemology or methodology that operates at a lower level of consciousness."

Probably the world's best-known abductee is Whitley Strieber, who wrote up his own experiences in the books *Communion, Transformation, Breakthrough* and *Secret School*. His story is largely similar to the claims of many others, and the reader is directed to those books for the account of his own exploration of his experiences. What is perhaps less known is that some of his abductions took place in his cabin in the countryside in an area of New York State which was undergoing an intensive wave of sightings (a UFO "flap")—including other abduction accounts. This flap has generally been known as the "Hudson Valley flap."

Philip J. Imbrogno, who has researched the area of the Hudson Valley, points out that Strieber's was one of a great many such reports from that area. He published his researches in the book *Night Siege*, co-authored with J. Allen Hynek and Bob Pratt. At the time, at Hynek's request, abductions were left out of the book, but following Hynek's death, and the recognition that in later life Hynek was increasingly interested in the "paranormal" side of the subject, Imbrogno felt able to release that aspect of their researches.

One account related by Imbrogno arose on 19 July 1984. At around 10.30 P.M. "Bill" was driving on Highway I-84 when he saw a UFO. It was bright, white and circular. He soon lost sight of it. Later during the drive he saw what seemed to be a large mass sitting in a field some 200 yards from the road. While he watched it, the object silently took off into the air. He became somewhat upset, aware that he was alone on the road. Bill's radio went "funny" and he decided to speed up and get out of the area. But he soon encountered the object hovering ahead of him, a few hundred feet off the ground. To avoid detection he decided to kill the car lights and engine. But the object also turned off its lights and drifted towards him, now a dark, triangular mass. It was silent, and perhaps 300 feet in length. But Bill did not see it leave; he was just suddenly alone, about 600 feet from where he had stopped the car, and the UFO was nowhere to be seen. He arrived home around an hour late, which suggested "missing time." Thereafter Bill underwent changes; he was afraid to drive at night, and even had to change his job-shifts to accommodate that. He had nightmares of being "pursued." Inspired by seeing Budd Hopkins on television, Bill approached Imbrogno and was hypnotically regressed. Under hypnosis it appeared that he was abducted and examined by small aliens with large heads and pupil-less dark eyes.

Imbrogno also relates the story of divorcee "Gail." During June 1987 she felt as if she was "being watched" at a time when she was alone in her house, lying on her bed. Her daughter was away at the time visiting her father. Gail heard a voice tell her, "We have come for you. You will not be hurt." She realized that she was paralysed and could only move her eyes. There were three "people" standing in the doorway to her bedroom. They were around five feet tall, with long arms. Their heads were large, and they had eyes that "looked like a cat's which wrapped around their heads." They surrounded her bed and during the next few minutes inserted something into her nostril. It was painful and she lost consciousness. The following morning she had a nosebleed; she felt as if there was something in her nose but could find nothing; also she had a rash on parts of her body. When she told her daughter about it, an extraordinary coincidence, or perhaps something more related, emerged. Obviously shaken, the daughter revealed that at the same time that Gail was having the encounter, she and her father had seen a large triangular UFO that had "paced the car." Imbrogno believes that the daughter and her father might have had a "missing time" and that, if so, perhaps all three were abducted at the same time. The same experience happened again to Gail, and Imbrogno considered examining the possibility of repeated lifetime experiences.

Catherine

To begin a detailed examination of the subject of abductions we set out below a case study that has been thoroughly researched, and which shows the range of the subject as much as any one case can.

The vast majority of UFO witnesses are surprised when they first encounter UFOs, not least because in many cases they have not given the subject much thought previously, and are not expecting to be involved even in a sighting, let alone something as close and personal as an abduction. However, one of John Mack's clients, Catherine, was an exception to that rule.

In late February 1991 she was driving to her home near Boston after midnight; instead of stopping at her home, however, she kept driving, thinking: "I guess I'll go for a drive." When she did reach home she discovered that there was a period of approximately three-quarters of an hour for which she could not account. The unusual nature of her decision to drive suggests what many abduction researchers have uncovered, that abductees seem to be abducted when under some form of compulsion or change of circumstance which many attribute to a direct intervention by the aliens. (On another occasion, when in Alaska, she was compelled to get up in the night and go out in the cold, about which she stated: "I did not choose to get up and go and do that.")

When Catherine awoke, at about noon, on the day after her drive near Boston, she saw news coverage of a UFO, reported the previous night by many people, and realized that although she had been in the right position to see it she had not done so. She found this ironic because, having read about UFOs, she was "halfway hoping to see one . . ."

It is clear that Catherine was also familiar with the literature. She approached John Mack as she was concerned about an unexplained nosebleed and had found herself answering in the positive to a questionnaire in a book about abductions, which was indicating a possible UFO encounter. She recalled dreams of strange beings and a time when she was in a spaceship with curved walls.

Hypnosis with Mack revealed that during that drive in February 1991 a strange being had drawn her out of the car. Mack reports: "She felt there was no choice." In her own words: "If I had my choice I would be speeding the hell away from there."

Interestingly, she also suggested one indicator which she is less likely to have read about, although a British UFO Research Association study of witness profiles shows that it is relatively commonplace. Mack notes that she was in a career crisis at the time and that she told him: "I'm not using all of the skills that I have." BUFORA's study reveals that abductees are often "status inconsistent," meaning that they hold jobs inconsistent with their background, education or cultural position. As a general rule such people hold lesser jobs than might be expected of them, as would seem to be the case here.

Catherine seemed drawn to the subject, having watched the film *Communion*, the CBS mini-series *Intruders* and having read David Jacobs book *Secret Life*. Indeed, in relation to *Secret Life* she herself wondered if "I am subconsciously picking up on stuff that's there." Furthermore it appears that some of her recollections were specifically triggered by these exposures. For example Mack notes: "The memories were consciously triggered—i.e. remembered without hypnosis—by a disturbing nightmare scene in the first episode of the CBS mini-series *Intruders*..." The memory triggered by *Intruders* is of a being similar to one in that programme, i.e. a creature with large black eyes, pointed face, a line for a mouth, small nose; a fairly classical "Gray."

Many motifs common across the UFO literature are contained in Catherine's story. It could be argued that Catherine knows which motifs are important to report, or that she is imagining some of them in expectation from her reading and television viewing. For example, one being "materializes at the end of the [blue light] shaft." The blue beam is a frequent characteristic in UFO reports and perhaps most famously associated with the Ed Walters sighting in the town of Gulf Breeze, Florida.

Under hypnosis it emerged that Catherine was about seven when, like so many abductees, she remembers being flown upwards into a flying saucer. "He is taking me up. We are flying up...I can see everything down. It's scary." She remembers a conversation with one alien when she asked why he was taking samples; the alien replied: "Because we need a sample...It's for scientific research...I'm researching your planet...We are trying to stop the damage...from pollution."

Catherine has one recollection of implants which is very consistent with the claims of such as David Jacobs. She recalls one being inserted up through her nose. "I could feel something breaking in my head. When he pushed it through, he broke whatever it was and he pushed it all the way through, up even further." Several abductees have made the same claim that implants are pushed into the brain area through the nasal cavity; often resulting in the spontaneous nosebleeds which are for some people the first suggestion that they have had an abduction.

Another of Catherine's recolletions is of a room with stacked cases covering one wall, all with identical tiny creatures in. "They're kind of deformed looking." It was a room which gave her very bad feelings during the regression in which her memory of it was uncovered.

Motifs

To explore abductions systematically we can divide the reports up into motifs which frequently, though not exclusively, recur within the claims. The pattern is an indication that something real—whatever it may be—is happening. (There are of course many other events which arise less frequently, or have less obvious importance, which should not be ignored at the individual case level.)

1 Controlled

Hopkins has stated that he believes the abductees are controlled more than we give credit for, and cites cases where people seem to have been "willed" into the abduction or a position from which they can be abducted. Jacobs supports this view. In *Secret Life* he comments:

> Sometimes the abductee will inexplicably get into her car and drive to a specific location where the abduction will take place. The abductee does not think about why she is doing this, or she invents a reason so that her behaviour conforms to logic and reality. For example, the abductee tells herself that she "wanted to take a ride" or that she was "going to visit friends." When asked where she went, she is at a loss to remember or makes up another excuse that she later realizes is not true.

The idea is not new, though it is being thoroughly explored in the United States for the first time by such as Hopkins and Jacobs. In the 1970s Jean-François Boedec studied UFO abduction cases in Brittany, France, and concluded that some abductees seem to act strangely for a period, sometimes as much as a week or two, before their abduction, resulting in their being in the location where the abduction takes place. They might suddenly seem to desire periods of solitude, or they would change their regular driving habits and use new routes, from where they would later be abducted. Whether this is under the control of the aliens, or is part of the process which creates the experience we call an abduction, is unclear.

Prompted by "a few memories" which were disturbing her, Patti Layne underwent hypnotic regression with David Jacobs which revealed a lifetime series of alien abductions. Aged 20, she felt a compelling need to get out of her apartment and drive into the mountains to be alone, though she could not quite undertand why. She felt a little depressed and believed that driving into the mountains would make her feel better. Even as she was driving, however, she was unclear why she was doing so. "Why am I doing this? . . . Why am I out here by myself?" In the mountains she stopped the car, the car door was opened and she was taken out and abducted.

On another occasion Patti was again in a remote mountainside area having a picnic with some college friends. Feeling the need to relieve herself, she went off alone into the woods. While kneeling down she saw a light shining on her and believed that it was one of her friends "bugging her." When she shouted "Cut it out," she not only failed to hear any response or the noise of her friends but could not even hear her own voice; she realized that something was wrong. Feeling scared she walked back to the group and saw "a whole lot of [aliens] standing there with my friends." Patti watched as the aliens, apparently moving very fast, touched her friends. She remained frozen and unable to move, just five feet away from them. "It's just everything standing still, including me."

Interestingly, Patti recalls that one of the aliens was wearing a scarf. A rare detail, but one first arising in the abduction of Betty and Barney Hill. Patti also recalled that the alien looked "military" and had an insignia, something that has arisen in several abductions previously. The insignia was "bird-like," a similarity to the Schirmer case of 1967. Despite the insignia, she believes the alien was naked and noticed that "he" did not have any genitals, "just kind of like a Barbie Doll." The aliens led the whole group into the woods and on to a UFO, "kind of like a bubble with a hatch." The description of the aliens moving the college friends is similar to that in the Hill case, the people supported by the aliens but basically half carried and half dragged along. At one point Patti questions, "I don't know why they don't float us."

Jacobs has also uncovered a series of abductions through the lifetime of Janet Demerest. At the age of nine she and several members of her Brownie troop were apparently transfixed, staring at something in the grass—"I think it's a bug or something." Janet backs away from the circle, but the rest remain transfixed. She goes over to a small figure—"he doesn't look like a person"—and together they walk away. Jacobs believes that this is an aspect of the aliens' controlling the abduction— by switching off the others. In order to distract them they are given some object which becomes the focus of their fascination while the abductee is removed. Janet and the alien walked through the woods to a UFO standing in a clearing, and together they walked up a ramp and into the object.

During one recollection Janet reveals that "I have no sense of who I am" during the abduction, as if disconnected from herself. Whether this is a product of the aliens' control, or whether this disconnection is part of the process which creates the experience we call the abduction, is unclear.

Another of Jacobs' clients, Jill Pinzarro, reveals that an abduction when she was nine years old seems to have been conducted while she was "under control." Pushing her bicycle home from the library one afternoon, she stopped in the park and then walked over to some trees. It's not very clear why she went to the trees. "I don't feel as if I can resist." Inside the trees she could see an object which she walked up to, and into.

Scott and Lee, a brother and sister who were examined by John Mack and who both have a history of abductions, played a lot together in what Lee remembers as a "little gully" near their house. She believed that this was one of the sites of their abductions and remembers that as a child she used to think of it as a special place that they loved. This might suggest that, however frightening the abduction experiences were, they also had a quality which was in some way appealing. Alternatively, perhaps their appreciation of the site was a "device" to attract them to it regularly so that they could be abducted; another case of "control."

2 Missing time

One of the commonest elements in abductions is the recognition of missing time. In the first recorded abduction that set the pattern for those that followed, the Hills' case, missing time of two hours was identified, and it was during this time that the Hills are believed to have had their encounter.

In June 1976, Hélène Giuliana was returning home late one night when her car cut out while crossing the bridge at Romans, in France. She saw a huge orange glow in the sky which then suddenly vanished; she drove on. When she arrived home she discovered that she had missed some considerable period of time. Subsequent regression hypnosis revealed that she had been abducted by small figures, tied to a table and examined in the area around her abdomen.

In August 1975, Alan Fallows was driving towards the village of Mossley, in West Yorkshire, when he was surrounded by a thick hill mist and saw a bright egg-shaped light. There was some evidence of paralysis and missing time, and when he fully came to his senses, he found he was clutching a screwdriver as if holding a weapon; but he does not recall picking it up.

On 15 October 1979, Luli Oswald and a friend were driving from Rio de Janeiro to Saquarema. They saw three UFOs and suffered from vehicle interference effects. The next thing they remembered was being somewhere else off on a side road; and discovering they had lost two hours of time. Regression hypnosis later revealed a "classical" abduction.

One of John Mack's abductees, Dave, seems to have had a number of missing time experiences. One such occurrence was when he was around 12 years old and walking along the path following a railway line near a lake. He looked up into the branch of a tree and the next thing he was aware of was walking back into the clearing where his uncle's cabin stood. Dave remembers a walk of a few minutes, but when he got home his aunt, uncle and cousins were very worried about him; there was a total of some 45 minutes of missing time. On another occasion he was in the back seat of a car driving in a rainstorm through New Brunswick, Canada, when he and his friend realized they had lost 90 miles. "Last time we knew we were 90 miles back down the road." None of the boys could apparently account for the missing time. An even more exceptional period of missing time arose shortly after Dave graduated from High School. He had just started at Penn State College. Both he and his room-mate went to bed on Saturday, woke up believing it was Sunday, and were then asked by friends why they had skipped chemistry class. They discovered that it was mid-morning on Monday and neither of them could account for the missing time period. Dave's case is further explored later in this chapter.

The case of "Tom" and "Nancy," examined by David Jacobs, combines missing time with a most extraordinary account of coitus interruptus. The couple had been making love when Tom suddenly discovered that they had been so engaged for some 45 minutes without his being aware of anything like that amount of time passing. Under hypnosis he recalled two figures coming into the room and his being "stilled," but remaining conscious. He was removed from his wife and left face down on the bed while it appears she was taken from the bedroom. "It was like they rolled her off. As they were rolling her off the edge of the bed, she just faded out with them, just like a flash." Tom remained aware but paralysed, unable to move even his eyes and only able to see what was in his field of vision. He couldn't move any limbs or part of his body. Later Nancy "comes into view" but Tom is unclear exactly how this happens. It appears almost as if she just rolled back on to the bed as if on a conveyor belt. The couple were then put back together, Tom discovering that throughout the whole paralysis he had retained his erection. Then Tom felt that they were "re-activated."

Nancy also recalled these events under hypnosis, though not

identically. She saw a blue light pointed at her. Tom was lying next to her, unmoving. She did not recall a sense of his being moved from her. She did recall, however, believing that the two of them were no longer alone in the room. She recalled a detailed abduction event before finding herself "returned" to her husband.

3 Screen memories

Several UFO researchers have speculated that abductees have failed to recognize their experiences because they are protected by a "screen memory" or substitute image.

Memories of cars, houses in fields, shops with "strange shop-keepers" have all been interpreted by researchers as screen memories covering images of flying saucers and their occupants. Vaguely discomforting memories or dreams of animals with large eyes—owls, deer, cats, and so on—are believed by many abductees and researchers to be hiding true memories of alien beings. One of Mack's abductees, Dave, has a screen memory of motorcycles with black-clad riders moving terrifyingly fast and unnaturally towards him but, during regression, he saw them "turn into the [alien] beings."

Whether the screen memory is the mind creating the image to protect itself from fear, or whether it is a "control device" of the aliens is a matter for speculation even among those who believe the abduction scenario can be taken at face value. For those who believe the abduction is largely an "inner" experience, the question is whether the screen memory is a product of or a trigger for the experience.

4 Out of body?

There are an increasing number of cases which suggest that at least some abductions happen as out-of-body experiences (OOBEs). For example, the lifetime experiences of Betty Andreasson, recorded in a series of books by Raymond Fowler, include a number of seemingly OOBE abductions. "I am standing there and I am coming out of myself! There is two of me there . . ."

she remembered on one occasion. She also recalled joint abductions with her husband where they both were out-of-body.

In Preston Dennett's excellent review of healings associated with UFOs *(UFO Healings)* he describes such a case. When Edward Carlos was aged five he suffered from severe respiratory pneumonia, had a high fever and was near coma. During this illness Carlos had an OOBE and, outside of his body, found himself surrounded by Grays. The Grays operated on his astral body rather than his physical body. Shining lights "like laser beams" went through his feet and hands, "expanding and changing colour as the light grew to fit the whole body interior, thereby healing it." Carlos was then returned to his body healed and well.

5 The elevator

Many abductees report that the direction of kidnapping is *upwards*. This did not arise in the Betty and Barney Hill case, where it seems clear that the flying saucer was parked on the ground from the outset, but a great many abductees have reported being lifted up into the air, and entering into a flying saucer through a hole in the underside. The "Linda Cortile" case investigated by Budd Hopkins and recounted in his book *Witnessed* is a case in point. In cases of abduction from city centres or otherwise built-up areas this seems perfectly logical—the saucer remaining where it cannot be detected, presumably. But even when abductions take place in remote locations it is becoming common. Whitley Strieber, for example, recalls being lifted up from a fairly remote area into an object. In the majority of cases the witnesses report moving up at high speed, as if in an elevator.

At the age of 21 Barbara Archer started the first of six regression hypnosis sessions with David Jacobs, revealing her abduction experiences. At the age of 16 she saw a light which seemed to be coming through her bedroom window and which illuminated her room. However, when she closed the shade, the light continued and on looking outside she could not see a source. Under hypnosis she realized the light was within her own room.

As the light "seems to be going away" she saw that there was
somebody standing in her closet. A figure came towards her,
touched her arm and she was lifted straight up fast, as if in an elevator, possibly through the window. She recalled: "When we
went out the window we went straight in between the two row
houses, my house and my next door neighbors'... And I go
straight up from in between there. So I can see everything. I can
see all the row houses on my street in the driveway." As she as-
cended she felt warm, and affected by weather, and looked up to
see that she was approaching the underside of a dark grey oval
shape in the sky. "We just go right in through the bottom." She
believes she was accompanied by the figure she first saw in her
bedroom and that she met other figures when inside the object.

One of John Mack's abductees, Jerry, used much the same description. Twenty or thirty "small beings" passed through her
window into her room and took her out the same way, "and then
I went up real fast." She was moving so fast that it took her
breath away and she found she was travelling up to a "big thing
above me" into which she was then abducted. As she was going
up she could see the top of the house, trees and ground below
her. She appears to be one of those abductees who accept a role
in the experience, Mack commenting that "Jerry feels that she
was somehow a participant in this process."

In 1974 Will Parker and his wife Ginny were driving through
Virginia late at night when for some inexplicable reason he
turned into a closed petrol and service station, killed the engine
and lights and waited in the darkness. Under hypnosis he revealed that while they sat there the two of them were talking,
but nervously, and that Ginny, heard a noise and then saw a
light. They saw outside the car a "little guy, he is outside the
car, and he is not human." Parker says, "I've seen this before,
but I didn't remember it until now." Switching his narrative to
plural entities, he refers to "them" taking him out of the car
while Ginny remains in the car apparently asleep. The four or
five figures take Parker into the dark around the back of the

building. Like other abductees Parker describes being lifted up into an object: "It's like we're on an elevator . . . We were on the ground a moment ago, now we are inside."

Perhaps the "elevator" is not a physical drawing up, but rather a "drawing out"; in short, the description is akin to reports of leaving the body during astral travel. Notably, most reports of out-of-body experiences refers to the "spirit" moving upwards. This would match the point in the section above and may be valid for many cases. However, it cannot be a full answer; in the case mentioned below the witness reported that a whole car was lifted into a flying saucer. Either we are presented with a physical lifting, or we might speculate that some illusion was devised to convince the victims that their car was being lifted (see "The holodeck," number 15 below).

In 1979 Tracy Knapp was driving to Las Vegas from Los Angeles accompanied by two girlfriends when they saw an unexplained light hurtling down towards their car. Tracy recalled under hypnosis that as the light flashed past the car there was a sensation of the car spinning round. She describes it as "like I'm in a teacup." Presumably this is an oblique reference to *Alice in Wonderland* or perhaps the fairground ride of spinning teacups based on *Alice*. She revealed that she believed the whole car, still spinning, was lifted up into the air. Her two friends seemed to have been "switched off." Tracy was removed from the car and only reunited with her friends when they were back on the ground.

6 Taller and shorter beings

Quite often abductees report one being who is taller than the others. The taller being is often regarded as the "leader," or sometimes as the "doctor," the "controller," the "captain" etc. Abductee Joe has referred to the taller of the aliens as "a head honcho." One of Mack's abductees, Jerry, described seeing different aliens; including a taller, lighter one she called "the leader." She described him as having a nice face and a smile.

Generally speaking, this taller being seems to give the orders or organize the examinations during abductions. Many abductees report that this individual is more clinical, "doctor-like" and authoritarian. Some relate to this in a positive way, seeing the figure as paternal or comforting, while others find it threatening. The taller figure is often referred to as a male, though not always. It is often the taller being that uses his or her eyes to calm, to remove pain, to control or to mindscan.

7 Alien knowledge

There is something curious in the lack of understanding by aliens of certain aspects of human activity. In the book *Perspectives*, John Spencer highlighted the many inconsistencies associated with the Betty and Barney Hill case, for example that the aliens did not understand the word, or seemingly the concept of, "yellow" or "vegetables," while at the same time they could use idiomatic expressions like "in no time."

Melissa Bucknell, one of Jacobs' subjects, had dyed her hair between two abductions, and this was of great interest to the aliens, who set about comparing their subject with the last time they examined her. She believes that they examined her hair colour and thought it was the result of her being ill and needing treatment.

Karen Morgan had also undergone a change between abductions which was of interest to the aliens. In her case she had had braces fitted on her teeth, and the aliens immediately asked what they were for. She did not tell them, and they removed a sample of tissue from her gum for analysis, apparently to discover the answers for themselves.

8 Eyes

Interaction with the aliens appears to depend a great deal on the eyes of the beings. Almost no abductee has failed to describe in great detail the dark, almond-shaped eyes of the Grays, and indeed the eyes of other aliens, with much more emotional intensity than they would describe, say, the nose, mouth, ears, etc. With respect to the "classical" Grays the details some abductees have gone into on what would appear to be fairly black doll-like eyes is quite extraordinary, with some abductees trying to describe texture, purple shades of light flowing within the eyes, and so on.

Apart from simply being fascinated by the eyes, several abductees have reported that when they are afraid or alarmed the alien looks directly into their eyes—and they into its—and they feel calmed and unafraid. This is reported so often that it would appear to be a motif of abductions; perhaps a "mechanism" used by the aliens to control their subject. Similarly, several abductees have reported that when the aliens move up very close to them and stare at them, any pain they are feeling diminishes or goes away. Again it would seem that this is possibly some sort of mechanism used by the aliens.

David Jacobs also examines a process he calls "mindscan," an extension of the above which he describes thus: "Mindscan entails deep, penetrating staring into the abductee's eyes. Abductees commonly feel that data of some sort is being extracted from their mind. We do not know what the information is, how it is extracted, or what the Beings do with it. One abductee thinks that they transfer it to other Beings' minds." It is apparently a process which requires proximity, abductee Will Parker recalling: "He is right up in my face. Not quite touching my nose with his face, but he is almost that close." Patti Layne revealed exactly the same thing: the alien pressed as close to her nose as possible without actually touching her. Others reveal that actual contact takes place, face on face.

The hypnotic power of the aliens' eyes is clear. "They are spell-binding, riveting," David Jacobs reveals. "He [the alien] locks eyes with the abductees. Even though she tries, she cannot close her eyes or take her eyes off his. Most abductees feel overwhelmed by the procedure." Karen Morgan commented, "Once you look into those eyes, you're gone. You're just gone."

Peter, one of John Mack's clients, comments: "In the eyes

there is a coldness . . . There is a coldness and a pure blankness, but behind the eyes—I almost want to say there is another eye behind the eye. And the other eye behind the eye is, I want to say it's sad and longing, and it's trying to comfort me, but at the same time it wishes I could help it. It wants to connect with me. It really wants to connect with me. It's almost like it's looking at an infant . . . If you were only a little older and a little wiser and we could have a relationship or something."

Abductee Sheila N., another client of John Mack, also commented on the power of the aliens' eyes. "The aliens," she said, "took my energy . . . There is power in those eyes . . . they are so big . . . they are different." She too said that the leader controls people with his eyes, and maintained even that the experience of "just their eyes and my eyes" was like neuro-linguistic programming; they "take control and then you don't have the energy to fight." She went on to describe what some abductees have said is like falling right into the eyes. As she looked deeply into the leader's eyes she felt "there is this black ball around me . . . covered with black stuff . . . I felt like I was in a black box."

Part of the process of mindscan, or possibly a related process, seems to be emotional experimentation on the abductees. In some cases abductees have reported a sweep of wondrous uplifting emotions which, as Jacobs reveals, can bond the abductee to the abductor. In other cases the close proximity of the alien can inspire fear, terror, anguish, depression and so on. For the most part the emotion is one of "bonding" or even love. Jacobs reveals from his regressions that abductees often feel that they want to help the aliens and "sometimes there is a romantic and even sexual quality to these thoughts." Barbara Archer, for example, at the age of 12, was subject to this close proximity "mindscanning" and revealed that, when looking into the alien's eyes, "He makes me feel happy. I think that he likes me . . . I feel wonderful. I think that he is wonderful." Interestingly, she accepts the suggestion that there is a sexual component attached to the feelings which, bearing in mind that she is 12 and therefore probably blossoming sexually, may be exploring her own feelings as much as alien-induced emotions. She states: "He makes me feel grown up, sort of. When he says things to me he talks to me like I'm really young, but I feel womanly . . ." This is precisely what pre-teenage and young teenage people seek: to be treated as adults and to be loved and respected; either the aliens know how to "tweak" our most important needs, or these feelings are part of an inner exploration of personal desires.

We should not lose sight of the importance of eyes to humans. We speak of "eye contact" being an important way of bridging between people, and our language contains many allusions to eyes: "bedroom eyes," "the windows of the soul," "eyeball to eyeball confrontations" and so on. The eyes, we are reminded, are the only living tissue we see when we look at another person; the top layer of skin is dead, as is the hair and the exposed finger- and toe-nail material.

9 Sperm extraction

No one facet of the abduction experience is as commonly reported as the interest the aliens have in the reproductive processes. Indeed many American researchers believe that this is the central theme of alien abductions: to examine our reproductive processes with a view to creating a hybrid human-alien species, presumably to add strength to the qualities of either or both of the originating races. For example, during mindscanning there are several accounts of eliciting orgasm often prior to gynaecological and urological examination, presumably the orgasm being part of what the aliens wish to examine. In the man, orgasm is an essential part of the normal reproductive process, but this is not the case in a woman who can become pregnant without having an orgasm. However, there are accounts of the aliens inducing orgasm in women as there are in men, which begs the question of whether they are examining the reproductive process *per se* or the emotional experiences associated with it.

Antonio Villas Boas reported many years after his abduction, which had involved sexual intercourse, that he had also been subject to sperm being removed; and the same appears to have happened to Barney Hill. Hypnosis on one of Mack's abductees, Scott, revealed that he too had had this experience. During one abduction a device was placed on his penis, wires or leads were attached to his testicles and a sperm sample was taken while he lay paralysed on a table inside a UFO.

Sperm is somehow extracted by a device clamped over the penis which may or may not cause orgasm. As reported by abductee Ken Rogers: "They hook up a machine on the tube, with a suction cap end. So now they put it on my penis. I don't remember this or feel it, but I can see it happening now [under hypnosis]." Will Parker revealed: "It looks like a polished stainless steel, aluminium, chromium I guess you'd call it. It fits over the penis and it's got a rounded lower section that fits up over the testicles. And it's like you're enclosed in this thing. It looks like a piece of machinery that no good mistress of domination would be without. Something rather kinky, in a different environment of course. But it looks, it's completely metallic."

Perhaps relating more to the emotional than the physical, there have been times when men and women have been abducted together and have been able to see the procedures on each other. For example, Melissa Bucknell was abducted she was making love with her boyfriend. They were both placed on tables and she watched as the aliens attached their sperm collection device to his penis. Jacobs reports that on another occasion a woman watched her teenage son undergoing the same experience, with the obvious emotional effect on her.

Another of Mack's abductees, Peter, related a story of sperm extraction which was, according to Mack, "one of the most disturbing episodes that I have encountered during the regression." Peter feels that he was aged about 19 and was lying on an examination table when a cup was placed over his penis, ejaculation forced and sperm extracted. Peter recalled that they did this to him frequently, and during the regression was crying and shaking at the feeling of utter helplessness during the experiences. He then recalled a time when he was abducted and taken aboard a spaceship against his will. He expressed his anger under hypnosis: "This little being off to my left . . . I'd rip his head off is what I'd do to it. I'd kill it. I'd struggle every ounce of my being." He was placed on the operating table, but on this occasion they cut under his testicles and drew semen from inside him surgically.

10 Reproduction

One commonly reported motif is the taking of eggs from female abductees. David Jacobs for example relates the case of Lynn Miller (real name Alice Haggerty) who recalled that a needle-like instrument was poked through her belly button to take an egg. Jacobs reports from his findings that sometimes the eggs are placed in a container and given to another alien who removes it from the room.

On other occasions female abductees report the insertion of a fertilized egg despite their own protests about not wanting to be pregnant. For example Karen Morgan, sister of Janet Demerest, believed an embryo was planted in her.

The third part of this procedure would appear to occur six to twelve weeks after the implanting, when the abductee is again taken and the developing embryo removed. Many abductees have reported this, and many have discovered, when they thought they were pregnant and perhaps have gone for an abortion, that the foetus has disappeared. Whether or not they have suffered a phantom pregnancy as a psychosomatic response to believing they have been abducted, or whether aliens have truly re-abducted the person and removed their foetus is one of the questions still hotly debated. Abductee Lynn Miller described seeing this operation on herself. Having had a probe inserted into her, and then withdrawn, she relates: "He seems to pull something out, and he puts it right in something else." Looking into the container she says, "I'm looking at a fetus." She was told that it was her child and they would raise it; they took it from her. Similarly Tracy Knapp remembered: "They removed something out of me. They removed like a, like a little baby or something. And they removed the sac or something. They removed the... but it's tiny, it's real tiny. It's not a baby." She also saw that her "baby" was placed where "they've got other babies there. They're in like drawers in the walls; it's like little drawers that pull out, and there's babies, like little, little somethings in these drawers that pull out like in a lab or something."

Mack's abductee, Lee, revealed under hypnosis a teenage abduction where "a probing instrument was inserted in her vagina, and some sort of tissue, perhaps an egg, was removed."

Another of Mack's abductees, Jerry, recalled under hypnosis watching the removal of a foetus, apparently when she was only 13 years old. She was abducted, stripped and laid on her back and felt instruments pressed deep inside her. She saw that one of the aliens was holding a "shiny horsehoe-shaped object with a handle on it as others bent her knees upwards and apart." She later recalled that something had been placed deep within her body, beyond her vagina, and compared this to when as an adult she had an abortion—it had felt something like the D & C procedure which had accompanied that. When she saw the horseshoe-shaped object being taken out of her body, she saw that it contained a tiny skinny baby some ten inches long. The aliens placed this in a clear plastic cylinder containing fluid. She believes that they seemed to think she should be proud of the baby, but she says she felt "angry, confused, used and betrayed."

Mack's subject, Catherine, recalls something similar. "He is cutting inside me. I can feel it... He has got it. He takes out this hunk... He takes out the thing he put in and there is something attached to the end of it. It looks like a fetus..." When asked to describe if the foetus looked human, her one comment was that it had "eyes like theirs," again a reference to the powerful impression the eyes create in anyone who encounters these beings.

There are several accounts of people being forced to copulate during abductions. For example a man being ordered to climb on top of a woman who is apparently "switched off" and to perform sexual intercourse. Somewhat chillingly, during orgasm the beings apparently close in on the person and stare closely eye to eye as if mindscanning. Jacobs emphasizes: "This is not a sexual fantasy situation, most men and women feel that it is an uncontrollable and traumatic event. One man tearfully said that he felt like he was raping a woman . . ." One young woman reported to Jacobs being on the receiving end of this experience: of being controlled by close eye contact by the aliens and then seeing at the end of the bed she was lying on "a man standing at the foot of the table, and his eyes are sort of cloudy, and he is erect, and he is just standing there, and I am afraid . . . He is absolutely out of it. His mouth is hanging slack, and his hands are loose at his side, kind of like an ape. And his eyes are glazed over, cloudy, unfocused . . . And this guy climbs on top of me, and he is moving, and it . . . doesn't make any sense, but it feels like he starts to climax and doesn't finish, or he gets to the point of coming, but what's the point of that? . . . They just pull him off, and they stick something up where he was, a metal thing it feels like."

The sexual overtones of abductions can have negative effects on the abductee's personal life. One of Mack's abductees, Jerry, reports that she is unable to have a normal sexual relationship with her husband. "My feelings during sex are like the feelings I have when I am abducted. I feel frightened, used, and feeling that I have to endure this." She has at other times referred to having sex in the same tones as she uses about going to a gynaecologist or being raped. Sometimes her fear of intimacy forces her to refuse to be touched at all, and she has often turned to alcohol to overcome her frustrations.

11 The family line

Hopkins, particularly in his book *Intruders*, was probably the first major abduction researcher to speculate that abductions follow a family line and that perhaps part of the aliens' purpose is to conduct their experimentation through family lines, perhaps tracking genetic code, DNA, etc.

One of Mack's abductees, Jerry, appears to fit that description. She has three children, all of whom, Mack suggests, "appear to be involved in the abduction phenomenon." Sally, born in 1981, had frequent nosebleeds, dreamt of UFOs and has even suggested to her mother that "maybe the aliens choose specific families." Sally has reported dreams of lots of creatures surrounding her and of an alien girl with no hair asking her to come out and play, whereupon she found herself aboard a spaceship. After a recent nightmare Sally was found on top of her blanket with her underwear missing, and more recently she had a time-loss of nearly an hour while reading a book when she was insistent she had not fallen asleep. Her brother Matthew, who was born in 1983, displayed a fear of puppets with "scary big eyes." He was also frightened by a yoghurt commercial which depicted a UFO. Colin was born in 1990, and Jerry believes he has taken part in some of her own abductions. He has asked his mother about "scary owls with the big eyes." (Whitley Strieber has referred to a screen memory where the aliens apparently "were disguised" as owls or at least where his own memory was of seeing an owl which he now believes was an alien.) One of the family's experiences with Colin was particularly distressing. At the age of three he was shouting in an angry voice: "I don't want to go back to the spaceship!" He claimed he got lost but he didn't like it, and also that "I was born there and fell from the stars." Asked to explain what he meant, he confirmed that he believed he was born on the spaceship. Asked how he got on the spaceship, his reply was only "the eyes." Colin's experiences have to some degree divided Jerry and her husband. A doctor to whom they were referred by Mack sought to explain Colin's problems in more conventional ways, perhaps related to his television intake and interaction with his brother, who had been sexually abused. Since the doctor could not be definite, the result seems to be that Jerry was further convinced that the difficulties were UFO related, while her husband took comfort from the search for a more conventional source and resisted the abduction as a reality.

12 Emotional testing

Both David Jacobs and Budd Hopkins believe that a central part of the work the aliens perform during abductions is to test human beings under situations of extreme emotional states, even creating false situations in order to see the responses.

Several abductees have reported being shown something like television or holographic images of atomic war, famine, the end of the world and so on. Jacobs points out that during this procedure the taller being "observes [the witnesses and seems] to want to analyse the emotional effects of viewing the images. The scenes themselves do not appear to have any prescient or prophetic value." When we spoke to Dr. Jacobs during a lecture in London we discussed this aspect with him, pointing out that many contactees had seen similar images but believed that they were being given warnings which they should pass on in the hope that people mend their ways. Dr. Jacobs believed that they were simply wrongly interpreting the images they had seen, and that they were interpreting in a positive and pleasant way these clinical examinations.

Jacobs lists other visioning. Some abductees are shown romantic or sexual fantasies, attractive or peaceful surroundings such as gardens, fountains, family life and so on. Occasionally abductees are asked to hold something, and always apparently with the object of being studied by the aliens while they are experiencing these emotional events. For example Lynn Miller recalls that at the age of 13 she was shown a list of names that the taller being handed her which she was told she must memorize because there will be a war and the names were important. As a result of the experience she "developed an intense interest in World War II and became a 'buff,' studying the battles and leaders." Jacobs points out that this is unusual for a teenage girl but even more so for a member of the Mennonites, a religious group who would find war abhorrent. Jason Howard is one abductee who was shown scenes of atomic destruction.

Jacobs reports that sometimes images are not brought up on the screens but somehow directly imposed into the abductee's mind or that somehow the abductee is forced to envision the images themselves. The abductee sees the scenes in his or her head. "Often the scene is so realistic that the abductee does not know until careful investigation that it is being played out in her mind." Abductees are often led to believe that they are with a friend on board the spaceship, but it appears that some kind of screen memory is being used to create the image of a friend when the reality is that the other figure with them is an alien. Karen Morgan at the age of 30 was abducted and during the abduction forced to envisage the scene of her mother's death. She could see herself in the room in which her mother had died, as if viewing from the corner. The alien made clear his intentions. "He is telling me that I have to feel the way I did then. He is telling me that I have to feel that again . . . It's not horrible, it's emotional. It's very emotional, and he is making me watch it." Throughout all of this it appears the alien was watching her to see her responses to the emotions.

One of Mack's abductees, Scott, indicates that he believes the visions shown to the abductees by the aliens might be more than just a diversion or test. He states: "There is a massive amount of information in my head that I can't even understand," and believes that the aliens are developing people so that we can comprehend them and understand them. "They are getting us trained to get us to the point where we can deal with them."

Jacobs reports that there is limited scope for resistance of the aliens' intentions. He summarizes his work on this aspect.

The abductee's ability to resist during the abduction episode is limited. The aliens meet resistance with either patience or exasperation. Because they can physically and mentally control humans, they treat resistance as a nuisance. If the abductee gets out of control, the Small Beings usually back off and let the Taller Being deal with the situation, and procedures for regaining control are instituted. Yet some abductees have learned the areas where defiance and self-assertion are possible. When they do resist or at least throw the aliens off their routine, they briefly enjoy a sense of control and mastery of the situation that allows them to feel they are fighting back and are therefore less victimized.

Jacobs cites a few cases of resistance which appear to have been successful. Evelyn Livingston managed to run away from her abductors inside the UFO, getting quite some distance from them. "I got a little way down the hall. It felt really good to get away..." Patti Layne managed to jump off an examination table and run away, which seemed to create some consternation amongst the aliens, who backed off, and for a while I was "calling the shots." She got into another room but found herself cornered and was recaptured. One extraordinary account is of Jason Howard, who was apparently abducted while drunk. He managed to break away from their examination, laughing, swinging his arms around and forcing the aliens to back off. It seems that perhaps they gave up; the next thing he knew he was standing in his underpants on the grass of his college campus about a mile from where he had been abducted.

But perhaps it is naïve to believe any resistance has been effective. Is it not possible that the aliens allowed a certain measure of resistance, or even perhaps the image of resistance, in order that the abductees should precisely feel that they were gaining some control of the situation, to see what they would do with that control? In short, the few triumphs which we seem to have gained in learning about the aliens' motives and methods may well be what they wanted us to learn in the first place, or to believe we have learned. If so, then what is our true measure of freedom in dealing with the aliens?

Budd Hopkins has related one account when an abductee was apparently given a gun and told to kill another human being. As the event played out, it appears that the gun was harmless and that the other human being was an alien disguised by screen memory. Hopkins believes that the aliens wanted to test the stress created by the situation and examine the emotional responses that resulted.

Similarly, David Jacobs reports that Karen Morgan was taken into a room where several human guards stood around. A friend to whom she was attracted was brought in, and she thought that they were about to make love. However, the scene dissolved and she came to realize that the guards and her friend were all aliens. Presumably they had wanted to see her responses to the situation.

Jacobs reveals the extraordinary circumstances of abductee Charles Petrie, who was driving late one night when a boy ran out in front of the car and was hit. (The story—thus far, anyway—has obvious parallels to the "phantom hitchhiker" stories of ghost lore which are abundant in the UK, but are also found around the world.) The boy ran away into nearby bushes, Petrie stopped the car and chased after him and immediately found himself confronting an alien, whereupon he was taken into a UFO where the aliens apparently were interested in studying his guilt.

Many abductees have reported a sort of bonding; of touching the alien babies, holding them and hugging them, as for example was reported by Debbie Jordan (in Budd Hopkins' book *Intruders* then using the pseudonym Kathie Davis), one of the first people to report such complex abduction situations. But holding the babies may be an emotional "trick" on the part of the aliens. As Jacobs reports:

> Abductees universally state that the baby does not have the normal human reactions of a human infant. It is almost always listless. It does not respond to touch as a normal baby would. It does not squirm; it does not have a grasping reflex with its hand. It is

lifeless, yet it is not dead. Most women think that there is some-thing terribly wrong with the baby. They feel they must hold the baby to help it survive. After holding the baby for a while, women report that the baby seems "better." It appears to have a bit more energy or to be thriving slightly.

This could well be another test, designed to create a sense of involvement on the part of the abductees or to measure their re-sponse to "generating life" in the baby. The babies themselves are described as "not like a baby alien, nor does it look like a baby human." Generally the description sounds more like a Gray: large eyes, small reduced facial features, pointed chin, long thin body, long thin hands, greyish skin.

13 Alien cures and healings

These are cases of abductees reporting that they have been cured of an illness or that wounds have been healed. UFO-based spontaneous healings and extraordinary cures have been reported for some time, but usually in a context which suggests the brotherly love of contactee-type experiences. Jacobs be-lieves that this is possibly a misinterpretation and that the aliens merely seek to "preserve the specimen for their own pur-poses." In an echo of the continuing theme that appears to come through abductions, of people being treated as machinery, one of his abductee clients reported that it was "equipment mainte-nance." Abuctee Lynn Miller had diphtheria, which she be-lieves was cured by contact with aliens. Her parents' religious persuasion prevented her from being vaccinated, and she con-tracted diphtheria at the age of six. On one occasion the doctor explained to Lynn's mother that Lynn was not expected to live through the night. That was the night when Lynn experienced an abduction and when she was told by the aliens that they were to cure her; a device was placed around her body and she was made to stand in a vertical machine and then illuminated by a blue light from above. She was told she was cured. The next morning she was found playing on the floor, her temperature back to normal and the diphtheria completely gone. Jacobs has other cases of apparent cures of pneumonia.

American UFO researcher Preston Dennett produced a very important and ground-breaking work called *UFO Healings–True Accounts of People Healed by Extraterrestrials*, which examined what Jacobs' client calls "equipment maintenance." If Jacobs is right, it perhaps explains the apparently random and personalized healings which Dennett and others have encountered. Dennett summarizes UFO healings into three scenarios:

1. A sick person is awakened in his bedroom by aliens, who then take him into a UFO, examine him and tell him that they can cure his disease. The aliens treat the person in some medical fashion and return him to his bedroom, whereupon he discovers that all traces of disease have cleared.

2. A person is hospitalized in the "normal way" and while in hospital is visited by a "strange doctor" who administers treatment to the patient, perhaps leaving pills. The patient discovers that the illness has disappeared, apparently more rapidly or more thoroughly than would normally be expected.

3. A person driving along a road is passed over by a beam of light from a UFO and suddenly discovers that an illness, injury or disease is cured.

Interestingly, there are differences between researchers in the numbers and qualities of UFO healings they have uncovered. This is one of many areas where we are forced to consider the possibility that the researchers play a part in formulating the detail of the recollections they derive from their abductee subjects. Jacobs has commented that most explanations for UFOs, other than the deliberate intervention of alien visitors, are not valid because accounts do not conform to any kind of standard.

Other explanations, he believes, are therefore possibly fantasy or psychological, and in particular he cites New Age beliefs. His belief is that the UFO abduction phenomenon is highly consistent because he has found many identical accounts containing similar motifs. We agree that he has found many similarities, and also that the results of his work are very similar to those of John Mack and Budd Hopkins. This is Jacobs' strongest point, but is also perhaps his weakest. For although there is consistency within his own work and the work of Hopkins and Mack, we must bear in mind that both Mack and Jacobs give great credit to Hopkins for basically teaching them their trade. We have seen already that there are certain differences between Mack and the other two; Mack seems more open to a "spiritual" interpretation and indeed his cases seem to emphasize this point more. With regard to healings, when we look beyond the work of these three we discover that other experienced researchers have produced different results. Hopkins indicates that he has encountered just a few healing cases. "We do sometimes, very rarely, but they do turn up." Jacobs has commented that healings are found "in extremely rare cases." However, Edith Fiore, PhD, who has done similar extensive research into the abductions, indicates: "One of the most interesting findings that emerge from this work was the many healings and attempts to heal on the part of the visitors . . . *In about one half of the cases I have been involved in there have been healings due to operations and/or treatments*" (emphasis added). This is quite at odds with her compatriots, yet her abductees come from the same cultural and media background, i.e. predominantly the population of the USA. So why does Edith Fiore discover that one half of her cases contain healings, while they are very rare for Jacobs and Hopkins? Mack, it must be admitted, refers to many more such cases. "Many abductees have experienced or witnessed healing conditions ranging from minor wounds to pneumonia, childhood leukaemia, and even in one case reported to me first hand, the overcoming of muscular atrophy in the leg related to poliomyelitis." However, he does seem to be discussing the wider study of healings rather than those from his own sample.

Meanwhile Eddie Bullard's book, *UFO Abductions—The Measure of a Mystery* reveals that in his research of 270 abduction cases he discovered only 13 instances of healing, nothing like the quantity reported by Edith Fiore.

Let's look at some examples of UFO healings which may after all be, as Jacobs' subject suggests, "equipment maintenance." Of the many accounts of healings reported by Dennett (and others) it is those of his first, and perhaps second, scenario that we are interested in. The third scenario cases, where people appear to have been cured more or less as an aside, perhaps by the emanations from UFOs, suggest something more accidental than deliberate "maintenance."

Perhaps something is suggested by Dennett's case #079. A family from Southern California were driving through a remote desert area and their car overheated. The father opened the radiator cap, badly burning his hand as hot water dashed out. They refilled the radiator and drove towards the nearest town, but on the way discovered what appeared to be a hospital in the middle of the desert. In the hospital a nurse sprayed a substance on the father's hand, telling him not to wash it, and then the family drove off. By the time they reached the town the hand was completely cured. Realizing something was adrift they retraced their steps to locate the hospital, but were unable to find it. Dennett speculates that perhaps the hospital and the nurse were screen memories, masking a flying saucer and an alien, and cites by comparison accounts such as those by Debbie Jordan in Budd Hopkins' book *Intruders*, where she described several encounters disguised by screen memory.

Dennett's case #056 also conforms to Jacobs' speculation. It relates to Fred X of New York City, who in October 1988 was abducted and whose abduction was revealed by regression hypnosis following missing time and inexplicable marks on his body. Under hypnosis it was found that Fred X had been abducted

aboard a craft, medically examined, and had had sperm removed. While in the medical room he watched healing operations of a surgical nature being undertaken on other individuals,
presumably abductees. For example, he saw a naked woman
"opened up and has a vertical incision from the top of her chest
down to the groin area." Fred X watched as Grays inserted their
hands into the chest opening, either as part of a healing operation or as part of an examination. At a later time an alien pointed
a light at the incision and healed the cut. He described it: "What
he is doing to the skin, as he pulled it together, is just sealing it
up as if there wasn't any cut. He uses the light, pulls the skin together, and you can't tell she was ever cut." Of course we might
speculate that this was an artificial scene presented to Fred X in
order that the aliens could study his responses. Jacobs has produced cases in support of his belief that the aliens staged certain
scenes precisely to gauge and learn the human response.

   Carl and Dagmar R., a farming couple in Iowa, were abducted in October 1982. They had for some time been watching
strange lights outside their farmhouse and seen circles of burnt
grass on the ground. On the night in question Carl, alerted by
the sounds of cattle noises, saw a landed disc-shaped object
and three entities entering his bedroom. The couple were abducted and underwent physical examination and removal of
reproductive material. Dagmar also recalled that the aliens
burnt off a mole from under her left arm.

   In case #054, John Salter Jr., Professor of Indian Studies at the
University of North Dakota was driving in Wisconsin late at
night together with his son when they experienced missing
time. This occurred on 20 March 1988. Hypnotic regression revealed a commonly reported type of UFO abduction, including
examination by long needles and so on. Following the abduction, however, Salter found many changes taking place. Within
two months he had lost the desire to smoke, although he had
smoked considerably up to that time, and stopped smoking
completely. He also found "improved skin tone, circulation, eye

sight, faster blood clotting after cuts or scratches, and faster and thicker growth of toe nails and hair." He believes his skin is much healthier, wrinkles and scars having disappeared, and that his body is slimmer to some degree, without skin "sagging." He also reports that his energy level is way up and he has not suffered illnesses since March 1988. His son also reports that his cuts heal at a rapid rate.

Dennett reports a little-known fact regarding the otherwise famous abduction of Carl Higdon, which is explored in detail in Warren Smith's book *UFO Trek*. Higdon had been deer-hunting in Medicine Bow National Forest and had taken aim to fire at a large buck, but to his shock watched the bullet slowly float out of the gun and drop to the ground 50 feet away. At that point Higdon saw an entity nearby "with yellowish skin, no neck, no visible ears, small eyes, a slit-like mouth, straw-coloured hair and two antennae coming out of his head." He gave Higdon some pills and Higdon swallowed one. Higdon was then taken on board a UFO, where he was subjected to images of futuristic cities and so on. Later he was returned to normality and recalled his story under hypnosis. However, Dennett points out that prior to his encounter he had suffered from persistent and painful kidney stones, but that after the encounter the kidney-stone problem was gone for ever. The doctor also pointed out to Higdon that a tubercular scar on his lung had disappeared, and Higdon feels he was probably healed while aboard the UFO.

Canadian Army officer John Cyr of Quebec saw a UFO and discovered strange and inexplicable marks on his body. Prior to the experience Cyr had suffered from severe multiple sclerosis requiring hospital treatment every two weeks. He was normally in a wheelchair and virtually paralysed. Following the encounter Cyr was completely cured. "All symptoms of the disease have gone, and he hasn't had a stroke since."

During an abduction Linda X (case #105) saw a cancer cured in another male abductee. The man with the tumour was lying on the table and the aliens were holding circular objects over the tumour, which began to disappear. She recalled: "They are pulsing it to shrink the tumour, and I can almost see the tumour shrinking as they are working on it." With the tumour gone, the man got off the table, to be replaced by another for examination.

Helen X (case #36) was diagnosed in May 1974 as having cancer in her hip bone, which was surgically removed. Later more cancer was discovered in her pancreas, which was also operated on. However, cancer continued to spread, this time to Helen's bowels, and she was told that she did not have long to live. One evening she heard her name being called and, despite barely being able to walk, got into her car and drove out of town. There she saw a large white UFO which came down to the ground and from which two small figures emerged. Helen was taken on board, examined and told she had cancer of the left breast, liver, right kidney, pancreas and spleen. The aliens performed various operations for quite some time, passing instruments over her body and also injecting fluid into her. She was then told that her cancer was cured and she was released. The following morning she explained to her son what had happened. He disbelieved her, but did discover a large depression on the ground where Helen thought the UFO had landed. That same afternoon, however, Helen was vomiting black material and was rushed to hospital, and her family were told that she was about to die. She was in fact violently ill for two days, and was offered various medicines but refused them, remembering that the aliens had told her not to take any medication. By the third day she had recovered. "It was just like I had never been sick." The doctors admitted that she seemed cured, her skin colour was returned to normal and her cancer cure was verified by the doctors. She is in fact one of many abductees who have reported cancer cures as a result of their UFO experiences.

One of the most famous cases, also covered by Dennett, occurred on 25 October 1957 in Petropolis, Brazil. A young daughter of a rich and influential family was dying of stomach cancer and suffering badly when one night a brightly lit UFO appeared outside the house. The girl's brother saw a disc-shaped object within the light, saw a door open and two small figures emerge. Another figure remained in the doorway.

The figures were described as short with large round heads, reddish ears, small slanted eyes and bright green skin. They entered the house and went over to the daughter, Lais. The extraordinary event apparently caused some consternation and a great deal of tension in the room, which also contained Lais's father and mother, her brother and his wife and a younger brother, as well as the maid Anazia Maria, who related the story. The figures placed instruments on the bed covers and shone a bluish light that seems to have acted as an X-ray, as all the witnesses were able to see inside the daughter's belly. They then operated on the cancer and after approximately half an hour they left. Apparently telepathically they told her father they would give her some medicine, handing him a sphere with 30 pills to be taken once a day for a month. After this period it is alleged that Lais was cured of her cancer.

But just to show how perverse and trying the interpretation of UFO reports can be, consider this case from Dennett (case #013). A UFO flew over a cockfight. Cockfights are particularly vicious and largely illegal confrontations between two roosters and are almost always fought to the death of one of them. The two roosters were apparently fighting, and nearly dead from their injuries, when the UFO directed a beam at the two of them. Then, in the words of the witness, Susan Morton, who was 13 years old at the time, "Their small broken bodies glowed eerily for a few seconds. Then slowly, they both got up on their little chicken feet and began strutting around with robust healthy enthusiasm." The beam of light retracted into the UFO, which then departed at high speed, leaving the roosters healthy and with no sign of injury. As a result the cockfight was cancelled. If the witness's memory is accurate over the thirty years which elapsed before she wrote up her story, then what exactly was involved here? Ecological concern? Emotional testing? Equipment maintenance? A sense of humour?

14 Geography of the flying saucers

On board the flying saucers there appear to be specific rooms into which the abductees are taken. One of these Jacobs refers to as an incubatorium. Abductees see many, perhaps hundreds of foetuses being incubated, the foetuses often floating in tanks of liquid connected to machinery. Abductee James Austino reported: "It's like a machine with 20 or 30 tubes. The whole room is like round with them . . . And they line the wall. It's like a big fish tank or something, each one of them's a little fish tank . . . It's like blue liquid. There's lights underneath each tube, shining up straight into it . . . There's little things in each of these tubes . . . They're got little black eyes, like curled up, floating in there . . ." Another abductee, Anita Davis, saw the aliens placing an embryo that had been taken from her into one of the tanks in an incubatorium. Generally the foetuses in the incubatorium are believed to be the hybrids, not quite human-like and with the striking dark eyes of the aliens.

Another room appears to be a form of nursery where more developed babies are "stored," often in large numbers and in rows, rather like nurseries in hospital maternity units. One experience by Karen Morgan, however, suggests that perhaps even showing abductees the nursery is more of an emotional test than a physical necessity—a separate motif explained below in greater detail. The aliens told her during her perusal of the nursery: "They need mothers . . . They have to have their mothers." And the alien goes on to say: "Don't you care about them? Don't you care?" Karen reports that the alien appears to become almost angry and tells her that some of the alien babies are Karen's own. Certainly it appears that the aliens are testing

Karen's emotions, and whether or not some of the embryos are hers may not be the important aspect of the question.

15 The holodeck

In the science fiction series *Star Trek–The Next Generation* the spacecraft, the *Enterprise*, is equipped with a recreation and training facility known as the "holodeck." The programme presents it as a location where artificial scenes can be created in which real people can then absorb themselves as if at a real location. For example, in the television series the "holodeck" can reproduce ocean-side beach locations, where people can take romantic walks in the moonlight, can reproduce the San Francisco of the 1920s or 30s, where Captain Picard lives out fantasies of being a fictional "Sam Spade"-like detective, and so on.

Curiously enough, this sort of situation appears to be coming forward as an increasingly common motif in abduction reports. Catherine's case contains two such indicators. In the first case, although believing herself on a spaceship, she found herself in "a forest" ... "There is like trees and rocks and dirt things off to the left.... How can I be in the forest?... It doesn't make sense!" Her confusion was derived from the fact that she could see both the forest and the curving walls of the ship. In the "forest" she could even smell familiar forest scents.

On another occasion the aliens wanted to have a conference with her and appeared to have created for her an appropriate environment precisely for that purpose. "The room seemed to transform from a typically sparce spaceship room with tables, curved walls, and perhaps a viewing screen into an ornate executive conference room complete with shagged carpeting, mahogany panelling..."

Of one of his abductees, Dave, John Mack comments:

> His story abounds with rooms, like the dining-room in his first regression, that are not quite the actual rooms of his house, and landscapes with caves and trails that are not there upon later

searching. There is something rather frightening about this. For it confronts us with just how arbitrary the physical reality is within which we happen now to find ourselves. All that is required for this to be abruptly changed is the choice on the part of some other intelligence with the power greater than our own to do so.

One of the early tales of abduction actually contained this suggestion, though it has not arisen frequently since. To set this into context the details of the case are given below.

The case arose on 30–31 May 1974 at Beit Bridge, on the Zimbabwe border. "Peter" and "Frances" were driving from Harare in Zimbabwe to Durban in South Africa. During the drive, at around 2.30 A.M. Frances saw a bright, blue, flashing light to the left of the vehicle, keeping pace with them. The car lights seemed to dim, though other electrical equipment seemed unaffected. They did notice that the interior of the car was exceptionally cold.

Then, as Peter tried to slow down from the fast speed he had been maintaining, he found he could not affect the car; he could not slow down. Nor could he steer the car. Peter was frightened but said nothing to Frances, who was still concerned by the UFO sighting. Eighteen kilometres later the UFO had gone and Peter was able to stop the car in a service station. It was now around 4.30 A.M. One hour later they left the station and found that the UFO was again in the sky and pacing them.

The fact that the road was deserted is important to the point in question. The route was normally a busy one, and the previous day had been a public holiday. There should have been a great deal of traffic, yet there was none.

Then, as they continued to drive, they believed they had perhaps gone off course. They did not recognize the landscape around them, with its low bushes, high grass, marshes and swamps. The car was also driving in a "cone of silence"; with no noise from the engine and none of the sounds of insect life that would be normal for the area they thought they were in. The road, which should have been twisting and turning, was totally straight. And again Peter had no control of the car, now moving at around 200 kilometres an hour. Despite the obvious danger, Frances fell asleep.

When the couple arrived at Beit Bridge they discovered some extraordinary things. They found they had lost an hour of time; indeed the car clock was out of synch with local clocks. The trip-meter on the car suggested they had travelled under 30 kilometres though in fact they had covered a distance of 288 kilometres. The petrol tank largely agreed with the trip-meter. It should have needed refilling, but in fact it took only 22 cents' worth of petrol to refill it. The tyres produced a strange analysis also; they were cheap and should have needed replacing after 1,200 kilometres; but much later it was found that even after 8,000 kilometres they showed almost no signs of wear.

Peter and Frances undertook regression hypnosis. This revealed that Frances had been deliberately put to sleep during the drive and that an alien had entered the car and stayed with them for the journey. The entity told Peter that he, the alien, could look like anything Peter wanted him to. The entity also told Peter that he had been abducted "out-of-body," an uncommon report for the time but one examined within this chapter. More significantly, the alien told Peter that on board their spacecraft was a room, a special abduction "unit," into which abducted humans could be taken and where they could be induced to believe, by some form of simulation, that they were still in an Earth environment.

So do we see here that the car was actually taken aboard the alien craft and placed into the abduction room "holodeck," and that a simulated journey was created to keep Peter and Frances occupied during which time they were "dealt with" in ways perhaps even they do not yet know of, and are perhaps similar to those revealed by Jacobs and others? Is this an early case which identified a common, yet until recently misunderstood, aspect of abductions?

Another curious aspect of Catherine's recollection also has its parallels in science fiction; in the TARDIS of time traveller Dr. Who. In that television series the main character, The Doctor, travels through time and space in what looks like a police box, the primary characteristics of which is that it is huge on the inside and small on the outside. During her abduction recollections of being in a "forest" Catherine seemed puzzled by the apparent size of the ship and the distance between the walls, given the overall size she believed the ship was. She stated: "I can see where the edge of the ship would be on the left, it is way far away—maybe 50 feet away. I don't understand how it could have been that far because the other room was only like 10 feet wide and this one is so really far away."

Another of Mack's abductees, Joe, makes a similar observation. "We kind of walked, kind of floated" into a spaceship which was, to use Joe's description, "much bigger inside than outside." Again, however, this is not unique to the UFO phenomenon and there is a case in the early literature. Hunter Carl Higdon in October 1974, coincidentally just months after the Beit Bridge encounter, had an extraordinary UFO experience in the Medicine Bow National Forest. The case was mentioned above in "Alien cures and healings," but of significance here is that Higdon saw a box-shaped object some 4½ feet wide, 7 feet long and 5 feet high which he then *found himself inside*. The relative dimensions between himself and the object had obviously changed, for he was able to sit in a chair in a room on board. He believes he was moved into the device either by being shrunk down or transferred into it by some kind of dimensional shift.

16 Multiple abductions

There is an increasing tendency for abductees to report seeing other abductees during abductions. Jacobs has probably uncovered more such cases than anyone else. In one recollection Karen Morgan remembers being strapped onto a bench on a UFO and seeing several other people sitting in alcoves nearby. She described one young man apparently "switched off" but with his eyes wide open, which she found "horrifying." She also saw a redheaded woman wearing pyjamas, implying presumably a bedroom abduction. She was apparently in a waiting room, a kind of purgatory before going through to the examination. While she waited, aliens came in, removed her clothes and then took her through to the main room. Each person was accompanied by two aliens. Inside the main room Karen saw many tables, shelves running round the room, instrumentation and so on.

Catherine also recalled the most extraordinary abduction room, with not just one or two subjects but possibly up to 200 people all being operated on during their abductions at the same time. Mack reports that Catherine saw "rows of tables on either side, separated by perhaps five feet, with many that were empty, and about a third to a half with human beings on them to whom procedures were being done. She estimated she saw between 100 and 200 humans in all in that room." This is not a unique account; Jacobs too has received a report like this from one of his clients.

These are rare reports, however, we might consider, apart from the possibility that they are factual as described, that these large rooms are a "holodeck" image for some purpose or another—as indeed could be the incubatoriums and nurseries. Linking several of the motifs, perhaps the purpose of all such geography is to provide illusory scenery for emotional testing. At the present time there is no reliable case of two "unconnected" abductees independently verifying seeing each other on board a flying saucer.

17 Aboard what?

Although in this chapter we have referred often to "the flying saucer," using it as a convenient shorthand for the location into which the abductees are taken, it is important to remember that many abductees do not clearly recall being taken aboard any such device. There have been cases of abductees clearly remembering the presence of a flying saucer during an abduction, of course;

Betty and Barney Hill were led to one, and Patti reports the same. But a good many assume they are on a flying saucer without actually seeing one; they simply find themselves in a strange room, or they are lifted up to a vague shape in the sky which they assume is a flying saucer. Perhaps it is one, or perhaps we are using this modern image to fill in an uncertainty. We might remember that most abductees report "doorway amnesia" which has been identified within the abduction phenomenon almost from the outset; put simply, they do not remember actually passing through a doorway on to the craft, but only approaching it and then finding themselves inside. We might also remind ourselves that there are few cases which actually link objects and lights seen in the sky with abductions, and the links are at best tenuous. There are few reports—and none without considerable doubts attached to them—of distantly perceived objects being seen by independent witnesses going to a location where those witnesses then see an abduction taking place. The "Linda Cortile" case in New York is a suggestion of one such case, but the evidence is so dependent on one witness—Cortile—that the case has not yet proved its reliability as the witnessed abduction it is claimed to be. We might consider therefore a curious but possible situation where we have a genuine UFO phenomenon (i.e. objects and lights in the sky) and a genuine abduction phenomenon (people having genuinely strange experiences in some kind of "other reality") without the two actually being connected, but being associated with each other by presumption and perhaps a dependence on a culture of science fiction to provide the imagery.

18 Spiritual dimension

A great many abductees have found that the experiences force them to explore what might be rather crudely summed up as "their spiritual side." Needless to say this can take many forms, so a selection of cases noted below gives something of the flavour of this motif.

One of John Mack's clients, Lee, did not feel that she was a vic-

tim even though some of the experiences she had had as an abductee were intrusive. Apart from the physical and sexual trauma
she herself pointed out that the experience had "provided a price-
less opportunity for spiritual growth and sensitivity to all sentient beings, ranging from insects to those of other dimensions
and planetary systems." She felt less like an inter-galactic rape
victim than someone who had had "an experience of something
which has nearly blown my head off with expansion of consciousness. I am strangely grateful." She seems to be someone
who was open to spiritual growth; shortly after her experience
she left for India, a trip which had previously been planned, and
studied Tibetan Buddhism and other spiritual disciplines.

Lee's mother Emily accepts the positive aspects of the abduction experience. Mack reports that "she feels a deep, intuitive
sense that the process that they are undergoing is one of personal growth and ultimate enlightenment." Mack does, however, comment that "this attitude, whatever its ultimate truth
may prove to be, is unique in my experience among the parents
of abductees." It is rare, indeed, though we found a similar level
of acceptance in one case, that of "Bryan," written up in the book
Gifts of the Gods?, by John Spencer.

Lee's brother Scott has also recognized a spiritual dimension
to his experiences, commenting to his support group that the experiences had "opened up something in me." He commented:
"It's almost like you are given an intense jump into a spiritual
realm you are not even ready for—like Yogis go through tons of
work to do to get to a certain point."

Catherine, the case outlined at the beginning of this chapter, is
also exploring her own personal development along with the experiences. Whether the experiences are dictated by the aliens or
are a device by which her own mind is creating ways to expand,
the effect appears to be the same. She claims that the experiences
were "not part of the normal consciousness" and that in order to
deal with them "I've got to change my world view . . ." Catherine
believes that the aliens are "more advanced spritually and emo-

tionally than we are" and that therefore "if I'm going to get anything useful from them I've got to deal with them on their level."

Leo Rutherford, a teacher of modern shamanism, who spoke
to one of Mack's abductees at a conference, believed that when
listening to the abduction account he was hearing something
very similar to the shamanic journey. If so, then the alien takes
the role of the "power animal" which teaches the individual
and joins him or her on exploratory journeys. This would seem
to be the effect with Catherine, whatever level of objective reality is involved. Certainly Catherine believes that the changes
in her own consciousness which she describes as both spiritual
and psychic growth are a product of the "life-shattering" result
of the abduction experiences.

Specifically she believes she had a greater psychological
openness, and Mack comments that "the abductions themselves
operated as a provocation." She believes that she has stronger
intuitive abilities, can "feel people's auras," can tell what their
intentions are. She believes, "This whole experience makes you
open up to so many levels, so many other possibilities." Mack's
own commentary on the case includes the point that "the acceptance of the actuality of her experiences, whatever their
source may ultimately prove to be, has permitted Catherine to
deal more effectively with the powerful effects and bodily feelings that accompany them . . . and to reach a higher or more creative level of consciousness . . . Catherine's shifting attitude from
antagonistic battling . . . to a kind of active acceptance has had
several results. It has enabled her to undergo considerable personal growth that has been manifested by a desire, which she is
already implementing, to help other abductees come to terms
with their experiences and by a deepening sense of concern for
the fate of the Earth's environment."

We can consider also the case of Whitley Strieber. Before becoming aware of his experiences he was a successful horror
writer, and his books perhaps reflect the inner feelings he had.
His accounts of his own abductions indicate that they were a life-

long set of experiences. For example, the blurb from the 1978 Whitley Strieber book, *Wolfen*, reads: "...they have existed for thousands of years in the midst of man"—an attribute Strieber also applies to what he calls "the visitors." *Wolfen* has many parallels to Strieber's abduction claims. The book starts with an unidentifed grey pack of (wolf) figures that are quietly identified to the reader as potentially supernatural. The first wolf creature properly identified is female. They are able almost to hypnotize their victims, such as happens to Officer Becky Neff in her first encounter. They have a strange "quality" or power that allows them to appear on the terrace of Neff's sixteenth-floor apartment. Quickly we discover that they have special intelligence and are seeking out Neff and her colleague Wilson. Later in the book is the speculation that the hunted plays a willing part in its own capture. This is demonstrated in the book by a scene which results in the death of a moose, but where the moose plays a part in its own capture by the supernatural wolf pack.

These are some of the most striking parallels between *Wolfen* and the 1987 alien abduction account *Communion*. Some have argued that this was Strieber's first try at *Communion*; that *Communion* is only another fiction story based on *Wolfen*. But the alternative possibility is that *Wolfen* reflects the author's lifetime contacts with aliens coming through in his fictional writings. Certainly there are major differences that probably suggest the latter: in particular the strong motif of "powerful eyes" in *Communion* is noticeably absent from *Wolfen*. That at least is Strieber's own feeling; he told us: "I think that the experience was unfolding in my consciousness throughout my entire career. You can see reflections of all of the forms I later saw in the 'Communion days' in my earlier work."

19 Past lives and reincarnation

Catherine seems to have experienced former lives while undergoing her abduction, possibly because the aliens felt that this was a way of educating her or making her connect with her own history. In particular she recalls what seems to be a former life in Egypt in the time of the Pharaohs. Mack reports: "What was striking at this juncture was the fact that the quality of Catherine's experience was totally transpersonal, i.e. she was not having a fantasy *about* the painter. Instead she *was* Akremenon..."

Past lives arise in several of John Mack's clients. Joe recalls something similar, in particular when he "was" Paul Desmonte, a poet living near London at the time of the Industrial Revolution. In his case also these "memories" allowed him to discover "my own fears. My own judgement. My own biases..."

We might consider therefore that the aliens are capable of triggering actual memories of former lives or that they are capable of creating false memories purporting to be former lives which enable them to trigger or study emotional responses, a theme to which David Jacobs is particularly attracted. Perhaps the "past life" scenarios are merely other forms of creating artificial situations in which to study humans.

One of John Mack's abductees, Dave, has recollections of what seem to be past lives. He apparently had feelings that he had once been in the American Civil War. Another abductee, Julia, with whom Dave feels a closeness, told him that the first time she ever saw Dave, in Mack's living-room, she saw him wearing a Confederate uniform.

Dave also has a close affinity with a North American native Indian sacred site, known as Pemsit Mountain. North American tradition has it that it is a place of magic and apparently many people living in the area describe it as "UFO base." At the age of 12 Dave would go there, commenting: "I think the Indians used to go there. I'm a modern day Indian." He recalls an abduction experience there. A tingling sensation was the start of the experience, then several beings floated up a trail on the mountainside. He was shocked, surprised and afraid as the beings floated him feet first along the same trail. Around the bend he could see a spherical ship suspended in mid air. He was floated aboard and laid on a table. On the table he was surrounded by many alien shapes and subjected to an intrusive examination including anal probes. "You can't do anything," Dave stated, the abductee being totally in their power. Despite the intrusive and aggressive circumstances, and Dave's fear, he felt "somewhat akin to them," admired them and obviously felt in harmony with them.

Dave has past-life memories of being a native American Indian boy. He was given the name Panther-by-the-Creek and was studying to be a medicine man of a Susquehannock tribe living near the Pemsit Mountain at a time before the white man had invaded the area. Dave described life by the river. "The eagle is real special. The mountain is like a special place. Medicine men go up there to get visions, do journeys." Clearly Dave is referring to the quest which all spiritual leaders, including medicine men, must go through in order to make contact with the spirits and spirit guides in order to lead their people. While up the mountain, during this past life, he met Velia, an alien figure that also features in his present life abductions. (Mack comments: "Velia appears to be a principal agent in the evolution of Dave's consciousness.") He recalled Indian wars with the Iroquois in which he took part, and indeed in which he was killed. He recalled being pierced through the heart by an arrow, of dying, of looking down on his body and seeing one of the Iroquois warriors scalping him and then drifting upwards and being contacted by Velia, not actually seeing her but feeling her presence.

Dave also recalled other past lives as part of his general personal voyage of discovery. Throughout many of these lifetimes Velia has been with him. His description of her is fairly "classical": "Grey skin, big head, big black eyes . . ."

Interestingly as Dave explored his experiences and his association with the magical Indian mountain he apparently discovered that "a book he was reading about a woman who was becoming a Shaman and had abduction experiences was leading him to connect Shamanism and abductions." Mack comments: "Native American spirituality, Shamanism, strange powers of nature, altered realities, Chi, karate, the mastery of dreams, UFO abductions, past life experiences, and a multiplicity of synchronisities are all part of a mysterious puzzle for Dave whose pieces . . . he is learning to put together."

20 Artistic effects

In *Gifts of the Gods?*, (by John Spencer) there are many accounts of what seem to be positive side-effects of abduction and close encounter experiences. Generally, many abductees find that the experience triggers in them both a desire and a talent for artistic expression in the form of painting, sculpture, music and so on. In many cases these become life-changing; several of John's interviewees had changed their career paths and were earning their living from their new-found skills. One of John Mack's subjects, Jerry, had abduction experiences which appear to have resulted in an astonishing outpouring of poems and complex information which intensified following an abduction experience in November 1991. Sometimes it has the quality of artistic expression, and at other times the information seems to have been "channelled." "I don't know where it's coming from," Jerry indicated, a phrase many abductees have used to us in describing artistic and expressive drives following such experiences. Mack comments: "Jerry felt that many of her ideas did not come from within herself but from some other source."

21 Turned into machinery / implants

Not all the side-effects or responses to the close encounter experiences are positive. One fairly consistent component arising from abduction research is a tendency for some abductees to regard themselves as being manipulated by machinery, being a part of machinery, or even being turned into machinery. Sometimes it is the overt description of being "wired into" machinery; at other times it comes through in the way abductees refer to aspects of their experiences. The following examples show this tendency. Whether it is because the abductees feel like machines being serviced, or whether it is a reflection of a criticism of our modern society which treats people "mechanically" is a question to be examined as this motif becomes more apparent.

Mack's client, Scott, described that during one occasion when sperm was being taken from him he had an out-of-body experience and was able to see himself while they operated on him. His description is one of being manipulated by machinery. Apart from the device over his penis connected to a box near the table he could see four prongs pressed into his neck which he believes might be like electrodes manipulating and controlling him. He could also see wires attached to his testicles and believes that he was mechanically stimulated to erection and ejaculation.

David Jacobs reports that he received accounts from two abductees of what appear to be the manufacture of what he calls proto-beings. Devices were fitted over one abductee as if to create moulds, and that same abductee later saw what looked like manufactured creatures which were "rough imprints of humans." They were like robots with wires attached to their backs and heads. This is perhaps the most obvious description of being "turned into machinery."

One of John Mack's abductees, Jerry, believes that an implant was left inside her to monitor her during one abduction. And also that she was partially paralysed by an intense vibration. She commented: "Like somebody turning you into a vibrating machine . . . like somebody put you inside a machine and you were part of that machine."

There is a well-known aspect of abductions that has surfaced over the years; that of implants. The belief is that aliens implant small devices into humans, often around the brain area, by inserting it into the ears, up the nose, or behind the eyeball (but sometimes in other parts of the body). The reason for these devices is only speculation: to track people; to stimulate centres of their brain; to develop aspects of the brain such as clairvoyance, telepathy, etc; to interface people to their own machinery, etc. The belief may not be so far advanced from our own abilities. We currently implant identifying tags into animals in much the same way as is being speculated for abducted humans.

Richard Sauder, writing in the July/August 1996 edition of the California *UFO Magazine* ("Alien Implants: The Realm of the Possible"), describes the work of companies developing such devices. He notes that three patents for such implant devices specify, "The primary object of this invention is to provide a system for identifying an object, animal or *person*."

22 Contactees/abductees

We have traditionally divided the close encounter experiences up between the contactees and the abductees; and there are a number of striking differences as the cases in this book show. However, not only are there overlaps, but there is an increasing tendency to find such overlaps in current abduction reports. For whatever reason, the "contactee era" looks as if it will get a boost and a rebirth within the abduction claims.

For example, in Mack's book he relates the case of Ed. It is a case which has many parallels with the findings of others such as David Jacobs but which is also much closer to the realm of the contactee than of the "traditional" abductee. In a series of flashbacks Ed recalled an experience he had when, as a High School teenager, he and some friends were on holiday in July 1961. Ed, his friend and his friend's parents stopped north of Portland on the coast of Maine overnight. The parents stayed in a cabin and the two boys slept in the car. Ed thinks that he slept and when he "awoke" he was naked on a precipice over the sea in a "pod" covered in a "glass bubble." With him in the pod was a small female figure with long silver-blond hair which seemed familiar to him, suggesting childhood abductions. The figure had a small mouth and nose, large dark eyes, triangular shaped head and large forehead.

This is an interesting description; it is similar in part to the Grays, but has parallels with the report of Antonio Villas Boas, the well-known abductee from Brazil in the late 1950s. At the time Villas Boas's account seemed to form a "bridge" between the Adamski-reported "Nordics"—human looking with long flowing blond hair—and the aliens reported by Betty and Barney Hill. This case falls within the same time frame. The Villas Boas account also contains references to sexual intercourse with the alien, as does this case.

Ed discovered that he was sexually excited and believed the female sensed this. They had apparently normal sexual intercourse, though he refers to it as being "similar" to human sexual intercourse and later still regarded himself as a virgin, although he describes the sex with the alien as both "fulfilling" and "great."

The female alien then started explaining various concepts to Ed, telling him that he would remember them later when he needed to know them. He seems to have regarded the sex as almost a preliminary "get to know you" before the real business of educating him. The information apparently related to politics, environment, human relationships and so on, with a warning that we need to conduct ourselves in a better way. This is very similar to the early contactee messages, and also very similar to the accounts of the contactees. Ed was warned that the damage being done on Earth was also endangering the aliens' planet, though this certainly seems unlikely, at least within known laws of physics.

The encounter permanently changed him, he believes. Interestingly, like so many people undergoing abduction—a motif to be examined—he relates this in very mechanistic ways, talking about himself more as a machine than a human. "The closest analogy I can give," he says, "is like changing some of the software architecture and some of the hardware in the computer." Following the encounter Ed apparently found himself involved in arguments on social, political and scientific matters which seem to have fascinated his friends and, according to Ed, intrigued his teachers.

He became interested in the history of human civilization, in nature and a closeness to trees and plants and the ecology, to

Eastern philosophy and meditation. His wife Lynn also seems to have abduction-related memories which perhaps have drawn them closer.

Exploring his abduction memory further, under regression hypnosis, it appears he was floated out of the car and to the object "flying" at high speed along the coast. (We might speculate on the increasing tendency of abductees to report out-of-body abductions, which matches some of the imagery described by Ed; if his abduction was not of his full physical body it might explain the dichotomy of his having appreciated "great" sex while still feeling himself to be a virgin.) The object he found himself in appears to have been very large; he described the room he was in as an amphitheatre.

Like many abductees, particularly those relating their accounts to Hopkins and Jacobs, Ed told how he had sperm removed by machinery as well as the sexual encounter (which also matches the claims of Villas Boas).

Then Ed was "educated," telepathically impressed with apocalyptic images of the Earth in anguish and pain. "You can talk to the Earth. The Earth talks to you," they told him. He recalled indeed that "things talk me . . . the animals, the spirits . . . I can sense the Earth." The aliens impressed on Ed that he had a "greater agenda" to do with harmony with nature, and at one point he actually saw spirits as "mirthful little playful creatures . . . just bounding around." Interestingly, one of the spirits appears to be very similar to the alien in his description, with long silvery hair, oversized head, and just a foot or so tall. She told Ed: "I put myself like this so you could sort of look at me and relate to me. But I don't have to be like this if I don't want to be like this, and I can change myself into a multitude of forms." (This would mirror the claims of abductees Peter and Frances in Africa, who were told by the alien they encountered that he could look like anything he wanted to.) Ed was given the task "to teach those human beings who will listen . . . There are those who will listen before it happens, and prepare themselves." The "before it happens" presumably relates to the cataclysmic and painful future of the Earth, which can be avoided if the human race changes its ways. When John Mack expressed his confusion about the overlap between the spiritual and the physical, Ed commented: "A person has to spiritually re-balance themselves." This is very much the stuff of contactees rather than abductees, but it may be that Mack's approach is less targeted than that of Hopkins or Jacobs and is actually getting deeper into the abductees' true feelings. On the other hand we must take account of Jacobs' and to some degree Hopkins' view that these visions are just experimentation and that the abductees are wrong to attribute anything of deep futuristic significance to them. The effect on Ed is very clear, however. "Love is the key, love and compassion for the Earth or the beings on the Earth, be they corporeal or incorporeal—not love in the mush and gush sense, but there is a deeper sense of love."

Mack's subject, Scott, also had visions of a destroyed world, but one which he felt was the aliens' own planet, and he believed that part of their mission was to stop us destroying ours. Scott believes that as a result of destroying their own planet the aliens now have to live in an artificial environment and that their goal is to live on Earth, either without humans or together with us if the humans change.

23 Equipment failures

One of John Mack's abductees, Dave, experienced a poltergeist-type event at the age of 25. He had just built a small cabin in an isolated area and had moved in there. One night he placed a brown paper bag full of empty beer cans outside the front door and then went to bed. Later he heard what seemed to be an animal approaching the house and then heard banging and crashing noises which seemed to correlate to it running into the beer cans. He continued to listen, hearing noises as if the animal was kicking the cans. When he shone the flashlight out of the window to see what mess had been made he discovered that the bag was still standing where he had left it and no cans had been dislodged. At the time apparently Dave considered that "a spirit of something" might have been involved and did not relate the incident to UFO experiences. There are many cases in poltergeist literature of, for example, people hearing whole cupboards of glass crashing in the kitchen, and running in to find nothing disturbed whatsoever. It appears that something similar happened in this case.

There are many accounts of close encounter witnesses also reporting other paranormal activity, poltergeistery being one of the most common. It is therefore interesting to see that the electronic investigation of both have had their parallels also.

One novel approach devised by David Jacobs to deal with UFO abductions was to monitor repeater witnesses continuously, using video recorders. As Jacobs offers: "The camera makes it impossible for the aliens to maintain secrecy during an abduction, and in some cases it is able to effectively forestall the experience."

Mack's subject, Scott, attempted to use electronics as a defence mechanism. Because of his abductions "Scott had wired the house where he lives alone with a radio alarm he activated at night, mounted surveillance cameras in several locations as a 'deterrent,' and a microphone by the front door with a speaker next to his bed for night monitoring."

Jacobs reports the case of Melissa Bucknell, who at one point was having abductions on an almost daily basis. Jacobs and his team set up a video camera and recorder on a dresser, focused on her bed. For several days there was no activity, and when the tapes were viewed Melissa was found to be sleeping throughout. Once, however, she reported that she believed something might have happened to her during that morning. On that occasion she had gone to sleep late and had slept until noon. The investigators discovered that the tape had run out at 6 o'clock in the morning and concluded that the abduction had taken place between then and noon. They regarded it as a "near miss."

On another occasion the video camera again just missed an abduction. Melissa had been sleeping on a couch, driven there by the noise of neighbours arguing, and again therefore the camera had

missed the abduction. It is easy to infer that the aliens knew that
the video tape was not recording Melissa, which enabled them to
do their abduction, but there are many objections to this. Not the
least is that if there are aliens with such abilities, they could presumably interfere with the camera in some way if an abduction
was necessary. We might also speculate that actually Melissa's
neighbours were not arguing, but that the argument was "created"
as a way of driving her away from the range of the camera. But we
cannot argue these possibilities without considering the further
possibility that the abduction experience is an internally generated image, and that it was suppressed by the knowledge of the
video cameras being present and allowed to generate again when
the abductee/subject knew that the camera was not on her.

Jacobs relates that Karen Morgan also used a video camera
and was never abducted while the camera was on her. She was,
however, abducted when away from her home visiting friends or
relatives, and even when she was staying on a friend's yacht. As
Jacobs reports: "When she 'forgot' to set up the camera or VCR
for the night, there was a good possibility that she would be abducted." Some such problem occurred surprisingly often:

> We began to notice that the video equipment would sometimes
> mysteriously malfunction or be turned off—and an abduction
> would follow. Unusual power outages that affected only the im-
> mediate surroundings (sometimes not even other rooms) would
> cause the VCR to go off and an abduction would take place. After
> one abduction Karen noticed that the camera wires had been
> pulled from the back of her VCR. Another time she noticed in the
> morning after her abduction that the video camera was off when
> she had specifically remembered turning it on and seeing the red
> light indicating that it was in the "record" mode.

If Jacobs and Hopkins are correct that the aliens control their
abductees, then perhaps that explains why one abductee felt an
otherwise inexplicable urge at five-thirty in the morning to get

out of bed and turn the camera off, all of which was recorded on the tape. She later remembered that there were beings outside of the camera range "directing her to do it." On another occasion a woman abductee felt nervous and had the irresistible urge to get out of bed and sleep in another room, and she was abducted while out of camera range. And on yet another occasion one woman had the urge to go to bed three hours early and was abducted before the camera was programmed to switch on.

However, consider the times that this has happened in poltergeist and other investigations. We attended one poltergeist-vigil where we set up a concealed video camera to point at an object that was said to move frequently from one room to another while the witnesses who lived in the house were absent during the day. The witnesses did not know about the camera. They were due to arrive home at nine o'clock; the tape should have run to nine-thirty. Just after nine o'clock we got a call from them to say they had arrived home—and the object had moved! Whatever was going on, we thought we would now be able to prove it. We would either have film of a spontaneous occurrence, or we would have caught the hoaxer. When we arrived at the house, we discovered that we had loaded the wrong tape in the machine; it had run out at eight-thirty.

Another experienced poltergeist researcher, Guy Lyon Playfair, did exactly the same thing with an audio recording at the famous "Enfield" case. Activity took place after a short tape left by Playfair had run out. He states: "This had to be the night I put in a sixty-minute cassette instead of my usual ninety-minute one."

Yet another poltergeist researcher we spoke to reported the same thing. Colin Davies set up video equipment overnight in a poltergeist-affected shop to try to record some of the events. During the day prior to that experiment Davies had himself witnessed some phenomena, so he had high hopes for the test. Two cameras ran for nine hours but did not record any events. Minutes after the last moments of recording, a pen, a bulldog clip and a plug and lead were seen to move spontaneously.

The link between the two phenomena suggested by this similarity is one that must be explored before the true nature of either can be understood with certainty.

Psychological Testing

The question of the reliability of witness reports has obviously been central to the debate on abductions. John Mack decided to ask Dr. Stephen Shapse of Harvard's McLean's Hospital to put one of his subjects, Peter, through a battery of psychometric testing. "My thought was that if this impression were affirmed by a qualified clinical psychologist, it could help to dispel the notion that the reports of abductees are the product of some sort of psychiatric disturbance." Mack believed that there was no "manifest or underlying psycho-pathology that could explain, or even shed much light, on the experiences [Peter] was having." Peter went through several tests: The Wechsler Adult Intelligent Scale-Revised (WAIS-R), which is an intelligence test; The Bender Visual Motor Gestalt Test (BVMG), testing for brain dysfunction; The Thematic Apperception Test (TAT); The Minnesota Multiphasic Personality Inventory - 2 (MMPI-2), and the Rorschach Inkblot Test (RIBT). Shapse concluded that Peter was "highly functioning, alert, focused, intelligent, well spoken, and without visible anxiety." The tests indicated that there was no basis for a belief in organic neurological dysfunctioning. Shapse could not relate the findings to the abduction experiences. It seemed that whatever was triggering the abduction reports, it was not any aberration on the part of the witness.

Hypnosis

The question of hypnosis is one that has divided the abduction debate. BUFORA has for many years worked under a moratorium, not using regression hypnosis as a means of research. Its value as therapy is clear, and there are many cases of those who have benefited by using hypnosis to "work through" anxieties. But is the information they retrieve of value, or is it fantasy? Some experiments conducted by the authors some years ago, written up in, for example, *Gifts of the Gods?*, indicate that people can lie or fantasize under hypnosis. The hypnosis can bring forward fears and wishes as well as memories. Similar work by colleagues in past life regressions had indicated the same. But on the other side of the coin leading researchers such as Mack, Hopkins and Jacobs disagree.

Jacobs states that hypnosis is "an indispensable tool in unlocking the memories of an abduction." He recognizes the possible problems, and sets out the methodology he uses to avoid those problems, or deal with them constructively.

John Mack, in working with Ed, believes that the hypnosis clarified a great deal of the imagery which Ed was confused about in his fragmented memories. Mack concludes: "All this suggests that, at least in Ed's case, the information recalled painstakingly under hypnosis is more reliable than the consciously recalled story, which seems to have been unconsciously adjusted to be compatible with Ed's wishes and self esteem." Mack also concludes that "there are other details obtained during the hypnosis session . . . which made the story obtained during the regression more believable, or at least more consistent with other abduction accounts." Mack states:

> The narrative which Ed was able to recover in an altered state of consciousness appears, from what we know of the abduction phenomenon, to be much more plausible than the account he could provide from conscious memory. This supports the argument for the power of hypnosis to recover memories of abductions that are both meaningful and true to the actual experience . . . and suggests that, at least in the case of UFO abductions, hypnosis may be more of a clarifying than a distorting tool.

11

Abductions— A Personal Account

The previous chapter shows that the abduction phenomenon is a complex field of study. To understand what it can mean to the experiencers themselves it is important to hear their own words, uninterrupted by interpretation and analysis. This chapter represents Ros Reynolds' own account, in her own words, of her experiences. It is based on our own interview with her, and she has approved the text as an accurate reflection not only of what happened to her and what she believed happened, but also of the after-effects, which can be difficult to come to terms with.

Ros was born in 1961 and had a UFO encounter in 1982 at the age of 21. Mark is her current partner. Other people are referred to by initials only. The interview was conducted in May 1997.

The first thing I ever knew about UFOs was actually seeing the darned thing I saw. It was 1982, around September I think. It was about seven-thirty or quarter-to-eight in the evening. [Ros and her boyfriend at the time, P, were driving towards Sudbury, in Suffolk.] There were warehouses to the right, and fields on the other side. This is going back before the bypass was built. I think it's a bit more built up now.

Researchers of the paranormal will be familiar with the area, one of the most haunted localities in Britain according to some studies. Borley, and its infamous rectory that was investigated by Harry Price, is just a few miles from Sudbury.

> The first thing I noticed, while we were driving along [P was at the wheel], was this fast-moving horseshoe shape of lights coming over the High Road; a horseshoe shape in all different colours. It was coming so fast, and straight at me. I swore it was a helicopter or plane crashing. I thought, "Christ, it's going to hit the power cables." In fact it actually went between the power cables and us in the car; that's how low it was. Then it sort of swerved and shot over a hedge beside the road.
>
> What was interesting was, it didn't make any sound. We saw blue tendrils of light bouncing off the pylons. The whole thing threw us really; one minute you're playing the radio and the next minute this thing flies over and, well, it changes the topic of conversation somewhat.
>
> So we carried on through Sudbury, and beyond. We were due to get to Corby, in Northants, by about ten o'clock. We always went through the back roads; P didn't like the main roads. We went towards Long Melford and on to the Clare Road. The roads there are, like, you get little blocks of houses and a little village and a few more houses and a farm; it's a bit like that. A few fields, then a few houses, a few trees, then a little bit of a wood, then lots of hedges and so on. It's a boring road.
>
> Then it came back. For it to come round and pick us up on the Clare Road it had to do a complete U-turn. It went straight over the top of us. And that's when it started getting a bit scary. It went over and then it swayed backwards and forwards just over the top of us. Just floating. It did that two or three times.

Ros described with her hands a "falling leaf motion" which is often reported in UFO sightings; the object oscillating back and forth as it descends.

> That really got my attention. It was weird. The only way I can de-

scribe it, it was like a whopping great big sting-ray with a horseshoe shaped group of lights around it, and this light in the centre. But it wasn't a light; it was more like a light that was "turned off," dark but you could see it. And then as it came down parallel to the car, and level with my eyes as I was looking out of the window, it turned into, like a big oval white light. It had like a white light around it.

It kept pace with us. It went in and out of trees, it went over hedges, it disappeared round the backs of houses, and at the end there was a great big railway embankment and these telegraph poles and you could see the electric lines behind it, so it must have been close to us. So it certainly wasn't the moon! Or a barrage balloon. Or a plane. It kept pace with us for about six miles.

I started arguing with P. He was just holding on to the steering wheel, like he was wearing blinkers. He refused to look at it. Just staring straight ahead and saying, "Whatever it is it will go away." But then all of a sudden the car started faltering, like it was running out of petrol. For a while it was like a joke; I thought he was winding me up—I'd seen Close Encounters [the UFO-based film], where the car stops in the middle of the road. But I looked out of the window of the passenger door and it was just hovering there. It wasn't up in the air, it wasn't landed on the ground; it was just in the field, hovering there. There was no sound, no humming, no nothing, just one big blob of light. Then it wasn't funny any more.

We argued about this damn car. Never mind the light, worry about the car, get the car started. But we were worried. I remember in the end we said, "We'll count to three; one, two, three, then we'll get out of the car together." I kept an eye on the light and he went round the front to open the bonnet. Then we got back in the car.

I remember it was like watching a film that you've seen before and you realize they've cut something out. And the more I thought about it, the more something felt wrong, because when I was back in the car it wasn't like before. Now I wasn't scared, I wasn't nervous, I wasn't excited. It was like being drugged. It was like we were both in the car, then the engine is starting, the key is in the ignition, everything is working fine, the lights are on, we are both sitting there drugged and I sort of looked at him, sort of oblivious, and I said, "Let's get the hell out of here."

But the more I thought about it later the more it seemed I said, "We'll count to three and we'll get out of the car"—and I didn't! Well, I did get out the car but not like we'd planned. I remember I looked out of the window and two, maybe three, heads were looking in. They were actually looking in the window. And that is the bit that was blank; from then to getting back in the car. Totally and utterly blank.

As far as Ros knows P has not had any regression hypnosis therapy and has no other memories of the incident. They are no longer together. In April 1996 P confirmed the sighting aspects in a letter to Ros which included a UFO report form she had sent to him. He described his car, a Mark II Cortina Estate, being drained of power. He felt excited and afraid, and confirmed the sighting of the lighted object as described by Ros. Of the car blackout he confirms: "The engine died, it wouldn't start. It was like the battery was flat. I had a look under the bonnet and could see nothing wrong. When I (then) tried to start the car it was perfect as it always had been for the past two years."

[Ros continued:] All P can remember is that the car stopped, he got out of the car, he went round to check under the bonnet, he got back in the car, we started and we drove off. It followed us again, it shot into the sky and we ended up in Corby. We'd lost about three and a half hours. But it never bothered him. As far as he is concerned they never touched him, they have never done anything to him. He never went on board the ship. They never abducted him. But there was missing time.

Bits of my memory of what happened kept flashing into my head. One of the most distinct recollections, and one of the earliest ones, is looking out of a window that's not a window. I am standing there looking at P, he is leaning over the bonnet of the car, the bonnet is open, but I'm up here somewhere looking down on him. I'm not standing next to him. I distinctly remember this sort of like a bluey, negative haze about. Everything has like a blue "negative" effect. I'm not above in that sense, looking right down at him, I'm looking at him from the same angle where that ship is sitting. But it's slightly up in the air. P was frozen in mid-action. With one hand reaching out towards something.

It was ten years later that Ros had regression hypnosis to explore these memories further.

For the first three years after the incident I threw it to one side. When we got home we noticed we had this period of missing time and we had a blazing row about it. He refused to talk about it. He didn't want to know about it. He took the view that it was all a bad dream that would go away. Then he started drinking, then he started taking drugs, then he started drinking and taking drugs. Then he started getting nasty, nasty violent. By the January following the incident we were a couple no more; I got a court injunction and got him out of my house.

I was having very bad nightmares, had a very bad rash, screaming headaches, fierce nosebleeds, my periods stopped, I lost weight like you wouldn't believe; it dropped from a little bit less than what I am now to a walking skeleton. I stopped going to dog shows.

This represented a major change in Ros's life; Ros breeds and exhibits pedigree dogs, but because of illness she gave up attending dog shows for some time.

I suffered for three years, and I got nowhere with doctors. Whenever I went to see them I felt like a complete idiot. How do you explain to them what happened? They just say: "Why don't you pull yourself together?" I never could say the UFO part. When they saw the rash they would say, "You've obviously burnt yourself" but I'd say "No, I haven't." For the headaches, they'd suggest Mig-relieve. I said, "No, it's not that kind of a headache;

it's like somebody is driving a nail in my head," but they'd just say, "Take the Mig-relieve." I had this irritation in my back which got worse and worse and worse; I went to see my doctor, he just gave me painkillers. After a while I said, "This isn't getting rid of the problem. If I've got a pain in my back aren't you at least going to look and see what's causing it?" In the end, in total agony, my friend took me off to an osteopath and he found I had a disc out of place. So he put it back in again. But he found a puncture wound in the area which he couldn't explain.

So this is how it went for ages. I had given all the dogs away and I was just sitting in the house. Every night I was having nightmares. And this was still within months of the incident with the UFO. Then one night my Mum's ex-husband came in blind drunk and told me I was possessed. I was trying to make sense of whatever was going on and he was saying I was possessed. He broke into the bedroom and raped me. "I'm going to drive the devil out of you," he told me, "I've been sent by God." This was still just the end of 1983, November.

Ros then described how she felt compelled to be up through the night either drawing or writing. She was, she believed, channelling information from the extraterrestrials.

I was stuck at the typewriter writing tons and tons and tons. I was able to have question and answer sessions with them. I asked them where they were from: they said they had returned to Earth, but they were originally from Reticulum. They returned here for the first time in the 1930s. I asked them if they were inter-dimensional: they said yes. I asked them, "Why do abductees become more psychic?": they said it develops the mind having trauma and stress. I asked, "Why are the Grays here?": they said for interbreeding. I asked, "Will they harm us?": they said yes. I asked, "In what way?": they said, "Control, slavery." I asked, "Can we stop them?": they said yes, by using the power of the mind, ESP.

Then I went into further and further details. "How does their engine work?": I got details of how the engine works and I got pictures of the engine.

I wasn't conscious when this stuff came through. I'd "wake up" and just find another pile of typing and eventually I would shrug and stuff it in a file. I've got this whole box file of stuff I received over time in that way.

Ros's mother described the time she thought Ros had been having a breakdown. Ros was speaking in foreign languages that she was not familiar with, and describing medical terms she was hardly likely to know. Her mother recalled:

I found Roslyn started to sleepwalk. She was just walking around the house trying to find paper, pens, pencils, anything. And she was drawing and drawing and drawing in the daytime. None of the drawings made any sense to me whatsoever. But it was the night-time which worried me. This is why I wanted her to go to a doctor. I thought her problems related to the break-up with her boyfriend. She was in a highly emotional state, although she had assured me that she didn't love him any more, she didn't want him in her life any more, but what one says outwardly doesn't always give the inner emotions. But of course it wasn't that; it was because of this experience she had had. But she was waking up and screaming. I would come into the lounge in the middle of the night, I would put on this dimmer light very low, and I could just see her lying on her belly on the floor, or sitting under a table, writing or drawing. She also wrote in ones and zeros which I now know is called binary code but we didn't know at that time what binary code was. She had a glazed look in her eyes, so I knew she wasn't awake, and I didn't want to wake her because I had been told you mustn't wake somebody up in a trance-like state. And she would eventually just walk herself back to bed. She spent days just being in her bedroom. She might come out for a meal or something and then go back there. And that's why I bought her a little television. I thought at least she would have a television in there.

And the first computer games came out and she got into that. I thought that would give her something to do. She wasn't agoraphobic; she just didn't want to go out. She was frightened of something which was out there. I couldn't find out any reason for it at that point of time because she hadn't disclosed anything to me. Had she confided in me maybe I could have had a different insight and could have maybe helped her at that point in time. I just knew I had a different daughter on my hands to what I normally had. I thought she was heading for a nervous breakdown. She didn't want to wash her hair. She didn't want to dress up. She just wanted to slob around. She just wasn't the same girl. She'd get up, maybe wash her hands and face but that was as far as it went.

Ros continued:

Just before I would get these communications it would be like a fax machine going off in my head, that was the sound. The first time I heard it I hadn't heard a fax machine, so I didn't understand it. Then, when I heard a fax machine signal on the telephone, I recognized it as the sound I got in my head—so I nicknamed it my fax machine.

We asked Ros about the "fax machine" noise. There are many reports of abductees referring to themselves using "machinery"-like phraseology during these encounters: did she feel that she was in some way "becoming" like machinery used by the aliens?

I don't know if it's a signal to relax me, or a signal to start downloading stuff into my head, or what it is. That's how I try to describe it now. It's the only way I can think of it.

[Of the encounters themselves:] Sometimes I see myself as a laboratory rat; what's the point of doing an experiment if you're not going to follow it up? What's the point of tagging something in the farthest reaches of Africa if you are not going to go back there and find out how it's getting on and how its babies are getting on? This is just me trying to make some sense out of what happened: I see myself as one of their experiments. What "they" are is still an open question for me. It's only "UFO people" that have said it's "aliens."

I came to the conclusion I was going nuts. And I went to the doctor and of course now I had a beautiful excuse; I could tell him it was all because of the rape. I could tell him it was all the stress that caused me to be scared to go out and scared of people and scared of anything, scared to look under my bed in case there was anything under there. The doctor sent round this woman who sat me on a couch and tried to get me to do these relaxation techniques.

But that triggered more of the memories off. I would be sitting there trying to relax when I would suddenly feel I'd got all these beings around me with long creepy fingers trying to poke me. I'd start screaming "I can't do this." So that didn't work.

Then in 1988 a "freebie" newspaper came through the door and there was an article in there: "Have you seen lights in the sky?" It was by a local UFO research organization. It gave a telephone number in Clacton, which I phoned. I left a message on the answerphone just telling them a light had chased me down the road and asking them what they thought it was. W phoned back and eventually came round to my house, and I told him up to date what I knew. I was still frightened to actually mention that I thought it was UFOs, and I didn't show him all the channelled messages; just told him the basic nuts and bolts bit [of the sighting]. And I asked him if he had any answers. Incidentally he tried to record the interview and it wouldn't come out on the tape.

I wanted answers. Was I going nuts? What else? I was trying to avoid admitting to myself that I thought it was UFOs, because if I thought it was UFOs I might be going mad, so I didn't want to admit that. There was this crazy battle going on with myself inside my head.

He suggested using a hypnotist. I didn't like the idea. I thought: "I'm not a performing animal. I've seen it on TV, I've seen these acts." But he assured me this was a proper hypnotist.

He wasn't going to make me act like a fool, pretend I'm riding a horse or anything ridiculous. So I agreed.

The hypnotist arrived; he brought a sceptic with him. But the hypnosis session never happened. In fact the hypnotist has told me that he won't go near me again. What happened was he got all his equipment set up and all I know is that I laid on the couch in the back room and went to sleep. But apparently what happened, so I was told, was this beam of light appeared in the middle of the room. All the clocks stopped. The sceptic got thrown to the wall, got mauled by something and had four claw marks on both arms. All sorts of weird and wonderful things started exploding, electrical phenomena and light bulbs going off, things flying round in the air. It's really spooky.

The UFO group brought SC into it (another UFO researcher) and I told him about the engine, and I gave him my drawing of the engine.

The group showed me pictures of "aliens," most of which I didn't recognize. But I came across one I knew from when I was about three years old. That really hit me, that did; I don't know why. It was like a massive dose of homesickness. I knew that person. He was like a little kid, humanoid. Very large head, beautiful big eyes and a little pageboy haircut. Ever so sweet. I'd even drawn a picture of him. I got all emotional when I saw his picture. But they showed me the "Grays" and I didn't recognize any of them.

After the session the channelling of pictures got more intense, I did several more in detail. [Ros's mother described landscapes that she thought might have been of an alien world, and pictures that joined together to make patterns only when you looked at them from a distance.] And I started getting the messages again. I started being told: you're going to see a UFO, it will be at two o'clock in the afternoon on 3rd February, or whatever. It will be at St Osyth's Point, or wherever. We went there, and there it was. I got another message and we set off there but we got there too late. Another time I was going to one of these "meetings" and I saw, blocking the road, this blooming great black car, two people in it. A great big black car with bright headlights, all the chrome trim. Like in America. They were just sitting there. [Ros is referring to the "Men in Black" reports, received mainly from the USA.] I'm shouting to them, "Move your flipping car. I've got to be there for 3 o'clock." But they wouldn't speak to me, wouldn't say anything. Wouldn't do anything.

Another time I was blocked by a JCB [excavation vehicle] on the road and he wouldn't move it. The same kind of person driving it. Dressed completely in black. Black glasses. Dressed like the blokes that walk alongside the President's car.

After that I took my camera. The next time I wanted to be ready so we went about an hour early. But the thing didn't arrive, there was no sign of the thing, so I just—bored I suppose—ran off a roll of film out to sea. And blow me down, when I developed it there were these three triangular lights in perfect formation over the sea.

But things went wrong between me and the UFO club. I think they decided I was possessed, and I got really ratted off with this. I'd already been through it once with my stepfather, I wasn't going through it again. I said, "I don't care what it is. Whatever it is, I am not possessed." I got really turned off UFO groups. I knew I wasn't possessed, I was sure it wasn't aliens. I felt it had to have some kind of grounded explanation.

I had met Mark and we started going out; he'd accompanied me to some of the meetings and seen these things, seen the men in the black car and so on. After I cut away from the UFO club we carried on together and things still kept happening.

Ros described several intriguing poltergeist activities that had happened in the house; objects that had been thrown away turning up suddenly, objects disappearing, things moving, and so on.

Then I met this chap called G who wanted to do a second hypnosis session. Because, of course, we still hadn't got to the bottom of what happened at the time of the UFO sighting. We had come to the conclusion something had happened. The UFO people were saying it was aliens. The sceptics were saying it was piezo-electric lights, or I'd seen the moon, or Venus. Someone else was spouting off about it being my brain misfiring. So we tried a second hypnosis session. It was either just before or just after that that Mark tried to show me this film about Betty and Barney Hill [The UFO Incident]. But I only watched a few minutes before I got very hysterical. After just a few minutes it was like someone had opened a door, let me have a look in and then shut it again, and said, "There you go; that's what happened." Under hypnosis, I remembered being in the ship, put on a table. I know I had a conversation with the people there. I know I had a guided tour. I also remember being in a waiting room. The room was like a pinky colour. Everything was "moulded." As far as I know I was on my own. And then we went through into a much larger room. There was a pedestal in the middle of the room, not a table with four legs, just a solid perspex pedestal. To one side was this great big hole in the wall which, when I went over and looked outside through it, I could see down to where P was at the car. It wasn't like a window. It wasn't glass or anything like that. There was five, maybe six, little fellows, about three foot six, big heads, big eyes. Not like your classic "Gray" with the funny-shaped triangular eyes but bigger, rounder. They were still very weedy, a little mouth, a little slit for a nose. And there was one of them much taller than the rest. The place smelt awful, That was the first thing that hit me; a smell like rotten eggs. And there was a funny, claustrophobic atmosphere. It's hard to describe. It was like being underwater but you're not. There is an air around you, an atmosphere that's very thick. It's hard to breathe and there is a strange feeling like you're on a big dipper and you are going down the dip. You think you are going to fall and suddenly you feel heavy and then you don't. That seemed to be going on all the time; it was strange. I don't know where the lighting came from, it was light but not bright light, it was very dim and you couldn't make out the edge of the room at all.

I don't know how I got in there, I can't figure it out. Because I didn't have any mud on me or anything [NB: the UFO had been hovering over a muddy field.] But I don't remember any beams of light "beaming me up, Scotty," or anything like that.

I had a conversation with the tall fellow. The little fellows sort of got me sitting me on this perspex thing. Inside I was screaming blue murder but outside I was just doing what they were telling me to, which isn't like me. With the tall fellow I was asking questions: "Why the hell am I here?"; "What am I doing?" Just a whole load of common sense questions really. He just said "We need you" and stuff like that. I can't remember it well. But we got to the part where "kids" were involved and I'm very anti-kids. I don't want kids. I shouted that at him.

Ros has not had any other successful hypnosis sessions since. There have been attempts sponsored by television companies covering her story, but they have not worked. She remembered one done in Canary Wharf tower where equipment was blowing fuses all around her and she felt she had to keep apologizing. She did not mind the lack of hypnosis, fearing that it could be suggestive and produce false memories. She believed that a more gentle, slower process of memory recall would happen if she took her time. She said that whatever was going to come out should come out naturally. It seemed like good common sense given the doubts about hypnosis that have arisen over the years, and the recent work into False Memory Syndrome. Of her experiences, she speculated:

I feel there is truth in it. According to my channelled messages I think it relates to a dying race, dying people, coming back— whether it's from outer space, inner space, the future, or whatever—coming back. They've got problems reproducing. They can't survive with us because we'll never accept them the way they look. But if they cross breed with us and produce other beings that look more human than like them, and put them back on this planet, then they are going to integrate into our society and quite happily be accepted. This will keep their species going. I think somewhere along the line they wanted me as part of their project, but I don't want kids. It's just a species looking after itself, life trying to find a way to survive. I suppose that explains why there is an awful lot of abductions.

We asked Ros if she believed it could all be a dream, or a fantasy.

I wish I could, but I can't because of all the evidence that's backing it up. The rash and illnesses, and so on.

On 21 August 1996 Ros had an experience which she felt was probably an abduction. Certainly it corresponds in many ways with the reports of such experiences from around the world. She was staying away, during a week-long dog show.

I went by coach, there were loads of us, and we were staying in a group of houses. They had a shared kitchen and utility and general meeting area; each person has a bedroom. Everyone has their own bedroom key and a front door key which not only lets you into the house but you need it to let yourself out of the house as well. All the windows in the place are sealed except for a tiny slit at the top which you can open to get air in. The dogs were all kepts in cages in the hallways.

I had my Sheba, my dog, outside my bedroom door. It was about nine o'clock at night. We had returned from the show and were sitting down relaxing, reading the catalogues and working out what was happening for the next show, things like this. And the next thing I know I am standing in the street. It's three o'clock in the morning and I'm stark naked; I haven't got anything on and I haven't got any keys to get in the house. So I rattled the door and somebody opened it and let me in. I told them I'd probably been sleepwalking; what else could I say? But they asked: "How did you get out without your key?" I told her the door must have been on the latch. I don't know where my clothes were; I never did find them.

The woman that opened the door then told me that she'd had trouble with her dogs all that night. She couldn't get them to sleep; they'd been restless all night. She'd had to bring them into the room with her and they'd still been restless. She told me they'd just settled down about an hour earlier, and that I'd just woken them up again.

The following morning we were told that someone had seen blue lights over the area that night. I suggested perhaps it was police activity and tried to just pass it off. There were two footnotes to this event. The first thing was that afterwards I found that I had a "thing" in the edge of my ear which two researchers are arranging to get examined by doctors. [NB: a small lump could be felt where Ros indicated.] The second thing was my hairdresser noticed I seem to have a big bald patch; my hair was falling out.

I think I might have been abducted. I really think something might have happened again, but I have got absolutely no recollection of seeing anything, any lights, anything.

III

Aliens into the Future

12

Evidence Retrievals

In the first section of the book we looked at the scientific searches and evidence for intelligent life beyond the Earth, and found that while the logic is supportive of such a likelihood, the likelihood of actual contact and meaningful communication is much lower. In the second section we set out the evidence for actual contact having been established not once but many times over by individuals who claim to have encountered visiting aliens. There is a recognizable contradiction between the two; between the science and probability on the one hand and the anecdotal evidence on the other. This section of the book examines these claims with the view that if the contradiction cannot be reconciled then it must be explained in other ways. We begin therefore by examining what many believe is the "hard" evidence for alien visitation.

In doing so we must assume that we are dealing with aliens that are reasonably like us in that they use technology as we do, albeit in a more advanced form, and act more or less as we would act in given situations. If this were not so, then we would probably be at a loss to comprehend any clues. Indeed we might never recognize them all around us if they were sufficiently beyond our frame of reasoning. We are therefore also considering beings with something akin to our form of reasoning.

Firstly, we can be sure that they know of our existence. If they are similar enough to us then they would have picked up our "leaking" radio and television transmissions as they approached the Earth and they would have been able to study us in some rudimentary form. Although human beings actually occupy very little space on the planet we would be instantly recognizable to a like culture; they would see our city patterns, detect aircraft and other forms of vehicular travel. They could choose to contact us, or they could choose to ignore us. They could land in remote places where the possibility of being spotted by humans was low. In the early days of "flying saucers" the reports state that they were doing just this. Many cases indicate that the aliens were going about their business in a clandestine manner and, when spotted, fled the scene. Let us first look at the validity of this so-called clue.

On 24 April 1950, Bruno Facchini, at Abbiate Buazzone, in Italy, came across figures standing near a hovering UFO. He approached them to offer help but they shot him with a beam of light, and then boarded the object and flew away.

On 11 October 1954, three men driving near Taupignac in France saw a round object with a dome hovering some 30 feet above the ground, silent and motionless. They watched it then move towards a wood, where it landed. Two of the witnesses went towards it and saw four small figures, approximately three feet high, working in the vicinity of the machine. As the witnesses arrived the four figures rushed into the disc, which then took off vertically at high speed.

At Socorro, New Mexico, in April 1964, policeman Lonnie Zamora saw an object descending into a valley, gave chase with his police car and arrived in time to see two figures standing next to the object, now landed, seemingly only just having stepped out. Alerted by his arrival, they quickly got back in and flew off.

On 1 July 1965, farmer Maurice Masse, at Valensole, in France, came into his lavender field and saw a landed object some 15 feet across standing there. As he got closer he could see two small figures standing nearby. On seeing him approach they fired a white beam at him which immobilized him, then they boarded the object and flew away.

Similarly, at Loxton in South Africa, on 31 July 1975, Danie Van Graan walked over a ten-foot-high bank of earth and saw in a field below him an oval-shaped object with four figures moving about inside. As he got to within about 15 feet the figures suddenly looked up, as if startled by his arrival. Van Graan heard the click of a flap opening, and he was hit in the face by a beam of light. The machine then took off and disappeared from view very rapidly.

Some accounts of "surprised" aliens go back to before the "official" start of UFOs, in this next case to the 1909 European wave of "airship" sightings. In the *Daily Mail* of 20 May 1909 there is the story of Mr. C. Lethbridge, who was walking home over Caerphilly mountain late one night, pulling a little travelling Punch and Judy show with him, when he came across a "tube-shaped" object being attended to by two men. They were wearing heavy fur coats and caps. Lethbridge related: "The noise of my little spring cart seemed to attract them, and when they saw me, they jumped up and jabbered furiously in a strange lingo." The object rose into the air, the two men jumped into a carriage suspended beneath it, and it flew away towards Cardiff. The object was apparently pushed by a propeller.

But we should consider these reports in the light of earlier accounts that have not made their way into the UFO literature. For example, Jeremiah Sullivan, writing in *Cumberland and Westmoreland Ancient and Modern* in 1857, refers to the time that fairies were last seen in the Lake District. He describes the experience of Jack Wilson, who was returning home in the evening over Sandwick Rigg. By moonlight Wilson saw a large group of fairies and noticed also a ladder reaching up from among them and into a cloud. They spotted him and —shy of interaction with mortals—ran up the ladder, drew it up after them and "shut the cloud," and then disappeared. When he saw them going up the ladder Wilson had dived towards them with the intention of following them, but clearly they wished to thwart that.

Whatever the context, perhaps it is naïve to accept these actions and the apparent clue they offer at face value. Let's revisit the Socorro case again and look at some of the details. The object landed, and the two humanoids emerged, less than one thousand yards from the southern edge of the town of Socorro. Why? They had a whole desert available. Furthermore, they had just flown so low over a car that the occupants of it had become alarmed, so surely the "aliens" must have seen the car. It was almost as if they landed to encourage the car driver to stop and look at them. But in fact that driver did not; he had seen a police car "giving chase" and continued into town. Then, once landed, the object waited just long enough for Lonnie Zamora in his patrol car to reach them. When Zamora saw the object he also saw the two small humanoid figures standing next to it. But instantly they saw him they appear to have been shocked: "One of the figures . . . seemed to turn as if it heard or saw my car coming," Zamora said. "It must have seen me 'cause when it turned and looked straight at my car, it seemed somewhat startled—almost seemed to jump somewhat." Zamora lost sight of them and the object momentarily as he bounced along the dirt track in his car towards them. He heard two bangs, possibly the aliens re-entering their vehicle, and then he saw it take off. Later examination showed that there were a few "footprint"-like marks consistent with a very short and localized excursion on the part of the aliens. But for what purpose? They must have known they were going to be interrupted. What were they doing? The conventional thinking in the early years of UFO research was that the aliens were sometimes caught repairing their craft. If so, they broke down a lot. But not in this case surely? They were able to fly away immediately they were interrupted, so presumably they could have set down a mile or so further into the desert where they stood less chance of being interrupted or "caught." The implication is clear: the purpose of the landing and the excursion must be *to be seen*! But why?

Fairy Exchange

Let us look at the "clue" offered to witness Joe Simonton. On 18 April 1961, Simonton was alerted by a noise outside his house like "knobby tires on a wet pavement" and on going outside saw a

UFO "brighter than chrome" hovering over his land. A hatch opened and Simonton saw three people inside. They were human looking; he described them as resembling Italians. They held up a jug and asked him for water, which he provided. Looking into the saucer, he saw that the three men were having some sort of on-board barbecue! They were sitting round a flameless grill, cooking food. Simonton indicated that he wanted some of the food, and they gave him three small "pancakes." Shortly afterwards they closed the hatch and took off, leaving Simonton with his clue.

But what a useless clue it turned out to be. Simonton had eaten one and confirmed that he thought it tasted like cardboard. The Food and Drug Laboratory of the US Department of Health analysed the pancake Simonton gave them and found it to be made of terrestrial material—"hydrogenated fat, starch, buckwheat hulls, soya bean hulls, wheat bran"—and lacking salt. In other words, there was nothing that could not have been manufactured on Earth, so even if the "Italians" were aliens they had apparently picked up their groceries on Earth—which therefore proved nothing—or their planet produces exactly the same materials as Earth, which again proved nothing. Of course the food may have been given generously and not intended as a "clue," so we cannot accuse the aliens of mischief.

A Gift From the Stars

But perhaps that is not true in the case of Betty Hill. The first "true" abductee, she was granted two clues which must have looked very meaningful; but turned out to be equally useless. If aliens were involved, then perhaps these were a little more mischievous. One clue—sight of a "star map"—will be dealt with in some detail later in this chapter. For the moment let us look at the other clue—a book.

While aboard the flying saucer, and speaking to an alien she identified as the leader, she asked for proof of her experience which she already knew would be precious to her. Betty Hill recalls: "He laughed, and he said what kind of proof did I want?" Betty asked for something she could take back with her that people would believe. She was offered the chance to look around and find something she thought was appropriate. She found a book. The writing in it went up and down rather than side to side and was unlike any writing Betty had ever seen. "It had sharp lines, and some were very thin and some were medium and some were very heavy. It had some dots. It had straight lines and curved lines." The leader agreed that she could have the book. "This was more than I had ever hoped for," Betty said. But as she was being escorted off the flying saucer the leader took the book back—the cup dashed from the lip. He explained to Betty that others aboard the saucer objected to her having the book. "They don't want you to know what has happened," he explained to her. "They want you to forget all about it."

Dr. Benjamin Simon, who undertook the hypnotic regression, considered it possible that the recall was the material of dreams Betty had had. If so, then in the book we see a basic insecurity theme coming out in symbolic form. Betty fears that her experience either might not be real or might not be believed, she dreams of the proof and then fears it taken away from her. But what if the experience was real? Perhaps the exchange happened exactly as she recalls it. In fact it is the sort of dispute that we might expect among a typical crew—in this case of a flying saucer—but it is at odds with the sort of aliens that we find in later accounts. Those encountered by Strieber seem to be from the same stable as those encountered by the Hills, at least they act in a very similar way with their abductees, but argumentative bickering as described by Betty just does not seem to fit Strieber's appreciation of them. Perhaps then the argument is a set-up. Researcher Budd Hopkins, as we have seen, believes that the aliens are interested in studying our responses to emotional tests; perhaps Betty Hill was involved in just such a test to see how she would react when "the cup was dashed from the lip." It makes as much sense as a real argument; but the possibility of dream material being involved cannot be ruled out. In the end, the clue that might have been valuable was not to be.

The same applies to the similar clue nearly obtained by Antonio Villas Boas when he was abducted in 1957. Not quite as polite as Mrs. Hill, Villas Boas spotted a device rather like a clock and "shoplifted" it. Unfortunately he got caught, the object was taken from him, and he was fairly brusquely thrown off the saucer. Again, so near, yet so far.

Lost Proof

But suppose they had got hold of the items and retained them? Would we have our proof then? Perhaps not; Betty Andreasson exchanged books with the aliens she encountered. She gave them a Bible, they gave her a book which sounds not dissimilar to the one Betty Hill describes. But Andreasson managed to keep it. (And interestingly there are many parallels between the two cases; they both underwent the same needle-in-the-navel operation, for example.) But, almost unbelievably, Betty Andreasson lost the book. An artefact from another world, and proof of what is surely the most important event in her life, and apparently she threw it in the back of a wardrobe and lost it. We could almost blame Andreasson for such carelessness were there not such a pattern here that we must assume that the denial of proof is a factor of the experience. We could speculate that the book Andreasson got was "programmed" to disappear into thin air after a certain period of time, though that is perhaps being too simple-minded and too "science fiction" led. But we might consider that this so-near-yet-so-far syndrome is a deliberate aspect of the abduction experience, whether it is alien-designed, a factor of the imagination, or a more obscure result of the true nature of a not-yet-understood experience. There have been other losses: metal fragments that were recovered from the landing site at Socorro were apparently purloined during the official examination and no trace of them is now known to exist; the whereabouts of the

fragments of recovered magnesium following an airborne explosion of an "unknown" at Ubatuba, in Brazil, are not known. The
literature contains a whole list of "nearly" clues. We could be dismissive and file the stories along with the traditional fisher-
men's tales—the one that got away!—but that would frankly not
give due credit to the sincerity of some of the witnesses involved.

No, we face two clear points here. Firstly, that the experience
seems to be of a deeper and more confusing nature than is perhaps even now suspected. Secondly, that we are denied proof of
it in concrete form.

Let's look in detail at what once seemed to be the most important clue of all—indeed many today still believe that it is.

The "Marjorie Fish" Star Map

During Betty Hill's abduction of 1961 she was apparently presented with a valuable clue as to the origin of the aliens visiting
Earth. During one session she spent with the "leader" of the
aliens, she saw a "star map," and under later hypnosis she was
able to draw it.

The sighting of the "star map" happened following a medical examination during which a needle had been inserted into her navel.
It had caused her great pain and she had been grateful to the alien
she perceived as the leader for calling a halt to the examination.
She spoke with him for a time, while they waited for Barney (who
was elsewhere on the saucer undergoing an examination of his
own). She asked the alien where he came from. "I knew he wasn't
from the earth," she said. After establishing that Betty Hill's knowledge of space was limited, the alien produced a "star map." The
exact way in which this was produced is unclear. In Betty's hypnotic regression she recalled: "He went across the room to the head
of the table and he did something, he opened up, it wasn't like a
drawer, he sort of did something, and the metal of the wall, there
was an opening. And he pulled out a map . . ." When the time came
to end the session with the map: "The map rolled up, and he put it

back in the space in the wall and closed it." However, Betty's hypnotic recall was subsequent to spontaneous dreams which she recounted to her hypnotist, Dr. Benjamin Simon. For the most part these dreams mirrored the hypnotic recall, but in the matter of the map there was a slight difference. In her dream she remembered: "He went over to the wall and pulled down a map . . ." and to put it away: "he snapped the map back into place." Jacques Vallee comments in *Dimensions*: "She remembered it as a flat, thin display giving an impression of depth. Since she didn't move while viewing it, she couldn't tell if it was truly three-dimensional or just flat like a television screen." John Rimmer in *The Evidence for Alien Abductions* describes it as "a screen-like object on the wall." So was the map on paper, on a screen, or was it a hologram? If we take her hypnotic session as the most reliable source—true or not, a great deal of reliability has been placed on this recall—then we seem to have a map capable of being rolled up and stowed away, seemingly in a manner that Admiral Lord Nelson might have recognized at his own map table. A curious device for a high-tech flying saucer.

Whatever its form, its use is even more suspicious. But we shall come to that shortly.

Under hypnosis Betty was able to draw the map as she had seen it. It showed several stars connected by varying thicknesses of lines. The heavy lines represented regularly frequented trade routes, she was told, and broken lines represented expeditions. But the map seemed to be a sterile clue; Mrs. Hill, in no recollection, remembered any words or symbols that might have identified the stars shown.

Then Mrs. Hill saw, in the 13 April 1965 edition of the *New York Times*, a map depicting the location of CTA-102, a radio source in the constellation of Pegasus which the Russians believed might have been the source of an intelligent transmission. She believed it was the same display of stars, and put the names from the map on to her own sketch. From that she believed that she had identified the home star of the aliens: one of the stars Homan or Baham. (It is often said that Betty Hill identified the home star as Zeta Reticuli;

this is incorrect and a point often overlooked in examining this case—Zeta Reticuli was the result of a subsequent analysis.) The degree to which wishful thinking and expectation clouded judgement here is clear; Betty recalls a pattern of stars under hypnosis, draws it, and within a short time a national newspaper—reporting on a quite unconnected matter—happens to publish a pattern of stars that Betty believes are "her" stars. The fact is that the pattern is not a perfect match, and it is clear that there must be thousands of near misses that might represent the right stars.

The next development is probably equally speculative, but it did hold a few surprises. And it eclipsed the idea of the stars in the Pegasus constellation. Amateur astronomer and teacher Marjorie Fish became interested in the so-called star map. Drawn to the subject of UFOs by reading Jacques Vallee's book *Anatomy of a Phenomenon*—which only mentions the Hill case briefly and does not deal with the abduction material—she decided to try to find her own match for the stars.

Her first observation was that there was not a pattern of visible stars that matched Betty Hill's star map. But she then assumed that there was no reason why a map on a flying saucer should draw a pattern of stars from a perspective as seen from the Earth; that possibly it would be drawn from the point of view of the home world. (Or, presumably, from any "neutral point" that allowed the map to contain both the home world and the other stars that needed to be included—our own maps view the Earth from a "non-existent, neutral" point somewhere in the air.) She engaged with help of astronomer Dr. Walter Mitchell and constructed a spatial model of stars, using as a criterion those stars thought likely to have evolved planets. They arbitrarily restricted their search to stars within 55 light years of the Earth. The choice of stars, based on their likelihood of developing planets and life, was to locate those which were stable, not varying in intensity, rotated slowly enough to allow for planetary formation and which were not thought too hot or too cold. All of this is of course making an assumption about planetary formation and the development of life which has yet to be proven. Given these criteria, 46 stars were found. These were then plotted to see if a pattern conforming to the Hill's map could be located. When a match was found, this seemed to suggest that the home star of the aliens was Zeta Reticuli in the constellation of Reticulum—virtually on the other side of the sky to Pegasus as viewed from Earth, incidentally.

When Betty had drawn the star map in 1964, she had drawn the home star as a double star—but at that time Zeta Reticuli was thought to be a single star. Nine years later it was discovered—by the astronomer Van de Camp—to be a double star, which seemed to offer more support for the star map. An article in the respected magazine *Astronomy* indicated it was impressed: "Ten of the sixteen stars (in the Fish reconstruction) are from a compact group that we selected earlier based on the most logical direction to pursue to conduct interstellar exploration from earth," the article stated, going on to add that "both Zeta Reticuli 1 and Zeta Reticuli 2 are prime candidates for the search for life beyond earth." Further interest was generated by the comments of Dr. Frank Salisbury, Director of the Planet Science Department of the University of Utah. He stated of Fish's work: "The final map has sixteen stars that form a flattened rather than a spherical cluster . . . The final breakthrough came in September of 1972, when Miss Fish assumed that the star Zeta Tucanae was directly behind Zeta Reticuli. This further refined the viewing position. Thus when one views the model from the proper position, only fifteen of the sixteen stars are visible—matching the number on Betty's map."

The Grays—the commonly reported visiting aliens—are today often known as the "Reticulans." The implication is clear: many people believe that the identity of the home star has been located, that the evidence of the star map is persuasive, and that by implication the data Betty Hill found are reliable.

In support of the belief, it has been pointed out that of over 100 stars that could have been selected by Fish all of the ones similar to the Earth's sun are included in her model, and the "routes" that link them are logical from a three-dimensional perspective.

Other arguments have pointed out that binary stars like Zeta Reticuli may not be conducive to planetary formation—one of Fish's own criteria—though that is also speculation.

But a good few other questions have been offered by more challenging researchers. The first is one asked by Jacques Vallee in his book *Dimensions*: "From how many positions in space can we look at the forty-six star model and find as good a match with the original map?" Vallee suggests that there may be many positions from which the map could be viewed, and that therefore even if the map reported by Betty Hill is valid it does not truly identify Zeta Reticuli as the home star.

We would add a good many questions to that general starting-point. One Vallee himself begins to ask: since the map was not drawn to scale, how do we know the distances and spacings involved? The map may represent a few selected, "favourite" stars over thousands of light years—assuming that the map represents stars within our own Milky Way, this galazy is approximately 100,000 light years across. If the map takes in a sizeable portion of the galaxy, then there would be almost limitless "matches" available. On Earth, we can have a map of a few surrounding streets or a map of several countries; so presumably can the aliens. It is often assumed that the lines between the stars represent flight through "normal space"; but perhaps the aliens travel through "black/white holes" or some other, unknown, method of movement. In that case any scale is possible.

The assumptions about which stars are to be accepted and which rejected may be wrong, and if more, or different, stars were valid then the actual match could be very different. Carl Sagan criticized the match in any case, believing it was not that close. If the "travel routes" lines were removed, he felt many people would not recognize the two patterns anyway.

One important piece of evidence needs to be considered, however. Sol, the Earth's own star, must be somewhere on that map. If we are to believe that Betty's recall is accurate enough to loate the stars sufficiently well for a "match" to be valid, then we have a right to assume her other recall is equally valid. And she recalls her conversation with the alien leader. "So I asked him where was his home port, and he said, 'Where were you on the map?' I looked and laughed and said, 'I don't know.' So he said, 'If you don't know where you are, then there isn't any point of my telling where I am from.'" The implication is that Sol was on the map somewhere. So surely it would have been easy enough to have pointed at the dot that represented Sol and say to Betty Hill: "That's you." Betty asked him to, and all he did was laugh.

What about the technology? Vallee points out that the map is an anachronism, that "we already fly spacecraft by software and telemetry, not by maps." But even if they had a map for some reason, would it be a piece of paper that could be rolled up? Would it not be an interactive screen—touch a particular star-point and get details on screen about that star, or get navigational information, etc.—or something our science has not yet devised?

We can summarize this "clue" from two perspectives: but both of them indicate that the star map data are useless.

1. *Betty was genuinely abducted by aliens and saw a real star map on board the flying saucer.*

Without meaningful symbols that indicate the stars involved, or the scale of the map, or the region of space, there is no way of knowing what stars were represented. Vallee's other point is absolutely correct; if the map existed then it did not seem to be serving any useful purpose to the aliens from the point of view of navigation; its only purpose was that it could be shown to abductees! If so, then was it used to convince Betty of the beings' other-worldly origin? Or to distract her while they did something to her—perhaps a mental scan of her brain? Or distract her attention from something else they did not want her seeing?

2. *Betty dreamt the whole abduction, and then recalled her dreams through regression hypnosis, believing them to be a reality.*

Benjamin Simon believed that possible. Fuller reports: "The

doctor believed this (abduction reality) to be too improbable, and much material was similar to dream material." What purpose does the map serve then? There is every evidence that Betty Hill believed her dreams represented a reality, and at the time and subsequently it is clear that she wishes others to believe so too. There are many indications in her account of her recall "proving" that the aliens are indeed real aliens. They speak idiomatic English, yet they do not know what the colour yellow is, what vegetables are, what old age is or what a year is. All of this allows for meaningful communication while at the same time defining their "alien-ness." The map is just another such image; it proves to Betty that her experience was not only real—but alien. That she could have fantasized it as part of a larger overall fantasy is obviously possible.

There are other indications that Betty's experience, while not actually an alien abduction, might represent a reality at a different level; the abduction experience could be something akin to a shamanic experience. But Betty Hill would not agree with that and does believe her encounter to have been with aliens, so, whatever the reality, her quest for proof, and the mental creation of dialogue and maps that support her belief, applies in any case.

Anti-Clues

When we consider the overall view of the aliens who visit the Earth in flying saucers, we are faced with what we might loosely call "anti-clues." For example, the aliens are clumsy. The crash retrieval incidents, which some researchers believe run into double figures, indicate if true that the aliens are far from technologically infallible. These incredible machines suddenly become prone to being struck by lightning or whatever other problem brings them down. Despite apparently being very active in and around major cities, according to the many reports, they always crash their saucers in remote desert locations where they can be retrieved in secret by government and military agencies. The cover-up of a crashed flying saucer would be difficult if one came down on Manhattan Island, or in Central London! Other than believing that crash retrievals are something of a modern urban myth, and assuming that they are genuine, then we must look for another reason why these incidents should be happening as they are reported.

The aliens treat people, whom they seem to recognise as sentient creatures, with less respect than we know that we should treat others. We ourselves of course do not have a much better track record even in our recent history, but at least that shows that for all their perceived advances they do not have much to teach us ethically.

They are bad doctors and bad scientists. They keep repeating their abductions, as if they have not learned from what they did previously. And many people, such as Jacques Vallee, have pointed out that they seem to be gaining little from their medical samples that they could not obtain by invading any one of several research laboratories. On the other hand, we have been performing experiments on animals for decades, and those animals—were they aware of that—might see little difference in what we do to them. Perhaps we need to know more about the nature of the aliens' experimentation. This matter is covered in some detail in Chapter 10.

If these aliens are real, then one thing it seems we can be certain of is that we do not understand their motivations. Many researchers claim that they do, but the coherence in their argument often depends on overlooking absurdities that need to be taken into account.

The tentative conclusion of this chapter is twofold.

- It may be that the belief that the Earth is being visited by aliens is a mythology based on a variety of experiences which have been collected together under the umbrella-term of UFOs. If so, then the absurdities arise because people are reading the data according to what they wish to believe, and they are ignoring "awkward" topic areas because they do not fit.

- The second possibility is that there really are aliens visiting the Earth. They really did abduct Betty Hill and act as she reports they did. They landed in front of Lonnie Zamora and then ran away once he'd got close enough. They crash their flying saucers in designated desolate areas where they can be recovered for research by military groups. If so, then we would tentatively suggest that there is only one reason for such absurdities: they are deliberate. The saucers crash where they do because they are designed to, possibly to provide us with technology to study, and to watch our responses in much the same way as we watch mice run down specific maze-runs in search of the cheese we have deliberately left for them. If so, then we should be very wary of the information we think we are learning from the retrieved saucers; deliberate "plants" are usually designed to provide false leads or to decoy us from something else. This is exactly the same conclusion that we reached in considering the star map.

The answer therefore may be that what we believe we understand about the aliens is false. The remaining question would then be whether the falsehoods are being created by aliens, or by humans.

There is one other possibility which would perhaps put the aliens in a more positive light. Budd Hopkins believes that they are examining our responses to emotional situations. It may be that they seek something for themselves that we have. But it could be that they are seeking to improve us for our own sake. If so, then perhaps their purpose is consciousness-raising; they are here to bring us to a new level of understanding. We might consider the UFOs as psychic toys for our benefit.

The Problem for the Aliens

As a last point we might consider a dilemma that we face as researchers. And one that considers the possibility that the aliens are more alien than we presently seem to think. We are justified in this assumption because our reconciliation of the absurdities may be that we are interpreting actions anthropomorphically, and getting it quite wrong because of the alien-ness of the encounters. If we are looking for clues that are absolute proof of alien technology, or alien intelligence, then we face a problem of knowing how to identify them. Even if they sought to offer us such proof, what could they possibly hand to us that we ourselves could not have faked? If Betty Hill had kept her book, would it not have been possible to have falsely created it anyway? If it contained terrestrial materials—like Simonton's pancakes—then it would have proved nothing. If it contained something so alien that it could not have originated on Earth, then would we recognize it? The answer might be that—by definition—we could not know the answer. Any answer that we can come up with is essentially anthropomorphic, and we could create it ourselves. The aliens, if they seek to offer proof, must come up with an answer that we cannot conceive of but which can be recognized when seen and is unambiguous. If they are deliberately offering clues, it is their job to ensure we understand them.

If they are sufficiently like us, they might choose to land on the White House lawn and engage in dialogue with us, using our own mass communications media. But think of the scale of the problem if they are as advanced as many believe, but very unlike us even in concept. Suppose an ant has an intelligence quite different from our own, but on a similar plateau. If we decide to impress that ant by demonstrating our intelligence, then how do we do it? It would be useless to show it our poetry or digital watches. We have to know what will astound the ant. And that may be an impossible gulf to bridge. And even if somehow we crossed that bridge, how would we know from the ant's reaction that it had understood?

13

Crash Retrievals

The "hardest" evidence of all that aliens have visited the Earth would be the retrieval of actual hardware manufactured by the aliens. If we had one of their flying saucers, or pieces of their saucers, or indeed if we had the aliens themselves, it would seem that we would not be able to deny their existence.

Crash retrievals, therefore—and many believe that governments and military have indeed captured crashed saucers—should be one of the most important areas of evidence in the claims for the existence of alien life.

The basic story of crash retrievals, of which Roswell is the primary example, is that flying saucers have crashed and have been recovered by military and government forces and stored in secure locations. In those locations, or at specially designed facilities such as the much speculated about "Area 51," these saucers are then "reverse engineered" to find out how they work. Along with the crashed saucers, alien pilots are supposed to have been discovered. For the most part the rumours have it that these aliens are dead, but there have also been claims of the recovery of live aliens. It is even claimed that the US government has been instrumental in forming alliances between humans and aliens, and are of course concerned to keep those alliances secret from the population at large.

Roswell

The most famous claim is that of the Roswell Incident. We can start by recognizing two undeniable facts about Roswell. (1) That something physical definitely crashed in the desert and was recovered—the military even displayed debris which they claimed was the material. (2) That they lied about what they re-covered—and that is now evident from the GAO (General Ac-counting Office) report which was released in 1995, admitting that the weather balloon story was a cover-up. The GAO report suggested that the actual recovery was of a listening dish strung under a special lifting balloon. Many people think this is just the latest lie.

The basic story is so well known it does not need repeating in detail here. Briefly, on Thursday 3 July 1947, rancher William "Mac" Brazel and his neighbour's young son Dee Proctor discov-ered a mass of fragments of material scattered across the Foster ranchlands. It was strange material, lightweight yet strong, re-sistant to attack, and seemingly covered in hieroglyphics. On Sunday 6 July, Brazel reported the find to Chaves County Sheriff George Wilcox, who in turn notified Roswell Army Air Field. They sent Major Jesse Marcel and Sheridan Cavitt of the counter-intelligence corps back to the ranch with Brazel to retrieve the material. The base issued a press release stating that the field had "come into possession of a flying saucer." The release described a very basic, flimsy dish—not a flying vehicle, it should be noted. As more detail was released, it was announced that what had crashed was the remains of a weather balloon. Major Marcel was photographed with weather balloon debris to verify the story.

At the time in 1947 there were no reports of alien bodies, now a prevalent part of the Roswell claims. What seems to have hap-pened is that Marcel became personally interested in the origin of the material, believing it possibly to be extraterrestrial. The flying saucer craze had just started in the USA, following the Kenneth Arnold sighting of two weeks earlier, and perhaps Mar-cel was caught up in the excitement. He seems to have played a part in the initial press release, which was perhaps more dra-matic than would normally be associated with the military.

Marcel did not claim to have seen alien bodies, or even a near-complete disc, just the fragments.

The story attracted some attention in the in-house UFO press, but not a great deal. *Flying Saucer Review* asked in its first edition: "Do the Americans have a Flying Saucer in their possession?" Writers Brinsley le Poer Trench, Brad Steiger, Frank Edwards, Harold Wilkins and Kenneth Arnold all mentioned crash re-trieval stories in a small way in their books, some obviously re-ferring to Roswell, some to other similar stories that were "doing the rounds" at the time, but generally the subject of capturing a flying saucer was handled with restraint. It was almost as if such a claim was too wacky to handle, even without the "alien bodies" claims that were to arise shortly after Roswell.

The most extreme claims were publicized in a book by Frank Scully, who seems to have been taken in by stories circulating about a near-complete disc being recovered along with the alien pilots. These stories were hoaxes, as quickly became apparent in the 1950s when he published his book *Behind the Flying Saucers*. They had arisen when the *Aztec Independent Review* had started a hoax story that a flying saucer from Venus had crashed near Aztec, New Mexico. A detailed account of how Roswell evolved because of these spoofs is given in our book, *Fifty Years of UFOs*.

Research into Roswell and crash retrievals started in earnest in 1978 following political disasters such as Watergate, which produced a climate of distrust and suspicion about what gov-ernments—and particularly the US government—might be capa-ble of, and such interest was certainly boosted by the release of the film *Close Encounters of the Third Kind*. By that time, of course, many of the people alleged to have been involved at Roswell were dead, and their stories were being retold by oth-ers, including their children. The principal story, that of Grady Barnett, who allegedly saw the crashed disc and bodies, was re-lated years after his death by friends recalling stories they say that he had told them. Even claimants telling their own stories were searching back through their memories to 30 years previously, when at best they could remember being involved in various "retrievals" in the area. Considering that Roswell is in the area of the most secret development sites on Earth, where the Space Race hardware was developed for example, and that many thousands of crashed experiments had to be recovered, it is hardly surprising that there are people with stories to tell. Few seem very reliable, and none have effective documentation with traceable pedigree to support them. But the Roswell Incident has become a myth with its own inertia now; most people believe what they want to believe.

The subject was given something of a boost when the MJ-12 documents were discovered on 11 December 1984. They seemed to be the evidence that was being sought showing that the government had in fact recovered alien bodies at Roswell. In fact, they boldly stated so:

> On 07 July, 1947, a secret operation was begun to assure recovery of the wreckage of this object for scientific study. During the course of this operation, aerial reconnaissance discovered that four small human-like beings had apparently ejected from the craft at some point before it exploded . . . All four were dead and badly decomposed . . . Civilian and military witnesses in the area were debriefed, and news reporters were given the effective cover story that the object had been a misguided weather research balloon . . . It was the tentative conclusion of this [study] group (30 November, 1947) that although these creatures are human-like in appearance, the biological and evolutionary processes responsible for their development have apparently been quite different from those observed or postulated in homo-sapiens . . . Since it is virtually certain that these craft do not originate in any country on earth, considerable speculation has centred around what their point of origin might be and how they get here. Mars was and remains a possibility, although some scientists, most notably Dr. Menzel, consider it more likely that we are dealing with beings from another solar system entirely.

Very strong stuff, and hardly ambiguous. Unfortunately the origin of the MJ-12 papers is anything but authoritative and satisfactory. They were sent, anonymously, to a group of UFO enthusiasts who happened to be committed to the belief not just in extraterrestrials but in the reality of the Roswell Incident itself. One of the team, Stanton Friedman, had long plodded the lecture circuit on that one subject. (Subsequent, similar documents have since come to light, all lacking an effective pedigree. For example, Stanton Friedman in his latest book, *Top Secret/Majic* describes the surfacing of the "Majestic 12 Group Special Operations Manual: Extraterrestrial Entities and Technology, Recovery and Disposal." In December 1994 a roll of film not unlike that containing the photographs of the original MJ-12 documents was sent to Don Berliner, co-author with Friedman of his previous book, *Crash at Corona*. On being developed it was found to contain pages of documentation dating from 1954. But as before, the source was anonymous.)

If the original documents are genuine, a far better pedigree needs to be established before they can be relied on. That pranksters have "set up" the Friedman/Moore/Shandera team that received them is a possibility. It has to be recognized that it would not have been impossible for one or more of that team to have manufactured them themselves. If, on the other hand, the documents are not genuine but were sent by government agents, then the possibility that they represent disinformation is high. The government could have its own reasons for wanting to test the passage of rumours among UFO enthusiasts who—after all—spend a great deal of their time spying on secret military locations, which must be of annoyance to the authorities. That they might want to discredit particular researchers is possible. It is also possible that they want to attract attention to the Roswell Incident in order to deflect it away from something else the researchers might stumble on.

There is even a possible scenario in which documents are genuinely from the late 1940s or early 1950s, as they claim to be, but not actually true. American researcher Don Ecker believes that the US government may have had reason to promote Roswell at the time—hence the nature of the press release perhaps—to suggest that the US military was in possession of advanced technology and biology. It might have been hoped that this would stay the hand of the Soviets, who had become the enemy following the end of the Second World War.

Quite possibly the "hardware" truth of Roswell is that the material was the remains of a top secret listening dish carried aloft by balloon to listen over the horizon in the days before satellites were in orbit. That is consistent with the witness accounts of the time. But the myth has now become so great, and so much time has now passed, that no truth is ever likely to be forthcoming—at least not a truth that will satisfy anyone except those who want to believe it anyway.

That said, there is a growing sense of "tiredness" among those who genuinely seek the truth of this case. Kent Jeffrey, for example, who has long promoted Roswell and the "Roswell Declaration," seeking to force the government to "come clean," has now decided that he does not think the case involves an alien spacecraft. He gave interviews on American TV in April 1997 and stated that his four years of investigation had ended in "a major disappointment for me. I started out here in a quest for the truth. Unfortunately, that truth ended up to be different than I thought it might be and hoped that it would be."

Jeffrey had believed that the key to Roswell lay in Jesse Marcel Jr., who, when he was 11 years old, was shown bits of the debris by his father, Major Jesse Marcel. Marcel Jr. recently underwent six hours of regression by hypnotist Neil Hibbler. The result was that Marcel revealed only what he had already remembered and stated, and Jeffrey believes that hypnotically recovered testimony supports the contention that the recovered material came, not from an alien spacecraft, but from a Mogul balloon. Marcel, on the other hand, still maintains that the material he saw was more than just that, and believes there is a story yet to be uncovered.

The same TV story announced that Roswell Army Air Field press officer Walter Haut, who issued the press release claiming capture of a flying disc, now admits that he had realized just days after the announcement that "it was a screw up." Haut also thinks that the recovered material was from a balloon, presumably the sort used to carry the listening dishes aloft. Haut had been a Roswell enthusiast, indeed he was a founder of the International UFO Museum in Roswell, but he recently ended his association with the museum. Haut now states that he thinks the UFO claims are "just a bunch of hooey."

More recently a film has been released which purports to be of an "alien autopsy" on humanoids found at Roswell. There has been considerable controversy regarding the validity of the film, and at the present time most serious researchers do not consider it a worthwhile addition to the debate on extraterrestrial life.

Kecksburg

With regard to alien spacecraft remains, we should perhaps not let Roswell blind us to other claims that might have value—such as Kecksburg. Leonard Stringfield, author of *Situation Red: The UFO Siege*, believed that the Kecksburg case was "just behind Roswell as the most significant UFO retrieval case in history." It is one of few cases which do not just rely on documentation, and it is a case that has not been overly contaminated by speculation. It is more recent than Roswell, though itself now over 30 years old. Research into the case—principally by Stan Gordon of the Pennsylvania Association for the Study of the Unexplained—appears to have been thorough and grounded. (It was written up in *MUFON Journals* numbers 257, 258 and 274.) In the mid afternoon of 9 December 1965, a fireball-like object was seen in the skies over several states of the USA south of the Great Lakes region. It was visible in some locations for up to 20 minutes. Several witnesses thought they were watching a plane crashing into Lake Erie; there were also several reports of a sonic boom. Although there were reports of debris being located, it now seems that officially the only material recovered was foil-like strips which were identified as "window"—a radar blinding material being used by a military exercise in the area at the time.

In fact the object did not fall into Lake Erie; it was witnessed crashing into a wood near the village of Kecksburg, in Westomoreland County, Pennsylvania. The impact created a strong vibration felt over a mile away. One farmer, Dale Howard, felt "a vibration" and "a thump" at the time of the impact.

Two children told their mother, Mrs. Kalp, that they had seen something fall into the woods; she told them to go and find it, thinking it might be a weather balloon. Then she realized there could be danger and called for them to come back. She contacted the police at Greensburg and reported the crash.

Local radio stations were receiving a number of calls about the impact, and reporters got to the location quickly to interview witnesses. Roads around the area became jammed with sightseers who had heard about the crash on the radio. Police and fire officials investigated the area, and Geiger counter readings were taken. Then the military were called in, and the area was sealed off.

The local newspaper, the *Tribune-Review*, covering the incident the following day, immediately referred to the object as a UFO, quoted the military as saying "we don't know what we have yet" and reported that "no one is being allowed near the object."

When the military arrived they established a command post at the fire station, and a telephone link to NORAD in Colorado. The team stayed overnight and searched through the following day; they claimed to have found nothing and believed that the explanation being given by the Air Force that the object was a meteor was correct. But some witnesses later reported seeing lead-lined casks being brought into the area, as if to transport something radioactive. Others say that at least one flatbed truck was brought in and that something big was taken away under a tarpaulin. This seems corroborated by claims from other witnesses that, on investigating the site after the military left, they found "deep drag marks" in the ground away from the site and up to where the military trucks had been parked. Still other claims include that later the military shipped in shrubs and plants and re-planted the area to cover up traces of impact.

The investigation of the event has revealed that it may indeed be something of interest. Over time Stan Gordon interviewed "dozens of people who were involved..." from both the military and civilian population. According to eyewitness accounts he pieced together it is possible that the object changed direction in mid-flight, possibly making several manoeuvres. These accounts also suggest something moving much slower than a meteor. One witness described the object as circular and stated, "You could make out the individual flames around it, since it moved so slow."

The evidence that something tangible had survived the crash comes from one eyewitness, "Jack," who was one of the crowd that drove out to the scene on the night of the crash; he looked down into the woods and saw around ten people—apparently civilians— grouped around something, pointing to it. He could see where something had smashed through the trees. Jack walked down to the site and checked it over with a torch, describing "blue sparks" coming off the object.

Stan Gordon and researcher Ray Boeche later undertook to further their investigation of the Kecksburg crash through the Freedom of Information Act, and in 1984 requested documentation relating to the incident. They discovered that the unit that investigated the crash, the 662nd Radar Squadron, was at that time under the command not of the Army but of Aerospace Defense Command—later known as Space Command.

By the following year they had obtained a 31-page report on the case, issued by the Air Force. It contained confirmation that Project Blue Book—the Air Force's UFO investigation project—had been called in to the case; indeed the project head, Major Hector Quintanilla, dealt with the enquiry himself. But there was evidence of some sort of cover-up, or at least concealment of the work of that night in 1965. For when reports were obtained outlining the work of the 662nd, no mention of any activity for the night of 9 December 1965 was included. Gordon asks the question: "Was this operation of such a high security level that the report on the incident was transmitted to unknown agencies where the facts of the case could never be unlocked?"

Gordon and Boeche found unclassified memos showing that Houston Space Center, the Air Force Command Post, the Space Defense Center and others were all interested in the Kecksburg case; so what was it that was of such interest to the military? It was a remarkable degree of interest and high-level involvement if the object was thought to be only a meteor.

The fact that the 662nd was deactivated in December 1969, the same month as the Air Force "got out of the UFO business" by shutting down Project Blue Book, led some researchers to speculate that the unit was a specially trained UFO retrieval squad. One suggested possibility for the object was that of a test missile fired over Lake Erie, but that was discounted when officials stated there had been no such firings. Another possible explanation for the object, and the involvement of the Space agencies, was the re-entry of Cosmos 96, which re-entered the Earth's atmosphere on that date. It seems a remarkable coincidence that two such objects should blaze their way down through the sky at more or less the same time, yet the data for Cosmos do not tie up exactly with the Kecksburg object. Cosmos re-entered just after three o'clock in the morning; the Kecksburg object at four in the afternoon. Presumably one possibility is that a fragment re-entered separately, but there is no record to support this.

A letter from Space Command stated that "it is unusual for an object to survive re-entry. If in fact it does, and it is recovered, it is referred to the Foreign Technologies Division at Wright-Patterson AFB, Ohio." Research by Robert Todd indicated that this Division was indeed involved in the Kecksburg crash. Todd obtained an interesting document under the Freedom of Information Act, stating:

Peacetime employment of AFCIN intelligence team capability is provided for in UFO investigation (AFR 200-2) and in support of Air Force Systems Command (AFSC), Foreign Technology Division (FTD), Projects Moon Dust and Blue Fly. These three peacetime projects all involve a potential for employment of qualified field intelligence personnel on a quick reaction basis to recover or perform field exploitation of Unidentified Flying Objects, or known Soviet/East Bloc aerospace vehicles, weapons systems, and/or residual components of such equipment.

The researchers believe that the Kecksburg material was recovered in an exercise by Project Moon Dust—a UFO investigation headed by the FTD at Wright-Patterson.

The most intriguing speculation Gordon raises is that of deliberation on the part of the object that crashed. He believes that the object was not only moving slowly, as the witnesses indicated, but searching for the best place to come down. Gordon believes it selected "the deepest section of a wooded area." Of course if it was an unmanned out-of-control object, it had to land somewhere, and perhaps its location was coincidence. But as Gordon points out, "unless you were at the spot where the retrieval operation was taking place, you would have no idea as to what was really occurring."

But if that is true, and the object was, as some have speculated, an alien spacecraft, presumably it would not have been concerned to make life easy for retrieveal teams; more likely it simply wanted to hide while it tried to effect repairs. Either way, the deep woods might have provided a useful place for crash-down.

The witness description of the object is of a bronze-coloured, acorn-shaped object some 12 feet long and 10 feet wide. (So famous is the object locally that when the local truck station was presented with a life-sized model of the object used in a TV documentary they displayed it on the roof of the building. Indeed, the incident has become something of a local attraction and has inspired an anniversary dance in the town, and sales of branded merchandise.) Witnesses who claim to have seen the object at Air Force bases locally claim that there is a band of "unintelligible markings" around it. One Air Force man claimed that he saw the object being taken into a hangar at Lockborne Air Base, near Columbus, Ohio, after the base had been placed on "red alert." The truck bringing it had been brought in through a little used "rear gate." He also observed: "President Kennedy came to the base while I was at Lockborne and there wasn't as much security as I saw that morning." Another witness claimed he delivered bricks to the base and was warned not to talk about anything he saw there, virtually ensuring that his interest was high, and indeed he decided to "sneak inside to see what all the secrecy was about." He described the acorn-shaped object being worked on by 10 to 15 men in protective clothing, apparently trying to open it. Then he was turfed out, and told to forget what he had seen. The witnesses insisted on retaining their anonymity; perhaps there is a sense that the Kecksburg case is mutating into a "Roswell incident" with dubious sources and strange claims. Hopefully not; UFO research doesn't need two Roswells to its name.

Area 51

At the present time there is considerable speculation about the fate of alien craft believed to have been retrieved by the US government and military. It appears that the question of concealed alien technology is to be one of the "growth areas" of UFO research.

The most famous of the speculated locations for military study of retrieved alien hardware is Area 51, made even more famous by its highly inaccurate inclusion in the film *Independence Day*. Area 51 is located in Groom Lake, a dry salt lake in the high mountains of Nevada, a remote location where some of the world's most advanced aircraft technologies are devised. It was built in 1954 with the purpose of developing the U2 spy plane which featured in the Cold War in the 1960s. It was also the home of the "Blackbird," and more recently was where the Stealth B2 and the Nighthawk were developed.

As a dry salt lake it has the natural advantage of a stable, long, straight runway, while its isolation makes it highly suitable for top secret development and testing work. Because of its isolation it is inevitable that some of the clandestine activities undertaken by the military are housed there also. There are so-called "black projects" which are not directly accountable to the public, and on which many millions of tax dollars are expended.

One of those "black projects," UFO researchers believe, is the reverse engineering of retrieved alien spacecraft. The two main thrusts of evidence for this are the claims of those who say they have worked there, and at the neighbouring complex known as S4, and the high numbers of UFO sightings reported around the base.

The authorities are clearly concerned that prying eyes should be kept away from Area 51, though that would be understandable whatever top secret project they are undertaking, UFO-related or not. In 1984 they took control of over 90,000 acres of neighbouring land for no other purpose, it seems, than to prevent sightseers reaching within "viewing range" of the base.

There are several reasons why the government are thought to be reverse engineering flying saucers. Firstly, and assuming that the government captured the flying saucers as the result of accidents or even aggressive military action, the reason for such analysis is to find out how the saucers work and use that technology for military purposes against other terrestrial nations, or at least to act as a deterrent against them. The second reason is based on the belief that the work is not being done on accidentally retrieved saucers but rather that the authorities have entered into a pact with the aliens, their side of which is to provide technology to the American military. (Our side of the pact, rather gruesomely, is to allow the aliens to abduct humans and to mutilate cattle and other animals so that the aliens may explore terrestrial biology, presumably either to improve their own stock or to create hybrids.)

As far as the testimony of those who worked there is concerned, the principal claims are those of Bob Lazar, who claimed to have worked for some weeks, at the end of the 1980s, at S4, engaged in analysis of the propulsion systems of the flying saucers. Lazar saw, he says, nine flying saucers (one he christened the "sports model"), all apparently in working order. He was eventually sacked for taking UFO enthusiasts on "saucer spotting" expeditions to the locality.

Lazar has been the subject of some criticism. He has been unable to substantiate his claims of qualifications in nuclear physics, and of his having worked at Los Alamos. Lazar believes that the "audit trail" of his qualifications has been doctored or removed in order to discredit him. What has not been removed from his "record" is the fact that he was prosecuted for running a brothel in Las Vegas and has been declared bankrupt. His supporters argue that his convictions were more of a technicality and that his private life should not be held against him. Indeed there is a somewhat cynical argument that the government would seek out just such a man—experienced, qualified but with a "dubious" past—precisely because if they needed to discredit him later it would be relatively easy to do so. And, seemingly, they did.

Dulce

If Area 51 is the best-known location of alleged technological experimentation, then Dulce is the best-known base where biological experimentation is thought to be undertaken.

The claims for Dulce base are extraordinary, and highly speculative. While there can be no doubt that Area 51 at least exists, whatever is believed to be happening there, there are good reasons for doubting that Dulce exists at all, or at least on the scale speculated.

The scale is huge; the persistent rumour is that the base, concealed under the desert in New Mexico, is the size of Manhattan. It is allegedly several storeys in depth, and approached through a natural cave system which helps to keep it concealed. Thousands of aliens are alleged to work in the facility alongside humans. When told this, Jacques Vallee asked, "Who takes out the garbage?"—which may sound like sarcasm but is in fact a pertinent question. Such a huge facility must need all manner of servicing—Manhattan could not effectively cut itself off from the world for long without needing services and supplies—and such needs would open up the possibilities of exposure. Too many civilian people would need to be involved to keep a base of that size secret for long. Vallee felt that the reaction he got was dismissive, because he wasn't playing the game and asking the "philosophical" questions which UFO enthusiasts expected. Certainly it is apparent in UFO conferences that people—whether believers or sceptics—seek out "like minds" to agree with them and brusquely dismiss those who do not.

But perhaps the base exists on a smaller scale, and the rumour of its huge size is put out to encourage people to think that the whole thing must be an absurd rumour. If so, then what is alleged to be happening on the base is no less fantastic.

The base is an area where it is believed humans and aliens work together, a product of the pact mentioned earlier, to undertake biological work. Alien abduction victims are said to be taken there for "processing," which includes being used to produce not just alien/human hybrids but human/animal hybrids. A persistent rumour suggests sightings of a half-human/half-reptile. This is thought "logical" as some researchers believe the Grays are actually reptilian in origin. (One sculptor created a humanoid form of what she believed dinosaurs might have looked like had they evolved into an intelligent species instead of becoming extinct—it is uncannily "Gray" in many aspects of its shape and appearance.)

Another activity in which the humans and aliens are supposed to be jointly engaged is the creation of a race of humanoid zombies that can be used as slave-labour in dangerous situations, such as handling of atomic materials.

Dulce is also thought to be the centre of activity of implants, and perhaps the location from which implanted humans are monitored. Implant rumours have included the devices being used for tracking, or for mind control.

But both Area 51 and Dulce, not to mention the many other so-called bases, suffer from lack of hard evidence. Supporters of such beliefs point out that that is hardly surprising, as admission or documentation would not be expected. The facilities are, after all, secret. Sceptics find that all too convenient, and suggest that the proof is not available for the simple reason that it doesn't exist. It will take a trail of much harder evidence before the rumours and claims to date can be considered proof. At the moment the speculation feeds a growing mythology.

Despite the claims of UFO researchers over the years, there are few cases to support the idea of a crashed flying saucer having been retrieved by any government. The number of hoax claimants in this field is high; recently there were two such claims from South Africa. In America the most extreme claims list an almost farcical number of crashed saucers and retrieved alien bodies. Unless the alleged aliens are "dropping saucers" around the place to test our responses—we should not rule out any possibilities— then we should surely not expect capture to be other than a rare phenomenon. Roswell seemed to offer possibilities, Kecksburg remains open. Almost all other claims fall down quickly on the basis of hoax, wishful thinking, lack of witness consensus or reliability, and the failure to trace documents to a satisfactory origin.

No single area of the UFO subject is so popular at the present time as the suspected retrieval of alien spacecraft. Unfortunately, no single area is so full of third-hand reports, suspicious documentation and rumour. In the search for evidence of alien life it is not as useful as many would wish to think.

14

Humanoids, Hybrids
And Science Fiction

The interaction between science fiction and UFO reports is significant. We have examined this interaction in several books, most recently *Fifty Years of UFOs*, studying such overlap as the effects of films such as *The Day the Earth Stood Still*. With regard to the perception of aliens, as opposed to the UFO phenomenon in general, there are two interactions that deserve mention. The first is in the shape of the reported aliens themselves.

Humanoids

As this book has shown, the vast majority of visiting aliens seen have humanoid shape. The two principal alien types reported in Europe and North America, the Grays and the Nordics, are both humanoid, and the latter are so human-like that they are able to go about on Earth undetected. South America probably has the largest variety of aliens reported, but most are humanoid, including bearded, troll-like creatures (e.g. Gonzalez and Ponce's encounter at Caracas in 1954; Bebedouro, May 1969), "normal" human-like ones (e.g. Parana, Brazil, 1963) and several versions of Cyclopean entities (e.g. Familia Sagrada, August 1963).

This question of humanoid shape creates problems. If we consider the Earth as just one biosphere where life has developed presumably along the same random lines as we might expect elsewhere in the Universe, then we immediately face the fact that the vast majority of life on Earth is *not* humanoid. Of the millions of species of animal life only a fraction, including humans, have that shape. Consider the range of insect-types alone. If, as is believed, humans developed as a random result of evolutionary forces, and given the wide possibilities that the Earth displays, then in a completely different biosphere those random forces could presumably produce different results. The intelligent creatures might not be the humanoid ones. That one other humanoid race should evolve and reach a state of technology that would allow it to visit Earth in the brief time-span that we humans happen to be dominant seems coincidence enough; dinosaurs lived for 165 million years, we've only been around for a million or two, and technological for a very brief time. Yet in fact we have not one but a seemingly endless variety of visiting humanoids.

The variety of humanoid shapes alone causes problems. Do we assume that we are being visited by a wide range of aliens from various other planets? If so, do they know of each other? The claims of the experiencers would seem to indicate that they do not. If we divide the experiencers into the contactees and the abductees then we have two scenarios. Of the contactees many are given special messages from particular aliens. All of these seem to come from different planets, all have different messages, and not one refers to others or to other contactees. There is no record of, say, Daniel Fry receiving a message that included "When my mate was talking to George Adamski the other day . . ." Each contactee is raised to a special individual platform. We shall look separately at why this might be, but it does not give much support to the idea of a race, or races, of visiting aliens.

The abductees are a slightly more credible case in this context. Abductees do not get mentioned to each other either; Kathie Davis is not told of how "We were talking to Betty Hill just a few years ago . . ." but perhaps the argument that abductees are "laboratory rats" in the experiments of another species means that they simply do not consider us worthy of talking to at all. How many biology professors talk to their frogs and rats as they experiment on them? Of course, we have the slight hurdle that many, such as Betty and Barney Hill, *were* spoken to, seemingly on an "equal" level. But perhaps we have to—and elsewhere we will—examine the overlap between abduction and contactee claims. Budd Hopkins' reports seem to contain enough cases of cold, unfeeling, dealings with people to suggest the "lab rat" scenario.

What we can consider is that even if some of the claims of those seeing aliens are true, they may not all be. Yet the humanoid shape is predominant. Certainly it predominates in science fiction, and we shall examine this shortly. It is the shape selected for the Norse gods, the Greek and Roman gods and most other deities. The term "personification" indicates a natural leaning towards a "person-like" shape. Such a bias reflects an underlying need: there are reasons why people "constructing" aliens within a mythology seek to create humanoid shapes.

Firstly, it is anthropomorphic to show that the humanoid, of which humans are a type, is the "Master of the Universe." If we believe, as many claim, that the visiting aliens are displaying a superiority over humans (they can travel between planets, we cannot, etc.), then the fact that they look like us gives us grounds for belief that we will do one day what they can do today. This meets our basic need to feel superior as well as our desire for new horizons ("To explore strange new worlds and new civilizations; to boldly go . . .").

Secondly, to create a worthy opponent. We find in our most visible myths—those created in the cinema—that we need worthy opponents. The *Superman* movies starring Christopher Reeve, of which there are four, survived only one without such an opponent. In the first film Superman battles the forces of nature unleashed by the film's villain. But in the three subsequent films it was necessary to create an equally powerful enemy to make Superman's talents seem necessary: in *Superman 2*, it was three other inhabitants of his planet; in *Superman 3*, his own evil side made physical; in *Superman 4*, "Nuclear Man."

Perhaps most fascinating in film development is the mutation of the *War of the Worlds* aliens. In H. G. Wells's book, and in the 1952 film, the aliens are non-humanoid and indeed rarely seen; the real "enemies" were the walking machines (book) cum flying saucers (film). But in order to sustain a long-running television series where humans had to do battle with a "worthy opponent" the script adapted the Martians into humans. They learned to take on human form. This of course meant that they could do what we could do, and had to be battled on equal terms. This is certainly a travesty of anything Wells seems to have intended. His aliens were non-human precisely to show how different they were, but you cannot have dialogue with, or fight against, anything so non-human for long before it gets boring. And so the humanoids needed to be created again. The *Invaders* series of the 1960s—probably the first popular UFO fiction of that kind—had aliens taking human form for much the same reason.

Such thinking seems to have been behind the artistic analysis of presumed dinosaur evolution. On the basis that the dinosaurs might have been killed off by a one-off accident (incoming meteorite changing the Earth's environment too suddenly), then speculation as to what they would have evolved into had that not happened produced a human-dinosaur, clearly humanoid, as the end result. The fact that dinosaurs might not have been killed off but instead evolved naturally into birds seems almost an affront. Why did they not do the decent thing and become human?! This is human-centred arrogance at its worst.

Some suggestions of the shape of aliens have them more insect-like, though still distinctly humanoid. Strieber, for example, has indicated the insect-like impression they give. Scott, one of Mack's clients, remembered a time when he was three years old and while playing outside saw "two beings appearing from nowhere." When he ran to his mother—whether there is any missing time is uncertain—he reported to her: "I saw big ants out there." Interestingly these claims parallel science fiction very well. Early sci-fi was full of combat with insect-like creatures. But the "Superman" effect is still evident. In *Them*, for example, the threat was from ants, but huge ants (worthy opponents). In fact, a billion intelligent small ants would probably make a more formidable enemy than a few huge ones—but not an enemy that sustains itself very well on the movie screen. Another planet might well have evolved insect-like intelligences, but is it not human-centred arrogance to assume they come in human size and humanoid form?

There are arguments in support of the aliens being visiting humanoids. Perhaps, even on Earth, different intelligences of equal magnitude, but on quite different plateaux, may exist. Perhaps dolphins are humanity's equal in their own way. Perhaps ants and bees have a higher intelligence, but in a way none of us can comprehend. And perhaps these and other variations of high intelligence exist elsewhere in the universe. But perhaps it is only the humanoids that develop technology—and needs—that allow them to cross the gulfs of space. Perhaps it is not the humanoids' superior evolution that creates space travel but its inferiority. Perhaps all these other creatures are reaching—even travelling—between worlds mentally or spiritually. Perhaps it is only the poor old defective humans who have to build spaceships in order to do it. Other creatures have evolved most of the tools humanity has built; insects alone have evolved drills, saws and chemical weapons biologically. Perhaps humanoids are cut off from natural developments and create tools and machines not because they are superior but because they have lost the ability to do it any other way. Perhaps also humanoids just seek out humanoids because it is difficult to impress an ant with your type of intelligence even if we all have equivalent but different plateaux! This is a theme examined in Chapter 3.

Non-Humanoids

The above should not be taken to indicate that all reported aliens have been humanoid. There have been a few, though very few, exceptions.

In August 1968 at Serra de Almos, Spain, a chicken farmer was to report one such rather frightening variation. It was approximately six o'clock one morning when he saw a dome-shaped object hovering a few feet above the ground. As he approached, two entities ran back to and into the object which then took off. The entities he reported were octopus-like, approximately three feet tall and had several legs each. He also described them as being light in colour and disgusting in appearance.

In 1971, "John Hodges" and "Peter Rodriguez" were visiting an apartment in Dapple Grey Lane in South Los Angeles at two o'cock in the morning when they saw two objects like human brains on the road. Each was approximately three feet high, and seemed to be alive. Hodges drove Rodriguez home, then returned to his own home, but arrived realizing that he had lost two hours of time. Under regression hypnosis it appears that Hodges was telephathically contacted by the entities, who told him that they would meet again. There was also some imagery of humanoid entities. Seven years later Hodges had a further contact warning him of the dangers of nuclear war.

At 1.00 A.M. on 27 January 1977, Lee Parrish was driving home in the town of Prospect, Kentucky, when he was buzzed by a bright, rectangular UFO. It sped away at great speed. On arriving home he discovered he had lost over half an hour of time. Hypnotic regression was used to explore the missing time. It seems Parrish had been transported into the UFO. Three machine-like entities surrounded Parrish; he believed them to be alive despite their appearance. One of the entities was a huge black slab 15 feet tall. It has been compared to the "monolith" in the film *2001–A Space Odyssey*.

At Niagara Falls, in January 1958, a woman reported entities emerging from something near the road. They were like animals, with four legs and a tail, and feelers on the head.

We might also recall the "biological computers" described by Helga Douglas in Chapter 7.

If we assume that aliens have a common point of origin, then perhaps the clue to their varied appearances comes from a contact at Beit Bridge, in Zimbabwe. The witness reported: "They can make themselves appear in any form in our minds." This adaptability is something considered in Chapter 10.

Science Fiction Films

Aliens in science fiction have largely been humanoid, of course, but this has mostly been due to the constraints of cost (it's cheapest to put a man in a funny rubber suit) and technology (what is achievable on screen). As budgets have soared, and the technology to create astonishing computer-generated images for films has developed, so the aliens are becoming "more alien." Metamorphs, for example, are very popular in current films, displaying the special effects teams' abilites to "change" one image into another without any apparent break in filming. But perhaps there is still one reason why humanoids predominate: horror. To be attacked by an insect-like, acid-for-blood creature that kills apparently thoughtlessly makes for a tense thriller, but for psychological horror there is nothing like the exploits of an alien that could just as easily be a human. That way, film-makers allow us to explore our inner selves too. The fictional development of aliens deserves an examination if we are to understand the widespread beliefs about aliens.

The humanoid shape has prevailed where it need not. For example, robots in early science fiction films were often made to look human although the development of *actual* robots—say in car production line facilities—shows that the humanoid shape is far from useful. Starting with the end-need tends to produce robots with quite un-human shapes. And the human shape is hardly very stable unless supported by a complex array of balance mechanisms. Even if one day an android resembling "Data" in *Star Trek–The Next Generation* could be created, for whom would the shape be pleasing? To Data? Or to us? In fact, to us, it would be a symptom of "creating in our own image" and putting ourselves—in our own minds at least—closer to the position of gods. Early science fiction films contained several such humanoid robots. *The Vanishing*

Shadow, a film serial from 1934, contains the typical robot/human where various appendages, radio aerials and so on are arranged to form a face; *The Phantom Empire*, from 1935, sported robots that looked as if they wore trilby hats; the 1939 *Phantom Creeps*, starring Bela Lugosi, included a hideous robot with a demonic face. A memorable robot, of course, was Gort in *The Day the Earth Stood Still* of 1951; *Target Earth* (1954) was the story of a straightforward invasion from space by robots; *The Colossus of New York* (1958) was a human brain in a huge robot; and we should never forget Robbie the Robot from *Forbidden Planet* and a few other film appearances, nor his "lookalike" from the series *Lost in Space*. Apart from Data in *Star Trek–The Next Generation*, recent science fiction films have contained human-looking android aliens, for example Ash in *Alien*. In short, we love to make our robots human.

When we move into flesh and blood we find that humans and humanoids still dominate. The Emperor Ming who fought Flash Gordon was quite human, as was Lightning from *Fighting Devil Dogs* (1938). Even with modern special effects the humanoid shape is apparent; one thinks of *Species*, *Independence Day* and so on.

We find a significant number of aliens that take over and use human bodies for their own purposes. This is of course the cheapest possible alien from the point of view of special effects budgeting, but the reasoning might go deeper than that. A "monster" that is indistinguishable from your next-door neightbour, or your spouse, is obviously a good chiller. *The Purple Monster* from 1945 had the power to invisibly invade the bodies of his human victims; a similar theme ran through *It Came from Outer Space*, *Invasion of the Body Snatchers*, *I Married a Monster from Outer Space*, *The Beast with a Million Eyes*, *Not of This Earth*, *The Village of the Damned*, and of course most famously the *Invaders* television series—as well as more recent films such as *Cocoon* and *Starman*. Even going right back to *Metropolis*, a science fiction masterpiece from the era of the "silent movies," we have a robot designed to replace a human.

Within and without alien invasion we find that a good many "monsters" from the horror genre are humanoid: Frankenstein, the Wolfman, Manimal from *The Island of Lost Souls*, the Eloi and Morlocks from *The Time Machine*, the Creature from the Black Lagoon, the Gill Man, the Alligator People, the Thing from Another World, the Mole People, both the aliens and the mutant in *This Island Earth*, the Man from Planet X, the black robot-like humanoids in *Earth v The Flying Saucers*, the mutant from *The Day the World Ended*, the Selenites from *The First Men in the Moon*, no end of monsters from such series as *Dr. Who* and *Star Trek* up to and including the Borg. To continue listing the hundreds of other examples would be pointless.

There have been notable non-humanoids, of course—the Triffids, the insect-like creatures in *Aliens* and *Alien 3*, and so on—but it is clear that the humanoid form has dominated science fiction. That might change as special effects allow for greater variety. But even with filming techniques that are a vast improvement in putting "a man in a rubber suit," techniques that could easily produce non-humanoid shapes, we do not see evidence of significant diversity. Perhaps we are discovering that creating humanoids is more than just an expedience, it is an inner drive. Consider one episode of *The X-Files* where a mutated worm in the sewers grew to human size and began attacking people; the worm was recognizably humanoid.

Even in searching for the "Grays" themselves there are many forerunners, including David McCallum's character in an *Outer Limits* episode called "The Sixth Finger." "The Cage," an early episode of *Star Trek*, contains very similar beings that even abduct people and create for them an artificial world so that they can believe themselves to be living their former life—something similar to reports of abductions as shown in Chapter 10. There are also similar forms in *The Invasion of the Saucer Men, The Man from Planet X, Mysterious Island* from 1929, and others.

Hybrids

The claims of the UFO researchers themselves, working from a plethora of sightings, and the evidence of abductions gained mostly by regression hypnosis, at least reconciles the visitations by humanoids, though not the variety. They believe that the aliens are here to create a hybrid alien/human, presumably to add quality to one or both races. That being the case it seems reasonable that like creatures would be involved. But this hybridization belief presents its own problems.

Some researchers, such as Budd Hopkins and David Jacobs, believe that the evidence of their work shows that the aliens are primarily interested in our reproductive capabilities. Hopkins states:

> We know a great deal now about what's going on. Whoever, or whatever, the UFO occupants are they seem extremely interested in studying us on the physical level: human reproduction, our DNA, the way on the emotional level we treat one another in sexual or loving relationships. But most especially how we treat our children. And it seems to be, even though this sounds totally crazy, that they are interested in producing some kind of hybrid mix of themselves and ourselves.

These researchers believe that humans are being subjected to a series of experiments designed to "blend" humans and aliens. They point to the number of rape-like claims that are offered, to the number of intrusive surgeries into the reproductive organs, to the removal of sperm and ova, and to the direct claims that female abductees have seen hybrid alien/human foetuses removed from their wombs.

John Mack entered the field with similar beliefs. "The purely physical or biological aspect of the abduction phenomenon seems to have to do with some sort of genetic or quasi-genetic engineering for the purpose of creating human/alien hybrid offspring. We have no evidence of alien-induced genetic alteration in the strictly biological sense, although it is possible that this has occurred."

Mack's client, Jerry, saw the hybridization as part of a higher purpose. She commented that what the aliens are doing is necessary and has to do with "races, beings or whatever" making another creation. She felt that as a single person she should "look beyond [herself] and know that it's for the greater good."

In our book *Fifty Years of UFOs* we examined the "hybridization" motif in detail, setting out the science fiction background to the image, and the fact that such images were a very strong component of, particularly, American science fiction. Much of current science fiction is exploring the hybrid motif, probably, we think, because it allows for the philosophical questions to be asked: how would I react if . . . ? If I were an "outsider," how would I view the treatment my society gives me? And so on. The hybridization theory within UFOs also arose in America. That nation is probably more than ever exploring its "inner self." Technologically it is the only major world power now that the Soviet empire has fallen. It has contemplated its involvement in Vietnam. It has asked itself how it is treating its ethnic minorities, its native Americans, indeed its own history. The fascinating thing about hybrids is that Americans, possibly more than any other nationality, are hybrid. Hybrid native American and "white man"; hybrid technocrats and New-Agers; there are Polish Americans, English Americans, Irish Americans. And now there are alien Americans—as in the Star People.

Before examining this, it is important to consider the cultural overtones of science fiction generally. It is held by many to be escapist fiction, and of course to some degree it is. It provides for a way of ignoring, or setting aside, everyday reality and imagining worlds and situations, futures and dimensions, where our dreams, or nightmares, can come true, where we can be hero or victim, or whatever appeals. But in fact such escapism is limited; to escape into a non-existent world is, for all but the truly deluded, a shallow victory. We can be a hero in science fiction because we make up *everything*: the situation, the environment, our own abilities or technology, and so on. In fact a thriller or a drama based in our own time, in our own environment, offers more true escapism because we are required to fantasize within an external reality; and the achievements of heroism seem to become that much more possible. We can fantasize that we are a hero in a situation where maybe it could just be true. We can all be James Bond in our dreams and interweave that fantasy into our everyday lives. So it is probable that the wide appeal of science fiction is not only one of escapism. The true appeal of *good* science fiction—as opposed to futuristic horror or titillation movies—is that it is philosophical speculation. In setting up fantasy situations which are not constrained by "the real world" we can speculate the "what if?" questions that fascinate us all. What if we could achieve a Utopian world? What if we could develop into a super-race of people? Therefore we should view the influence of science fiction, which is a strong element in the background of "UFO-lore," as one of philosophic questioning.

In science fiction the theme of hybridization has long been tested. The super-heroes such as Batman and Superman all have their dual identities. We see them also in *Star Trek*, (Spock—half human/half Vulcan); and in *Star Trek—The Next Generation* (Data—machine trying to be human, and Worf—Klingon trying to adapt to human standards). The first episode of *Star Trek—The Next Generation* to introduce the alien humanoid/machine hybrids known as the Borg also showed their "nursery" room on board their spaceship—with many similarities to the "nurseries" reported on board some flying saucers by abductees; the Borg were described as born organic and then changed by mechanical implants.

The latest of the spin-offs, *Star Trek Voyager*, offers us a holographic doctor, a computer-generated assistant to the medical section who, in various episodes, gradually explores his feelings and experiences as they develop. In addition we see a certain "full circle" emerging. Commander Chakotay, played by Robert Beltran, is the descendant of a native American Indian who strives to reconcile his modern, technological environment with the "worlds" of his vision quests, sky spirits and medicine wheels.

Several episodes of the series relate to this duality, and the series is clearly exploring the American psyche as much as it is exploring Chakotay's inner learning. The episode "Tattoo" in particular explores Chakotay's heritage, while at the same time the holographic doctor gives himself a computer-generated flu so that he can suffer as a human and learn how to deal with human frailties.

The cultural "background" of a society steeped in science fiction with regard to beliefs about aliens cannot be overstated. It has created the image bank of aliens that has formed the background tapestry to the "space race," and to the expectations of the SETI programmes, and has created much of the imagery of UFO-related abductions and indeed to the UFO reports of earlier years.

In fact, UFOs have made their way into the "background" of science fiction much more directly in this decade than ever before. For example, the episode that introduced the *New Adventures of Superman* has him hunted down by government UFO researchers who have retrieved the craft in which he crashed to Earth. In one sequence of going through government files we can see folders marked "Voronezh" and "Gulf Breeze."

And, interestingly, *Star Trek* has "softened." It had always distanced itself from UFOs, with only one passing reference to the *Enterprise* becoming a UFO during a time-travel episode. (In fact *Star Trek 4* contains the line—during a visit to the twentieth century: "It's a historical fact that these people have not yet met an extraterrestrial," and this becomes the theme of *Star Trek—First Contact*, released in late 1996.) But in the *New Generation* episode "First Contact" the formula is clearly based on contemporary UFO reports, with references to UFOs-as-weather balloons, the social responses of people to UFOs, "people" working with the aliens, and so on. And an episode of *Star Trek Voyager*—"The 37s"—completed the "conversion," with the ship encountering a group of people who had in 1937 been abducted by aliens. The programme was clearly based on UFO-abduction imagery.

This brings the influences full circle, but since the UFO is still an evolving phenomenon it means that the science fiction images derived from UFO stories are now set to further influence future UFO imagery. Programmes such as *The X-Files* are now taking the UFO stories and feeding them back into fiction, and therefore into the belief systems that people will draw their images from in the future. The full circle is becoming a closed circle.

15

Mythology

C.G. Jung commented of contact with aliens: "We would be placed in the very questionable position of today's primitive societies that clash with the superior cultures of the white race. All initiative would be wrested from us. An old witch doctor once said to me, with tears in his eyes, we would 'have no more dreams.'"

There is mythology surrounding belief in aliens. Whether or not we have been host on Earth to extraterrestrials, there is no doubt that many people live their lives as if that were a fact. Not just those who believe they have made contact with aliens personally, for whom the belief must be a certainty, but also those who believe in the literal truth of their stories. Forty years ago, before the dawn of the Space Race, the idea of aliens was almost exclusively the purview of science fiction, and anyone who offered the suggestion that there must be life "out there" somewhere was thought to hold very curious beliefs. Today, there is an almost universal acceptance that in an infinite universe intelligent life must exist somewhere. We are living in a world that believes in aliens. As such there will inevitably be mythology surrounding the truth.

This is particularly likely in our present time, because for many people in the West the old mythologies seem to be dying. But all cultures need mythologies, or, whether they need them or not, it is a fact that no culture ever existed or exists now that does not have mythologies, so we must assume they are fulfilling a need. So when old myths die, new ones arise to replace them and fulfil the need.

Our present Western culture has promoted science as the True Word. That which can be measured, predicted and replicated under controlled conditions is real; everything else is of no value. Partly this is science justifying itself for a variety of reasons, partly it is science fighting against the widespread interest in the paranormal. There are many scientists, paramount among them perhaps Richard Dawkins, who believe that the richness of science is being ignored or not appreciated; that science is as full of wonders as is the "paranormal." He believes that the achievements and the possibilities of science should be more strongly promoted. There is concern among academics that fewer and fewer students are taking up the mainstream science subjects. This message that there can be more to science is undoubtedly correct, but it should not be allowed to overshadow other areas that are important to people, individually or collectively. "Man does not live by bread alone" is a universal truth. Starving people need food above all else, but when hunger is sated people soon look towards intangible areas of life: a sense of community, love, a sense of value and achievement, appreciation of art, and so on. These are not scientific concepts, but they are important. Myths are a part of that intangible way we understand the world, and we need them.

The belief in aliens is, it seems, partly fulfilling these mythological needs. They reconcile us to the present day inasmuch as we have gods again—superior beings from the skies, but with technological craft that are the product of science.

We can see that this new, emerging, myth is comparable to "old" myths in a great many ways. Consider Robert Graves's description of the two purposes of mythology: "The first is to answer the sort of awkward questions that children ask, such as: 'Who made the world? How will it end? Who was the first man? Where do souls go after death?' ... The second function of myth is to justify an existing social system and account for traditional rites and customs." A belief in aliens, and the attendant implications that there are other worlds, other sciences, answer some of his direct questions. Ancient astronaut theory, for example, helps us to "answer" the question, "Who was the first man?"

Interesting to consider his comment "to justify an *existing* social system." Mythology can help to create a social order, but Graves rightly points out that it starts by explaining the existing ones. There can be little doubt that one aspect of belief in aliens, that governments have deep knowledge of their existence and are covering that up from public exposure, is an "explanation" for many which "explains" why governments cannot be trusted. For many people this is just what they want to hear. What Nixon did with Watergate was not only to create distrust in governments—though he did that clearly enough—but also to create an excuse for almost every occasion. If something goes wrong, someone will say it must be a corrupt government, and if you can't prove that it is a corrupt government, that just proves how corrupt it is! Probably no example of distrust of governments is as well publicized as the belief that the US government has retrieved crashed flying saucers and is studying them in technological facilities within the US, even working with living aliens in top secret locations. The fact that the evidence supporting such belief is flimsy, to say the least, does not deter those who wish to, or need to, believe.

Graves also points out: "One constant rule of mythology is that whatever happens among the gods above reflects events on earth." Again, we must turn to ancient astronaut theory to see how this is being promoted at the present time. The gods treated the Earth as an experiment and created humanity; sometimes they come back to see how their experiment is progressing. Religion, myth and the scientific method all rolled into one.

Graves concludes: "Myth, then, is a dramatic shorthand record of such matters as invasions, migrations, dynastic changes, admission of foreign cults, and social reforms." In other words the major social, cultural and political upheavals of the time. In the present day we must assume that modern myths would encompass technology, politics, mass communication, and so on. In olden times gods threatened or protected seafarers—the great unknown areas of exploration. It is hardly surprising that the new gods are space gods—watching over our attempts to explore the "final frontier."

Mythological Motifs

We can even see similarities in the motifs of "old" myths and the UFO/alien beliefs.

· Domain

The gods lived in inaccessible places. The Greek gods, for example, lived on Mount Olympus. This was, at the time, thought by the Greeks to be the highest mountain in the world and quite inaccessible to mortals. The Japanese gods traditionally lived on high mountains, of which Fujiyama was the most sacred. Such domains were thought to be special in their qualities. Homer said of Olympus: "Never is it swept by the winds nor touched by snow; a purer air surrounds it, a white clarity envelops it and the gods there taste of a happiness which lasts as long as their eternal lives." Many contactees and abductees also claim to have been shown, or taken to, the aliens' home worlds; and they are usually very special worlds, with no disease, no death, no war or conflict. They are out of mortal reach—we need an invitation by the aliens to get there. Only "special" people get to visit there.

· Hybrids

In the previous chapter we have shown that the belief that aliens are creating hybrid alien/humans is mirrored in contemporary science fiction. We can also find parallels in mythology; the gods were prone to creating human/divine offspring. Zeus, for example, took several mortal women as his partners. The first of these was Niobe; their son was Argos—presumably therefore a hybrid. In the modern version we sometimes have artificial insemination, but this is only applying technology to an old theme.

• Screen memories

The Greek gods were masters of the art of disguise, of which screen memory seems to be a modern version. For example, when Zeus became enamoured of Europa he disguised himself as a bull so that he might approach close to her while she played at a water's edge. She was impressed by the bull's air of gentility combined with majesty. Europa embraced the animal, even climbed on his back when he knelt down for her, whereupon he leapt to his feet and bounded across the waves, abducting the girl.

• Channelling

The oracle at Delphi and many "wise women" parallel closely the belief that we today receive messages from the gods—in our context the aliens. Many of the contactee messages could as easily have been delivered at Delphi.

• Cleansing

The myth of the Great Flood, a myth that arises all around the world, often with a Noah-like figure in the starring role, is basically a myth of cleansing. The gods were unhappy with the impurity of mankind and sought to wipe the Earth clean and then re-populate it. Ancient astronaut theory takes this literally, but certainly it is a myth that many cultures have incorporated. Mesopotamian myths, for example, include a version in which four gods planned the flood but a fifth, Ea, revealed the secret plan to a man named Ut-Napishtin, the Noah figure. Ut-Napishtin, like Noah, built an ark to protect species. Greek mythology from the same general area has a similar tale in which the Greek hero Deukalion and his wife Pyrrha survived a flood sent by Zeus to destroy all mankind.

The contactees and some abductees have indicated that they believe that the aliens are warning us to mend our ways or suffer extreme consequences. One contactee, Marian Keech, even gathered a group around her, united in the belief that aliens in a flying saucer would come down and save the chosen ones from a great flood.

· **Greater and lesser gods**

Most mythologies acknowledge a hierarchy among the gods. In the reports of the abductees, as shown in Chapter 10, there are also hierarchies. The saucers contain leader-beings and doctors, examiners, workers, "robots" etc., suggesting a hierarchy. It seems that in both the mythology and perhaps the flying saucer accounts the same need is being addressed; a hierarchy provides for certain gods (or aliens) who maintain the "mission," while there are others who can "bend the rules" and sympathize more with mankind. Consider the alien leader who wanted to give Betty Hill a book to keep but who had to bow to "pressure" from his crew. For the abductee, there is the possibility of taking some element of control if there are fallibilities among the alien crew.

What will be the pantheon of gods embraced by a fully developed flying saucer mythology? It is not yet clear. Although we have a rag-bag collection of entities, they do not seem to have definitive purposes yet, as did the ancient gods. But perhaps we begin to see something in the Nordic (good) and Gray (evil) divisions: the Nordics such as Adamski's Venusian were beautiful and caring, while the Grays seem to be demonic and shadowy. Certainly the basic conflict of good and evil is begging to be catered for.

· **The underworld**

The way in which the afterworld or underworld has migrated is a lesson for us in flying saucer mythology. In Homer's *The Odyssey* Circe says to Odysseus, "The Afterworld lies at the extremity of the Earth, beyond the vast Ocean." The Earth was at that time perceived to be a flat surface surrounded by a River Ocean. Beyond that was the land of the dead, where the sun's rays could not penetrate, the soil was barren and no living thing could exist. Such was the tradition of the epic poems. But as navigators and sailors crossed the oceans and discovered in-habited lands there, so the afterworld was removed to a new po-sition. The Kingdom of Shadows was thought then to exist within the centre of the Earth. To reach the underworld re-quired exploration of caverns deep into the earth. Certain rivers were held to flow to the underworld.

In flying saucer mythology we were first told that the aliens came from Venus, sister world of the Earth as it was then thought to be, but as it became clear that we were actually able to explore such regions and indeed found them quite uninhab-itable, the realm of the aliens was moved further out of reach; either to other dimensions or to worlds in far-off places where we could not explore.

• The Greek hero

The Greek myths contain a strong presence of the hero. He was mortal, a man of strength, courage and wisdom who could more or less take on the gods—within certain latitudes. Did not Adamski share much with his aliens, and travel with them in their spaceships, even helping them to fight battles because of his great wisdom? Did not George King tell of similar acts? If you can't make yourself a god, at least make yourself a hero. But in fact some of the cult leaders hint that they actually are gods. Is this also perhaps an underlying claim of the Star People?

• Missing time

In the Celtic tradition of Ireland a supernatural world could be found within *sidhs*—burial mounds and tumuli. Time had no meaning within a *sidh*; a minute in a *sidh* could be the equiva-lent of several mortal years, or several months or years in a *sidh* could be only a minute in mortal time. In the Celtic otherworld

there was mortal perfection. Food was abundant, unpleasant-
ness did not exist whether in people or in nature, all were im-
mortal and could not suffer illness or wounding. In the myths,
man sometimes enters the otherworld by force or by invitation
of the gods. Humans were invited into the *sidh* to help the
rulers to fight an enemy, and were rewarded with the love of a
divine woman. Sometimes humans would break into the *sidh*
to steal treasure. All of these have their parallels within flying
saucer reports, as shown in this book.

If we seek parallels, then there is one question of particular interest to answer. Who will be the mischievous Loki? This Norse
figure caused a great deal of problems with both gods and mortals—does he have an "alien" equivalent?

16

Needs-Based Belief

Around the Christmas/New Year holiday break of 1996–97 John, as Chairman of BUFORA (British UFO Research Association), received what seemed to be a fascinating request from BUFORA's Director of Investigations, Gloria Dixon. What many people were alleging to be a dead alien had been located on a piece of wasteland in Israel, and BUFORA was being asked to assist in analysing the samples. Could the association provide support and funding for the work? We had been contacted by Debbie Segal who, together with Uriya Shai, was working for an Israeli UFO Research Group.

The finding had occurred during a wave of UFO sightings around 21 December 1996. On that day, in the Galilee farming village of Achihod, the "entity" was retrieved by a local kibbutz resident, Tziona Damti. The creature was described as being five centimetres in length, with human-like limbs but surrounded by a slimy substance. Damti alerted the police and two officers arrived to investigate. One story had it that the entity was alive when found but later died. Another related that when one of the officers tried to put the "alien" in a bucket, it jumped on his back. Officer Asher Ben Ezra told the press that the volume of bodily fluids left on the ground by the creature was abnormal, which led him to believe that there was something suspicious about it.

Contrary views were expressed. One theory was that the "alien" was "a lizard which hatched too early." The slimy substance around the creature was thought to be the gelatinous sac which, once shed, would have deposited amniotic fluid over the ground. Doron Rotem, who investigated the case for the Israeli Association for UFO Studies, said he believed the remains to be the embryo of "a chameleon or a salamander."

To believers in the extraterrestrial hypothesis of UFOs, the idea that a dead alien has fallen out of a flying saucer and been retrieved is not that illogical. Within a wider context, one that includes SETI and the variables of the Drake Equation, the probability looks less certain. In this case there were clearly many doubts, but there is a duty that lies with such groups as BUFORA. To fail to explore every avenue of investigation possible would be to let down the Association's members, for such research is the Association's *raison d'être*. On the other hand, it was obvious that a sizeable chunk of the group's research budget would have to be allocated to the work. Another consideration was the belief that BUFORA was dispassionate enough to undertake the work in a serious and scientific manner—something not all groups can lay claim to. And if another group decided to promote false stories, the subject would again be hit by the questionable publicity and circus-like fiasco that had just surrounded the release of footage of the so-called "alien autopsy."

But there were other considerations. Why was a British group, albeit one with a good international reputation, being asked to study material found in Israel? And would the Israeli authorities allow it out of the country? (We were later to discover that Debbie Segal had apparently been in regular contact with David Kelly, an independent researcher from Chesterfield, who in turn had contacted Gloria Dixon, the BUFORA Director of Investigations.)

John gave Gloria a list of criteria to be met by the Israeli investigator who had contacted her; only if this was acknowledged and agreed to would BUFORA become involved. Recording these criteria in this book is important; the purpose of this description is to show that BUFORA was able to conduct a fully scientific, proper analysis of the material under predetermined agreed conditions. The conclusions, and the resultant response of some of the people involved, is of interest when considering "needs-based" beliefs.

Gloria added one or two points of her own to John's list and the following conditions were imposed:

- Any form of physical evidence is not free-standing; it can only be considered in relation to the testimony of the witness, so that we must have access to all the evidence in the case.
- BUFORA will assist in the objective study of reports and materials which witnesses believe are attributed to the UFO phenomenon. However, a vast majority of claims turn out to have a perfectly rational explanation and have simply been misinterpreted by the witness. We would expect the right to make such findings, if appropriate, public.
- We are not prepared to undertake the work in secret; our function is to make public our research and we expect to have the right to do so.
- We must point out that we have no research facilities of our own and would ask credible laboratories or research institutes to undertake work on our behalf. Any material would have to be made available to them for their analysis.
- In any reports that BUFORA studies, all related matters are considered in order to determine the credibility of claims. It would be only fair to point out that the Israeli case has been immersed in reports and rumours, particularly that the witnesses possessing the material have sought payment for access to the material. If BUFORA believes such material may be of scientific interest, we would NOT make payment for access to it.
- We understand that some element of research has already been undertaken and the results made public. If this is the case we would request a copy of this report and its evaluation, and more importantly access to the research facility which undertook the study. We would expect to be able to publish these findings along with any of our own. Alternatively, we

would expect to be informed if we were denied access and would demand the right to make the explanation public.

· BUFORA is not prepared to transgress any national or international laws, and the presenters of the material to us in the UK will be responsible throughout for ensuring that export, quarantine and other laws and regulations relating to all countries are fully observed.

· With regard to a presentation BUFORA would be pleased to make available a public platform at a BUFORA lecture. However, any views expressed are those of the presenter and not of BUFORA which has no corporate stance.

Our concerns about being caught up in a circus were well-founded. Rumours were already running around that the famous psychic, Uri Geller, had offered the family $1,000,000 for the entity. Naturally, the whole story was becoming a favourite with the Israeli media. The Damti family, and the local UFO researchers, seemed to believe they had something of great scientific—and financial—value. We already knew of rumours that Israeli scientists had concluded that the entity was "alien." Perhaps needless to say, we could not always trace the source of the rumours, which were spreading wildly and whose factual basis seemed obscure.

Debbie Segal arrived in the UK on 15 January, with her son and a photographer, and with the material. It was sent to a laboratory, LC2 Ltd., as pre-arranged by Mike Wootten, another director of BUFORA. Debbie requested that BUFORA analyse three samples taken from the material that she had with her. Mike Wootten handled much of BUFORA's efforts this from this point on; the following is from his own report:

The lab took delivery of the samples on 16 January and completed the work on 29 January. BUFORA had asked for an initial study to ascertain whether the samples supplied could be of extraterrestrial origin and whether further work would be justified. It was agreed that the carbon and nitrogen signatures of the samples should be examined to see whether there was a marked difference from the signatures that all terrestrial life would produce. Each sample was analysed three times (enough for the results to be legally admissible in a UK court). The very latest, British designed, mass spectrometer equipment was used to conduct the analysis.

The work was undertaken and the laboratory report produced. "The nine conducted tests showed that each signature fell well within terrestrial limits," wrote Wootten. "Not included in the report is the assertion by the lab technicians that the signatures come very close to those expected from lizards and frogs."

The full text of the lab report was as follows:

LC2 Ltd. (Analytical Laboratories)
CERTIFICATE OF ANALYSIS
Certificate Number: LC97-006
Project Description: Analysis of Biological samples for Delta C13 values and N15 values by Isotope Ratio Mass Spectrometry.
Submitted: By Debbie Segal
Date received: 16th January 1997
Your Reference: Analysis and report commissioned by BUFORA Ltd. on behalf of Debbie Segal
Our Reference: LC97-006
Date of report: 0th January 1997
Project Summary

Three samples were received into the laboratory for analysis. The samples were placed into a liquid Nitrogen container for storage purposes and to minimize any possibility of cross contamination of sample integrity. Each sample was carefully removed from the liquid Nitrogen container and a small portion of each was removed for Isotope analysis and placed into a sterile pre-cleaned vial of EPA quality. Each sample was then subjected to Isotope analysis using a Micromass EA Isotope ratio mass spectrometer with both Carbon and Nitrogen measurement capability. Each sample was run in triplicate to establish good statistics for both the Carbon and Nitrogen components of the samples.

Project Results

Sample ID	Delta C13 value	Nitrogen Value
LC23741 (Brown Container)	-24.25	4.2
LC23742 (White Container)	-24.12	4.3
LC23743 (Black Container)	-24.35	4.2
Typical Values for Terrestrial Samples (depending upon diet)	-15 to –30	0 to 14

These values fall directly in the middle of expected values for terrestrially derived Carbon and Nitrogen and therefore we submit that these samples are of terrestrial origin and not extraterrestrial origin as originally anticipated.

For the attention of: Debbie Segal, Simat Ben Shabat, Shmuel No. 56b, Neve Yosef, Haifa, Israel

Signed on behalf of LC2 Analytical Laboratories:

Keith Hall

Director

Mike Wootten's report continued as follows:

This is the first time that a British UFO research group has had the opportunity to examine samples that are alleged to be of an alien origin and it is the first time in nearly 20 years that the study of any UFO related material has been objectively analysed in the UK (Livingston Case). Geller, who was immediately informed of the results by BUFORA, is said to be very disappointed with the Association's findings. So too are the Damti family along with their supporting UFO researchers. BUFORA is not disappointed with the results. We are an objective research organization who approach the subject with an open mind. We work to ascertain facts and although we have a negative result, we have done what we set out to do and establish facts.

But Mike was aware that belief systems don't surrender their hopes that easily. Perhaps less so if there is money involved, as it seemed there could be in this case. He continued:

However, to many this may not be the end of the story. Despite submitted expert and impartial opinion, there will be those who will argue that what we have presented proves nothing. It may be said that it is possible that an alien life-form may have the same carbon and nitrogen signatures as us. But the same argument may be posed if we had discovered that the samples had similar cell structures or indeed DNA. Indeed if we follow the popularist theory that we are all born from an alien origin then we would never be able to prove or disprove anything in this case irrespective of what analysis or expert opinion we sought. This is a circular argument that dogs the subject time and again. In the cold light of day, BUFORA is satisfied that this careful and precise analysis shows that what was discovered in Israel last December does have a terrestrial rather than extraterrestrial heritage.

Had the analysis suggested that we had even the possibility of non-terrestrial material to hand, we would have pursued the matter further. But with the findings very clearly within the range of terrestrial material we did not feel that more money could be spent on further expensive research. Our decision was in part determined by the attitude of some of the players involved. Debbie Segal requested that she be allowed to present her story to a public lecture of BUFORA—these are held in London once a month and around the country on an *ad hoc* basis. She was given a slot during the lecture for February 1997. Many in BUFORA were not overly impressed with the nature of the presentation. She related the story of the finding of the material, but then showed a film that had already been made for broadcast which more or less concluded that the creature was alien—made before the analysis had even been undertaken! It was a rather hyped film complete with the theme tune from *The X-Files* to introduce "the alien in Israel." John, who was present, gained the impression—fairly or otherwise—that the "terrestrial" conclusion on the analysis was not welcome—and certainly would not sit well with the film.

Then Debbie Segal rounded on the analysis, waving a copy of

the report dismissively in the air. It proved nothing, she maintained. The analysts did not have the right to comment on whether it was alien or not, they had only to present the findings, Segal believed. In other words, the lab, she thought, was within its right to publish the Delta C13 values and nitrogen values but not to express the comment that "we submit that these samples are of terrestrial origin..." Several BUFORA officials wondered whether her response would have been so critical if the lab had expressed the view that the material was *extra*-terrestrial in origin. She also castigated BUFORA for making the report public, despite the pre-warning we had issued that we would not act in secret and would make public any findings of whatever nature. At the most basic level, she ignored the fact that we had done the necessary work, and had funded the work.

John formed the opinion that what Segal seemed to be doing was "shopping around" for the conclusion she wanted. She hinted that she would take over the analysis herself, that there were other places she could go who would do the job "appropriately."

Barry Chamish, an Israeli journalist and consultant to *Sightings* who examined the case, seems to have been unimpressed, and supports BUFORA's contention that scientific analysis had now possibly been left behind against a background of other, and less worthy, considerations. The following is Chamish's report, reproduced in full with his permission.

It's a Bird, It's an Alien, It's a Fraud

On December 22, Israel Television's First Channel Evening News programme broadcast an exciting report. It seems that on a night of intense UFO activity in the Galilee farming village of Achihod, an "alien" fell from a craft and was captured by a local resident.

An attractive woman, Tziona Damti, was interviewed and described coming face to face with the alien the evening before, which was standing motionless just outside her father-in-law's barn. She showed her father-in-law the weird "being" and he said it was nothing. She went to sleep but in the morning returned to find the "alien" standing in the same place.

So she called the police, which sent two officers to investigate. According to the conventional story, journalists monitoring the police band picked up the call and this was the start of a media event. The cops arrived and when one bent down to put the "alien" in a bucket, it jumped on his back. Officer Asher Ben Ezra told the press that the volume of bodily fluids left on the ground by the creature was abnormal and persuaded him that there was something suspicious about it.

The police, apparently deciding the creature was no danger to the public peace, returned it and the media circus was on. Besides the report on TV, the newspaper *Maariv* printed a photo of the "alien" on its front page while Yediot Ahronot devoted two pages in the centre of the paper to the encounter.

On the night of the TV report, I called Michael Hesemann, editor of *Magazin 2000* and told him the news. He asked that I hire a cameraman and cover the story in depth. I immediately called Tziona's home and spoke to her husband Yisrael.

"You'd better hurry," he said. "The body is disintegrating quickly. Most of the head has melted away."

"Please," I replied, "put the body in a nylon bag and freeze it."

The next day, the *Jerusalem Post* reported that an "alien" was being kept in the freezer of the Damti home. The Hebrew papers also reported on UFO activity over and nearby the village. *Maariv* connected the UFOs with a recent wave of mysterious livestock disappearances.

I arrived on time, after a three-hour journey, and Yisrael Damti was not at home. Tziona invited me inside and called his cellphone. He was at a laboratory of the Technion Technological Institute with fifty journalists and observers, including Uri Geller. He apologized for not meeting me, but the "alien" was about to undergo a thorough autopsy.

"Are you filming it?" I asked. The answer was no.

"Well," I replied, "if you don't, the first link in the chain of evidence will be destroyed. You won't have a creature or proper proof that it was examined scientifically."

He told me that he would ask for permission to allow me to film the examination. Why he needed permission I don't know, but a few minutes later one Debbie Segal phoned back. I knew her as a UFO groupie who had organized a failed conference some months before. She denied me permission to film. I tried a new tack, which I came to regret very shortly after.

"If this is really a space being," I said, "it's about to be chopped into pieces and you'll have nothing to show anyone. Whole, it may be very valuable to science and the Damtis. It will be a huge loss if you cut it into strips."

She handed the phone to one Uri Avishai. "Yisrael only wants money, money, money," he explained. "I'm interested in truth. But let's talk money anyway. How much can he get?"

"I don't know," I answered. "My editor informed me that if I could acquire a real alien, he could bring a well-known financier of UFO research into the picture."

"We'll be back in half an hour. Give me Tziona."

He then instructed Tziona not to allow us to film her till they arrived. It was already 2.00 in the afternoon and we had two and a half hours of sunlight left.

I spent the next hour interviewing Tziona and talking UFOs. She told me the alien appeared out of nowhere and had large, black eyes. It was originally 20 cm. long but after purging itself of an enormous volume of body fluids, had shrunk to 5 cm.

The pictures I had seen had shown a green creature with lizard-like features. There were four limbs but no fingers. Five cm. is the length of a human finger, and Israeli ufologist Doron Rotem was quoted in *Maariv* and *Yediot Ahronot* saying no alien yet reported was only 5 cm. tall. The next day he was on the early evening news programme of Channel Two television debunking the incident point by point. He later told me, "After that interview I received actual threats from the UFO community. They want an Israeli Roswell and I had the nerve to say this wasn't it."

Tziona went on. The creature had a human-like face and jumped away whenever anyone tried to touch it. The same night, December 21, that she discovered it, blue luminescent discs were seen by numerous residents of the village. I took down the name of one witness. And that night, a sheep farmer, also from the Damti clan, lost fifteen of his animals without a trace. Again, I wrote down the name. Further, Uri Geller told her that in the nearby Arab town of Tamra, he was invited to see a small UFO flying inside someone's home.

Clearly, there was real UFO activity in the area. And why not? Since 1987, Israel has been in the midst of a UFO wave that intensified profoundly last February. In big cities and small towns, UFOs had been filmed, physical evidence left behind and one highly likely abduction widely publicized. Until now, almost every reported incident was factual. But there were probable hoaxes.

The best-known example was the silicon shards found in the famous landing circles of Kadima. Between March 1993 and February 1995, at least fifteen very real landing circles were identified in Kadima and one UFO successfully filmed. The flattened grass within the circles was imbued with a red fluid, later tested and found to be cadmium-based. Also found were shards of silvery rocks which the National Geological Laboratory director, Dr. Henry Fohner, found to be of "elemental silicon which does not exist in nature." While researching Kadima, two people reported that they saw a local resident spreading the rocks into circles. Further, I saw him lead a group of researchers to an obscure circle where he told them to dig in a muddy puddle in the centre. Lo and behold, silicon emerged. So I took samples to a microbiologist, Dr. Rachelle Fishman, who is the Israeli correspondent for the respected medical journal, *The Lancet*. She had them tested by two geologists, both of whom concluded that they were composed of industrial-grade silicon. One problem . . . Tsiporet Carmel, the first of five Kadima-area witnesses of an alien being, presents the best case for the validity of the silicon. "It was found in the very first circle, behind my house. He couldn't have acted that fast."

Or could he? In June of last year, ufologists found the likely source of the "alien" silicon; a dump outside an electronics factory near Holon.

Yisrael Damti returned with Uri, Debbie and two very strange women. The first thing I said to him was, "There's 90 minutes of sunlight left. We have to start filming."

Uri interrupted and said, "Relax, have some lunch first. Maybe talk to the ladies."

The ladies were allies of Yuri Isaacov of Nazareth. Last summer, he was abducted by small Grays who lifted him into their spacecraft and ultimately threw a yellow powder on him which made him pass out. The powder, composed of 55% aluminium, was unknown in Israel and made his case believable. But it turned out, the powder burns could not be cured by conventional medicine and he was in great pain. He needed expensive medical care. Could I help? I said I'd interview him and publicize his ordeal. That's not what the ladies wanted to hear. They wanted someone to pay for an exclusive interview. When I refused to become a chequebook journalist, they left.

Next was Uri's turn. He claimed he was in the Israeli UFO research business for the past 25 years, a good trick since the first recorded landings began ten years before. What he wanted more than anything else was the right to negotiate with my editor for the rights to the film and possession of the "alien" itself. I turned [him] down twice.

Clearly UFO madness had hit still another village. Last April, one Shula Cohen filmed a remarkable event in the town of Ramat Hachayal. At 3 A.M., a globe appeared in the sky which lit up the whole town as if it was midday. After local reporters publicized the film and I tracked down a copy, her attorney contacted me and presented me with a written pledge not to publish or show the film for less than $20,000. Needless to say, I have not shown the intriguing film publicly.

In August, the Shuah family filmed a UFO over their kibbutz, Hatzor, for two nights and mornings running. On the third night, a crowd of over 70 kibbutzniks witnessed the UFO but the battery of the family camera wore down. A neighbour with a professional video camera was summoned and it captured one of the most amazing close-ups of a UFO's structure ever recorded.

Word somehow spread that the film was worth $100,000 and that the television networks would start bidding. Hence, an ugly battle erupted over who owned the rights to the film, the Shuah family or their neighbour. Villagers who had got along fine for decades were suddenly at loggerheads.

The same madness had hit Achihod. Whoever Uri was, he had persuaded Yisrael Damti that he was going to make him rich. And it was Damti who offered to allow me to film the creature and his wife if I promised him future payment for selling it to my editor. I refused and explained that no one, including my editor, would ever offer money without a thorough preliminary report. He agreed to bring the creature to me to be filmed.

Again I waited half an hour, this time outside, until Uri announced that [he] would not be able to even see it, let alone film it, because I "would spread doubt about its authenticity."

At that moment, I knew I was dealing with a hoax. It was not the first time. To put things into perspective, I have interviewed dozens of witnesses and on only three occasions did I smell a hoax. The Kadima silicon was one, the alleged abductions of Yossi Ronen and Yossi Saguy were the other two.

The *Maariv* UFO column, called not too originally, *The X-Files*, had accepted both "abductees" at their word. But nothing of their stories or their behaviour convinced me. Ronen wrote me monthly with increasingly wacky tales of outerworld experiences, until I dismissed him as a nut. I was prepared to give Saguy a chance to appear on a segment of *Sightings* I was arranging, until his agent called to discuss conditions. It seems Saguy is an actor and being abducted was good publicity.

The Achihod "alien" incident appeared to be stage-managed. Yisrael and Tziona are simple villagers, and Segal and Avishai [from] the big city. Everything was aimed at making money. I refused to play the game and walked out of the play. The next day, Segal appeared on the news and announced that an "unnamed" laboratory would offer proof of the veracity of the alien nature of Tziona's creature soon. In the meantime, Tziona announced that the alien would be put on the auction block with bids beginning at $10,000.

On the way back, I stopped in Zichron Yaacov and visited Dr. Fishman. She had seen the "alien" on TV and pictures in the paper. "It's my opinion," she said, "that a simple biopsy would have exposed the whole thing in an hour. What you have here is a lizard which hatched too early. It is covered in a multi-layered gelatinous sac. When it shed the sacs, it left amnionic fluid. The jumping is the typical flexional and convulsional reactions of a trapped embryo, I think of a salamander."

Doron Rotem agrees: "I thought it was an embryo but of a chameleon. I reached the conclusion the whole thing was a hoax from Tziona's testimony. She told me the thing was dead from the minute she saw it. When she started talking to reporters, it miraculously came to life. And originally, she told me the creature was 5 cm. tall. Suddenly it's grown to 20 cm. but it shrunk later on."

My opinion is that initially Tziona was caught in UFO hysteria and imagined a lizard embryo to be an alien. Then [they] arrived at her door and the hoax began in earnest. Soon, a controversial laboratory opinion will be released, similar to that of the Kadima silicon, and a legend will be born. But a false one.

Whatever the truth of the Israeli "alien," whether it is an alien, a mistake, or an outright fraud, it triggered in many people an acceptance or rejection that was too quick for the data. Even during the presentation at the BUFORA lecture there were people in the audience aggressively shouting their support or condemnation for the findings. There were those who claimed the creature must be alien because it was similar to others found around the world—though that statement has no basis in fact at all. There were those who condemned BUFORA for producing a negative outcome, as if the organization had dictated the course of the laboratory analysis. There were those who inevitably charged BUFORA with covering up the truth—they assumed that the analysis had actually confirmed that it was alien, and that we were unprepared to admit that. And there were those who used the indication that the creature was not alien to "prove" to the world that therefore no aliens existed and that the UFO story was entirely one of hoax—an athletic and bizarre jump to a conclusion if ever there was one. We were reminded of the reaction in the BUFORA audience of August 1995 when the "alien autopsy" film was first shown; one man at the back of the audience stood up and declared to Ray Santilli, who was taking questions at the front, "You've got the real thing there, mister." Perhaps the film *was* "the real thing," but it was certainly nothing that could not have been produced by special effects, and the man doing the shouting had not had the opportunity of doing any analysis on the film. So why was he so certain? It is this question that we now look at.

Dissonance

UFO believers and sceptics tend to have passionate views; strongly held and aggressively voiced. Such passion is probably explained by the theory of cognitive dissonance. If something happens which is consonant with a person's beliefs, i.e. consistent with the beliefs that the person is committed to, then the person accepts that event or information without challenge. If an event occurs that is dissonant with a person's beliefs, in other words is against what he or she believes, then there is energy put into reducing the dissonance. This may take the form of denying the fact that those events have occurred or of constructing explanations—however bizarre—which reduce the likelihood of the reality of the unfavourable event. A further method of reducing a state of dissonance, which is an uncomfortable situation to be in, is to encourage other people to "see things your way."

In the case of the alien autopsy film, for example, those who want to believe it is real find excuses to ignore the mass of contradictory evidence offered by critics of the film. Those who do not want to believe the film augment the genuine doubts by adding unfounded rumours and speculation about the history of the main players in the release of the footage.

Dr. David Gotlib, from Toronto, Canada refers to this as "the ratchet effect," a reference to the ratchet screwdriver, where turns in one direction drive the screw in deeper whereas turns in the other direction have no effect at all. Evidence regarding UFOs is rarely analysed in a balanced way because it is being analysed against the background of a committed belief system, whether for or against their existence.

Experiments by Aronson, Turner and Carlsmith (*The Handbook of Social Psychology*) show that the reliability of the source of the data plays a part, though not the obvious one. Whenever the source of information *can* be derided, then if the information runs contrary to the expectations or wishes of the receiver the source *will* be derided. But not necessarily so if the information is acceptable to the receiver, even though the source is no more worthy. And the ways in which people can be derided are often unfair and imbalanced. They convince themselves that the person is foolish, stupid, uninformed, etc., though there may be little evidence for that. Or contrarily, where the source can be shown to be foolish or uninformed, this will be ignored if the information is acceptable.

Whether people are prepared to believe that UFOs represent aliens will in some part depend on their belief about the aliens in the first place. There will be one division between those who believe in aliens and those who do not. For those who believe in aliens there is then the problem of whether they believe the aliens to be benign or malign. Those who believe them basically malign will, again according to the theory of cognitive dissonance, disbelieve those things which seem to confirm that the aliens have good intentions and easily believe those things which point to their bad intentions. The converse will be true for those who believe the reverse. So even among those who believe in the extraterrestrial hypothesis there will be a distinction in the value of certain evidence, again according to belief rather than the evidence itself.

Furthermore social psychologists have discovered that most people tend to trust gifts when they can give something in return and distrust gifts given without the possibility of return. Therefore those who believe the aliens are good will only be able to do so if they also believe that the aliens themselves can take something from the Earth which is of benefit to them. This then leads to a conflict between those who believe that the aliens have a right to take something and those who believe that what they take would be far too great a price. This belief in gifts "trading" may refer back to the statements of such as Democratus, in the fourth century BC, who commented: "Accept favours in the foreknowledge that you will have to give a greater return for them." In other words it is wise to look every gift horse in the mouth despite the proverb that says the opposite! This is demonstrated quite well by a recent change in the UK tax system. For many self-employed tax payers one year of their profits would not be taxed. This was distrusted by tax payers who were unable to believe the Inland Revenue could be so generous. When it was pointed out that the Revenue gained a cashflow advantage, then people found it easier to believe that this was a "true gift"—because "the other side had gained something too."

Questions for those who believe in aliens then become: What is it we have got that they want? What is it that they are offering us? And what is the balance of value between the two?

Some other beliefs about aliens are equally ill-founded. Many people believe that public reaction to a landing of a UFO in a highly public place would be mass panic. To the "believers" this explains why the UFOs do not make the proverbial landing on the White House lawn. Yet there is no valid evidence to support this contention, and studies of panic largely refute it.

The classic support for the view that a landing would cause panic is the reaction to the *War of the Worlds* radio broadcast in 1938, when it is "well known" that panic ensued when Orson

Welles broadcast, as if "live," a so-called report as the Invaders marched on New York. As we have shown in *The Encyclopedia of the World's Greatest Unsolved Mysteries*, this panic actually never happened. It was a media hype, stirred up by the publicity-seeking Welles and supported by the media who recognized a good story. The study of the panic by Hadley Cantril is thought to have taken the few extremist reactions and incorrectly extrapolated them to a much wider population. The solid evidence does not support the notion of panic: vehicle movements on the night in question were not significantly different to other nights, nor were hospital admissions. Most of the irregular traffic movements in the countryside around New York turn out to be cars heading not away from the reported landing site, but towards it—sightseers who in any case did not for the most part believe that the radio broadcast was true but thought that the radio station might have staged something worth seeing at the site.

Mass panic in fact requires very special conditions. Summarizing the work of several specialists (Robert Hall/Baker and Chapman/Barton/Berkun and others/Fritz and Marks/Janis/Kelly and others/Wolfenstein), it appears that the following conditions are most important:

1. A likelihood of being physically trapped in an enclosed space.
2. A lack of opportunity for self-protective action to be taken, or an ambiguity about what action to take.
3. Loss of contact with family, friends, support group, or authority figures.

The landing of aliens would not necessarily involve any of these aspects. The probability is that some people would stay tuned to radio and television to keep up to date with developments, and they might telephone friends and so on to ensure that they too were fully aware. Most people would assume that someone else was going to deal with the situation. (Of course if the aliens came in "shooting from the hip," as in the more aggressive scenes from

Independence Day, then panic might well ensue as the above conditions might well be met, but we are considering here a responsibly handled landing with no overt aggression.)

An event which may seem rather tangential to the question of panic, but which reflects the fact that people do not always react as expected, was the SAS raid on the Iranian embassy in London in 1982. A terrorist squad—or freedom fighters, depending on your political perspective—took hostages inside the Iranian embassy near Hyde Park. The SAS, in the full glare of cameras and on live television, blasted and machine-gunned their way in and freed the hostages, killing all but one of the terrorists. People pay good money to go to the cinema to watch James Bond do that, but in this case the TV companies were receiving complaints that coverage of the raid was interfering with live coverage of a snooker match! If the aliens ever do land on the White House lawn they had better not do it at prime time on TV or they're in for a disappointment.

What we can be certain of is that a belief in aliens is basically "needs driven." Most people who have a strong opinion on the subject perceive themselves as having some stake in the outcome. Such needs or wants include the following ideas:

- the aliens will cure our ecological or famine problems (therefore we do not have to worry about our long-term future—someone else will deal with it)
- the aliens will show us how to be better people (therefore we have a great, Utopian, future)
- the aliens will make us part of a galactic brotherhood (perhaps one day each of us will have the opportunity to travel in space)
- the aliens are future humans—they are what we shall one day become (we shall survive the nuclear/ecological/ozone/whatever threat)
- the aliens are here to invade and enslave us (so I need not take responsibility for my future)

- the aliens are here to tinker with our minds (so any strange belief or behaviour on my part is not my fault)
- we can work with them (I can play a real part in humanity's future)
- we can defeat them (I can be a hero)
- our government knows more about them than it is saying (so don't trust the government on any issue: taxes, road planning, etc.)

And there are a hundred other reasons for believing one thing or the other. This is not some peculiar facet of belief in aliens. Conventional religion attributes the same possibilities to God and offers the same reasons for following or denying a path of spiritual growth. Belief in other paranormal areas often have the same basis; telepathy and remote viewing "prove" that as humans we are a good deal more effective than we are often led to think; ghosts and reincarnation suggest that we shall continue to live after death. Belief in science has its own version; that science will cure all ills one day ("someone else will deal with it"), that science is the pathway to a great future, etc. We hope that scientists are on the verge of curing AIDS even though there is not a single case of curing any virus; but we need to believe that something so devastating as AIDS is within someone's control. There is often no proof of a rational kind on offer, but the belief is strongly held.

Another aspect of the "aliens" debate concerns the measures of control. Contactees were largely rejected because their claims were non-scientific; indeed they were shunned even by UFO-believers because they were detracting from "serious" scientific debate. But there seems to have been another reason; that the contactee himself or herself becomes an Important Person without support from others. There is a stratum of "needs-based" activity within UFO circles where the investigator seeks to be the "main character." Some of them are living out childhood "David Vincent/*Invaders*" fantasies—they are the person chasing down the aliens and who will one day defeat them. Others see themselves as the witchfinder-general; the special person who knows a true abduction when they hear one and can offer support and help to the "victim." Not all investigators are so motivated, it should be said in fairness, but a good many are motivated by these and other "personal" reasons. The contactees do not need such a person, they are important in their own right, and to the aliens themselves—a big ego boost if nothing else.

By contrast, the abductees are much more "agreeable" in that regard. They allow the investigator to take control of their experiences—to tell them what really happened, to help them through the experiences, to support them, etc. Early abductees, or abductees "new to the subject," tend to throw themselves at investigators—which perhaps meets the needs of some investigators. And many of those investigators distance themselves from those abductees who take control of their own experiences (Whitley Strieber was shunned by mainstream ufology in the US for some time despite a world-wide following) and simply move on to find another person who does need them. When abductees start producing contactee-like revelations they become something of an object of suspicion. Are they putting themselves centre-stage instead of the investigator? But from the experiencer's point of view perhaps that is part of the point; they want control of their own experience. They want control of their own lives back, not from the aliens—they can surrender to them if they want to because the aliens are so superior—but from the investigators, whom they wish *not* to rely on. The interplay of belief and proof within the subject becomes, therefore, a very complex one.

What we must consider is that the image of alien visitation is one that meets needs in a great many ways. And if we are sensible, we will distrust anything that is so agreeable because we might just be making the facts fit the need.

As a final examination of what constitutes proof, we might ask ourselves what proof *would* convince the otherwise uninterested section of the public that aliens were real. It is not an easy question.

It cannot be simply numbers of claimants. There is no short-age of people claiming to have met aliens in various ways. Lit-erally thousands of people have told their stories in detail in books, newspapers, and so on. We have personally spoken to more people who claim to have stepped off spaceships than have returned from Australia; should we believe more in aliens than we do in Australia?

It cannot be quality of evidence. The stories can be remark-ably similar and as such therefore would seem to support the no-tion of objective reality. A detailed analysis shows that there is a great deal of scope for contamination when using hypnosis, where investigators have pre-determined beliefs, and so on, but this evidence is not broadly available to the public at large who do not read authoritative UFO books.

It cannot be the reputation of the witnesses. The witnesses claiming alien contact are a broad spectrum including figures of authority such as police officers. Their testimony in court as, say, witness to a traffic accident, would not be disbelieved *per se*, yet their testimony regarding meeting aliens is immediately considered suspect.

If we cannot determine what makes claims of alien contact un-acceptable, then let us compare the revelations of alien contact with something almost equally extraordinary that was generally accepted without question by the population at large. On 1 Sep-tember 1986 Robert Ballard announced that he had located the wreck of the *Titanic* on the Atlantic ocean floor. The lost *Titanic* as a subject is comparable to the claims of aliens in certain ways. It is a romantic notion that touches people without anyone being able to say for certain why that should be; there was the percep-tion that it symbolized the end of the Edwardian age; the belief that the "unsinkable" claim was an affront to God, who punished the sinners; horror at the awful revelation that some lifeboats were half empty while people drowned, and a host of other rea-sons. Also, following the Grand Banks Earthquake of 1929 in the region where the ship sunk, it was thought probable that it had been engulfed by rocks and sand and was lost for ever. So its discovery was thought unlikely, if not impossible. Yet when Ballard claimed to have found and photographed the wreck it was accepted as such by the media and the public largely without question. A few detractors had their "conspiracy views" but they were immediately regarded as "wacky." Yet Ballard could have faked the photos without great effort, and he could have put together a small team that could have contained the lie for quite some time at least. And of those who believed him almost none had any chance of actually diving to the location to check it out for themselves. Following his find Ballard published a successful book and became a celebrity, which for some could be a motive for a hoax. Yet it was not challenged. He was believed. Was it simply because people wanted to believe he had found it? Was it because they did not perceive a personal stake in the finding of the wreck? (Those who did have a personal stake, survivors or relatives of survivors, immediately accepted his find as fact.)

Perhaps the answer lies partly in the certainty that "the truth will out"; although no one had tested Ballard's claim at the time it was accepted, there was no doubt that it would be tested and that others would see the wreck. In the case of UFO claims an underlying distrust is that perhaps they can *never* be tested. Fifty years of research has amounted to little more than collecting more and more anecdotal evidence and forming opinions about it. The attempts to test the information inevitably lead to no satisfactory conclusion, and no likelihood of a conclusion. Even over individual cases or individual documents debates ramble on for years and the waters just get muddier; they rarely clear.

When we strip away prejudice (such as "UFO believers are all mad so why try to study their claims," as some scientists suggest), we need to know why these two situations are not viewed with the same rationality. Then we shall be closer to an understanding. But an understanding of what? Aliens? Or human motivation?

17

When Belief Is All

Whatever the basis of the belief of the contactees or the cults, it is clear that they are serving a purpose. Even if their messages are mistaken—as rational analysis would seem to indicate—they are fulfilling a need in people and are for the most part harmless. While it might be possible to debate the social wisdom of people holding such beliefs, the fact is that UFO-based beliefs are usually "one-worldly," ecologically positive, and generally peaceful. Such believers might be living in delusion but they are not usually violent people. Loutish, vandalistic behaviour by such believers is generally unheard of. But there was always the danger that such passionate belief could become harmful, as some other, non-UFO/alien cults, such as at Waco, have demonstrated. If people became convinced, for example, that governments were deliberately preventing alien contact, could they become violent, and so on? That has not happened at the time of writing, but in 1997 one cult went one step further than harmless belief.

Hale-Bopp: Those About To Die Salute You!

One of the most dramatic responses to cultist belief in recent times was the mass suicide of members of the "Heaven's Gate" cult. An examination of their history provides a fascinating insight into belief systems at work.

The original cult that was to develop into Heaven's Gate was headed by Marshall Herff Applewhite and Bonnie Lu Nettles.

Applewhite, like most cult leaders, was highly intelligent, very charismatic but greatly troubled in his relationships with others. He at first followed in the footsteps of his father, a Presbyterian minister, and attended theological school. But he turned to singing, and was a singer of some renown who taught music at college and performed with the Houston Grand Opera. He appears to have had difficulties coming to terms with his sexual needs and identity and was eventually discharged from his teaching job for "moral misconduct"; this appears to have started a disintegration of his sense of social self-worth. He was homosexual, or perhaps bisexual, but could not accept his own desires. He underwent psychiatric help to eliminate his homosexuality but finally resolved his personal crisis by having himself castrated. Interestingly, it was reported later that several members of the cult followed his example.

His social problems started before the cult, however. Applewhite was arrested and jailed for car and credit card theft in August 1974. In 1975 he was hospitalized, and reported psychic experiences including a near-death experience (NDE). In hospital he met up with and became attached to a psychiatric nurse known as Bonnie Lu Nettles. Between them they recognized their mission and the beginnings of the cult were being laid down.

At first the couple started the "Christian Arts Center" which specialized in healing, metaphysics, astrology and comparative religion. Nettles dealt with the astrology with the assistance of "Brother Francis." "He died in 1818," she explained publicly, "but his spirit stands beside me when I interpret a chart. There can be several meanings to a chart and, if I am wrong, Brother Francis will correct me." The resultant publicity resulted in Applewhite immediately losing the job he then had as director of music at St Mark's Episcopal Church. When the Center failed to attract sufficient members, the two analysed their situation and came to the conclusion that they were from "the level above human." This led to the foundation of the original cult.

The cult, based in California, was first named the "Human Individual Metamorphosis"; the two adopted the first of their "cult-names"—Bo and Peep. The basis of the cult was that humans needed to "metamorphose" in order to move on to a higher level of spiritual existence. Appropriately prepared members of the cult would be transported from Earth by a flying saucer. Although the cult mutated over time to some degree, essentially it remained true to this idea from the mid-1970s to what is presumably its end in 1997. Applewhite and Nettles basically believed that they were higher beings who had adopted mortal form in order to lead others. They had, they stated, come to Earth in flying saucers, were not of Earth, but were just using Earthly bodies for their work.

The cult achieved wide publicity almost immediately. There were various stories in the US national news media, they made a full page in *Newsweek*, and Walter Cronkite broadcast to millions of viewers on their activities. "A score of persons from a small Oregon town have disappeared," Cronkite reported. "It's a mystery whether they have been taken on a so-called trip to eternity—or simply been taken." The news coverage later reported that these missing people were the first 20 people to join the Applewhite cult which was awaiting a UFO to take them to the next world. As the publicity machine followed their activities the cult grew. At one time it was said that over 100 members were all travelling in a huge convoy across the United States, heading for a new home in the prairies of Colorado.

As cults go—and despite the tragedy of the ending—it was less oppressive than most. Members were not apparently put under any pressure to stay; indeed many left without any aggression from other members. But those who stayed had to submit to rigid rules of behaviour, even for apparently trivial operations such as the peeling of apples. Subsequent analysis of the group indicates that the loyal followers who stayed to the end were generally intelligent people, but like their leaders had difficulty relating to the world at large. The cult therefore, like so many sects within and beyond UFO-related beliefs, became a surrogate home and parentage for members. They accepted the leadership of Bo and

Peep as the highest wisdom. They accepted regimentation as a protection from evil influence; from Satanic intervention; from the manipulation of evil aliens, and—a cornerstone of much UFO-related belief—from evil government. If they became "more than human" these influences could not harm them.

Over time Bo and Peep adopted the names Do (or Doe) and Ti. It appears that Applewhite promoted his own belief that Ti (Nettles) was the more advanced of the two and he put her on a pedestal above himself for other cult members. In 1985 she died of cancer. For the cult this was a great sign; she had "gone ahead" into the next level "above human" to prepare the way for the rest of the group.

But even in the early years—certainly before 1977—one story emerged from former cult members that was a chilling forecast of the future. One former member explained: "Bo and Peep started saying that the entire group would have to die in order to complete the process."

The rumours that followed the group probably became exaggerated through fear; the inevitable result of secrecy and strange belief. One sheriff's deputy in Oregon stated: "We don't know what kind of people we're dealing with. Since these people moved into the area we've had a lot of cattle mutilations. If the people who disappeared would just get in touch with their families or friends. We don't know if the missing people are dead or alive, the victims of an elaborate con game, or—God forbid—maybe used for a human sacrifice." Still more hysteria linked the cult with the Charles Manson "family" that had in 1969 murdered Sharon Tate and others, though by this time Manson was already in jail.

By 1993 the cult had adopted the name "Total Overcomers Anonymous," having also been known for a time as the "Next Level Crew." The group advertised in *USA Today* with a virtually full-page advertisement headed: "UFO Cult Resurfaces with Final Offer." They also ran an article in "spiritual magazines," presumably targeting a certain audience. The article stated that the group was in its final stages; indeed that time was short. It warned that the Earth's civilization was to be "spaded under" (recycled). "Its inhabitants are refusing to evolve. The 'weeds' have taken over the garden and disturbed its usefulness beyond repair."

By 1997 the cult had become known as "Heaven's Gate." It appears that the cult—or at least a large number of the members—were running a successful computer-related business known as "The Higher Source" which designed websites for other businesses. The cult was based in a mansion at Rancho Santa Fe, near San Diego. An insight into the cult is offered by a former member, Behzad Sarmast, who had left some years previously and who has related below his story in his own words especially for this book:

> Roughly five years ago . . . and still seriously looking for a community of like-minded people, I ran into an ad placed by this group. It was in the last page of a popular spiritual magazine, full page and bold. They have definitely not been "hidden" for many years, as some suggest, I know. The ad declared the usual brouhaha about the spiritual poverty of the planet, the inevitable disasters looming, the need for community, and a method for reaching a "higher state." It was all very generic, didn't mention much about UFOs, and was carefully edited for "lowest-common-denominator" impact. I called to see what they were about, and two days later, via Fedex [Federal Express—mail service], I received a video. Again it was all generic introductory stuff, but being naïve as I was, not to mention extremely curious, adventurous, isolated, and reckless, I decided to check them out. A week later I received a call, saying that there were two members swinging by San Francisco, and that they would pick me up and drive to New Mexico, where they were holding a meeting. I agreed.
>
> The two men seemed intelligent, and driven, and I sat in the back seat of their car, and off we went. During the trip, I noticed the driver would repeatedly stop by a pay-phone, and call some-

one. At each point he seemed to be getting instructions as to where he should go next. He wouldn't tell me what the calls were about, and yet again, my "bull**** detector" began to activate. Somewhere along the line, they dropped me off at a motel they paid for, and told me to wait there till the next morning, where some other members would pick me up on their way to New Mexico.

The next morning an older man and woman, who were not a couple, came into the motel room, and asked me to tell them about myself. They seemed nice enough. From there we drove in their wagon, again with me in the back seat. I began to tell them about my affinity for a book called The Impersonal Life, and tried to show it to them. I did that because I already realized the importance of being led by the inner spirit, rather than some external source, which is what they seemed to be about. They told me that they were not to read books from the outside world. I knew then they were off-course, but I kept going.

Now I have to mention something peculiar. During the entire length of my stay with them (three days), we ate at, and only at, Taco Bell! For the life of me I couldn't figure this out. I was vegetarian, and ate pretty healthy food, and it seemed bizarre to me that they had to eat at Taco Bell—at least while they were on the road. I'm pretty sure that if I ate that stuff day after day, year after year, I'd want to commit suicide too! (sorry, gotta keep a sense of humor, or else . . .)

After reaching Albuquerque I met more of their members, totalling about ten for that meeting. They posted many flyers around about their meeting, and seemed very dedicated, and nervous at the same time. As I read more of their literature, I understood that these members believed that they were the present incarnations of the Apostles, and even referred to themselves by those names (Matthew, John, etc.). I'm pretty sure that Doe claimed himself to be the present incarnation of Jesus. At least that's what his followers claimed.

The meeting day finally arrived, and we went to a hall they had reserved, and waited for people to show up. And we waited, and waited, and waited. I think a total of seven or eight people showed up! The "apostles" sat in a row, facing the audience, and spoke of their previous lives, their current mission, and the benefits of living in their community. None of these people were very impressive, but they weren't belligerent either. From their confessions, it became apparent to me that the majority of these members simply couldn't function in the outside world, and even though some had deserted or doubted the cause, most of them eventually crawled back.

Their lives were orderly, efficient, almost mechanical. Each had a function, and the focus they paid to what they were doing at the moment seemed to be their principle discipline. For instance, they told me of one of their practices, back at their home base (then somewhere atop a mountain, but they often moved), which was to peel apples in a certain way. The angle of the knife, the attention paid to the procedure, and the efficiency of it, were supposedly there to prepare one for the efficiency of the "higher level" beings, who could not pick you up unless you already knew these things. Basically, their entire day was built around becoming prepared for this UFO rescue.

After the lousy meeting (and consumption of more Taco Bell), we went back to the hotel room, where five or six of the higher ranking members stayed, and I got to know them a little better. During my entire stay, telephone communication with Doe seemed a primary event. It seemed like he was a dispatcher, and directed even the details of each members' lives—they talked with him constantly. I remember the original two guys saying that this planet was ruled by the devil (or "Luci"—Lucifer), and that this personal direction by Doe was the only way they could be sure of being absolutely correct about everything—since he was divine. I specifically remember answering them: "But isn't everywhere the Kingdom of God?" They became silent, and didn't answer, and I believe they thought me a simpleton.

They also seemed extremely nervous about going outdoors, since they were sure they were being followed by the government, the Lucis, and the unfriendly UFOs. Like any good cult, they always travelled in groups. During my last day there, I got to listen to some of their phone conversations, and I asked them why they were so cryptic about giving info about their plans or whereabouts over the phone. They said that they did this to confuse the "Lucis," who were of course tapping the phone. Another man came up to me and said, "They're (the UFOs) monitoring us right now, Behz." That pretty much did it for me.

I told them I had to go for a walk, which I really did, and while objecting to me leaving the premises alone, they let me go. Believe it or not, a police car did follow me, pulled up beside me, and shined their power-light right on me as I walked. Being so macho and defiant as I was, I stood there and glared right back, which I guess surprised them, and so they left. When I got back I told them what had happened, and they all looked at each other and turned pale. They were sure they would be killed (again) because of their beliefs.

Anyhow, I got tired of the whole routine, and told them I'd need to go back. They all looked at me like a poor lost soul, who couldn't understand what he was giving up, and would be lost to the world. Very little was said to me after that point. They drove me to a bus station, and insisted on paying me $50 (which Doe had told them to do), and we said goodbye.

I believe there was a movie (not friendly) made about this group sometime in the 70's, but I don't remember the name—I think it was popular when it came out. [The movie to which Sarmast was referring was probably the TV movie Mysterious Two, about Applewhite and Nettles, which was shown in the 1980s.] They had been waiting for their UFO for a long time, some members staying with them the entire time. Of course, all had given their life savings, homes, etc. It's a strange feeling knowing that those bodies found probably included some of those people I met.

I pray for their souls. Peace.

Sarmast's observation that Applewhite ("Doe") believed himself to be the incarnation of Jesus may be inaccurate, though understandable. Applewhite hinted to many followers that he was "doing the same job" that Jesus undertook, or "following in his footsteps." His teachings suggest that he believed himself a spiritual leader, though not actually Jesus. To have believed he was Jesus would not have, in any case, fitted well with his statements that the higher leader was Nettles; there is no equivalent in the biblical teachings. Applewhite rejected the term "Messiah," though within the group he was obviously regarded in such a light. Many leaders and would-be leaders within UFO cults or beliefs that we have interviewed usually drop a non-specific hint or two that they once were great spiritual people from the past—Jesus is often hinted at—and therefore short-term cult members might well have picked up the hint slightly incorrectly.

Richard Ford was another member of the group who left after he heard they were contemplating taking their own lives. He parted from the group just four weeks before the deaths. On 25 March Ford—known as "Rio D'Angelo" in the group—received two videotaped farewell messages from the group, one from Applewhite himself. The following day he, together with one other person, went to the mansion and discovered the bodies.

The group had committed suicide, it seems, in order to complete their human metamorphosis, to discard their Earthly bodies and to move on to a higher existence. One member, in a personal video statement made just before the suicides, stated of the discarding of the human body: "We take off the virtual reality helmet. We take off the vehicle that we've used for this task." Police investigators are satisfied, from messages left, from the comments of surviving cult members, and from the information on the cult's own Internet website, that the suicide was a willing act on the part of those concerned. In the case of other cult-based mass suicides there has been evidence that "weaker" members might have been murdered by others before those others took their own lives; not so in this case. That is entirely in keeping with the cult, which does not seem to have forced anyone against their will.

It was the comet Hale-Bopp which was the signal to Heaven's Gate that their time had come. The comet was discovered in July

1995 by two American amateur astronomers, Alan Hale and Thomas Bopp. Rumours soon circulated that the comet was being followed by a flying saucer which was "hiding" within the tail in order to approach the Earth. Quite why this flying saucer was thought to be hiding is unclear; many UFO supporters believe flying saucers are almost constantly invading our airspace, and as for approaching the Earth, Hale-Bopp did not come closer than 120 million miles of the planet. In fact it is highly possible that some material was following the comet; pieces of comets break off when comets near the sun and experience thermal changes; those pieces continue in the same orbit at slightly reduced velocities. Rumours that the "companion object" was several times bigger than the Earth were clearly absurd, and this rumour was very quickly refuted by such as the SETI Institute.

But for Heaven's Gate the comet was special indeed; they believed that it brought with it, perhaps aboard the companion object, no lesser person than Ti—Bonnie Lu Nettles in her new incarnation, having paved the way for them and now returning to collect her companions. "Hale-Bopp's approach is the 'marker' we've been waiting for—the time for the arrival of the spacecraft from the Level Above Human to take us home to 'Their World,'" stated the cult's website, which went on to say: "We are happily prepared to leave 'this world' and go with Ti's crew." One rumour was that Ti might be the captain of the saucer/UFO. It seems that the religious overtones may have been more important for Heaven's Gate than the physics or the UFO rumours. They viewed the comet as a UFO in its own right, a sign perhaps which some have likened to the Star of Bethlehem. "Whether Hale-Bopp has a 'companion' or not is irrelevant from our perspective," the website stated. Perhaps the imagery was reinforced with the comet making its closest approach to the Earth near Easter.

The group's website stated:

We know that it is only while we are in these physical vehicles (bodies) that we can learn the lessons needed to complete our own individual transition, as well as to complete our task of offering the Kingdom of Heaven to this civilization one last time. We take good care of our vehicles so they can function well for us in this task, and we try to protect them from any harm.

We fully desire, expect and look forward to boarding a spacecraft from the Next Level very soon (in our physical bodies). There is no doubt in our minds that our being "picked up" is inevitable in the very near future. But what happens between now and then is a very big question. We are keenly aware of several possibilities.

It could happen that before that spacecraft comes, one or more of us could lose our physical vehicles (bodies) due to "recall," accident, or at the hands of some irate individual. We do not anticipate this, but it is possible. Another possibility is that, because of the position we take in our information, we could find so much disfavor with the powers that control this world that there could be attempts to incarcerate us or to subject us to some sort of psychological or physical torture (such as occurred at both Ruby Ridge and Waco).

It has always been our way to examine all possibilities, and be mentally prepared for whatever may come our way. For example, consider what happened at Masada around AD 73. A devout Jewish sect, after holding out against a siege by the Romans, to the best of their ability, and seeing that the murder, rape and torture of their community was inevitable, determined that it was permissible for them to evacuate their bodies by a more dignified and less agonizing method.

We have thoroughly discussed this topic (of wilful exit of the body under such conditions) and have mentally prepared ourselves for this possibility (as can be seen in a few of our statements). However, this act certainly does not need serious consideration at this time, and hopefully will not do in the future.

The true meaning of "suicide" is to turn against the Next Level when it is being offered. In these last days, we are focused on two primary tasks: one—of making a last attempt at telling the truth about how the Next Level may be entered (our last effort at offering to individuals of this civilization the way to avoid "suicide"): and two—taking advantage of the rare opportunity we have each day—to work individually on our personal overcoming and change, in preparation for entering the Kingdom of Heaven.

They were as precise about their deaths as they were about other details. Investigation showed that the suicides took place in several phases over three days, with the decreasing number of remaining members tidying up after the dead before taking their own lives. Just two remained to clean up at the end, and then take their own lives. These were the only two not found neatly laid out in purple clothing. Death was achieved by ingesting a mixture of Phenobarbital and vodka, and in some cases aided by suffocation with plastic bags. All 39 bodies appeared calm; there were no signs of struggle or injury. Applewhite's body was found alone in the master bedroom of the mansion. Each body was accompanied by a suitcase of personal belongings and all had identification and a few dollars cash on them. The arrangements seem to have been an echo of the ancient Egyptian rituals which treated the dead body as if it were itself to make a physical journey to the next world and might need earthly belongings for the journey.

The group had been meticulous in prior arrangements also. They paid their following month's rent before the suicides, settled a small library fine and, having made individual videotapes explaining why they were going to take their own lives, they then had an evening out, eating pizza and seeing a movie.

One member's video stated: "It's just the happiest day of my life. I've been looking forward to this for so long." Another declared: "I've only one regret, one regret. The time wasted outside this classroom, walking down paths that were dead ends. I know I'd be a fool to stay here. To me it was the only logical first step."

There were many former members of the cult who openly praised the act and proclaimed their admiration for the "transfer" of their former colleagues. Nick Cooke, whose wife was one of the 39 dead, stated on the CBS programme *Sixty Minutes*: "I wish I had the strength to have remained . . . to have stuck it out and gotten stronger and continued to be a part of that group." Cooke, and another known as "Sawyer," confirmed that they still believed the principles of the cult were good and true and believed many others would still hold that view. Even the Cookes' daughter, Kelly, whom the couple had abandoned 20 years ago to join the cult, accepted her parents' viewpoint. On the same programme she said: "I don't believe she [her mother] committed suicide. That's a strong word to use when you consider that . . . this is something she worked for all her life . . . She graduated to the next level."

This sentiment was echoed by Sawyer: "Suicide isn't the proper term for what they did in my opinion. They left their bodies. It was something they were preparing for for a long time."

Not all former followers were so certain of Applewhite's sincerity, however. One, calling himself "The Jody," commented that he believed that the real reason why Applewhite took that opportunity for suicide was that he knew he was already dying of a heart condition. "I think it would have changed some of the others' minds if they knew their leader was going to die anyway," he said.

Another sounded more desperate than rewarded in her last video statement: "Maybe they are crazy for all I know. But I don't have any choice but to go for it, because I've been on this planet for 31 years and there's nothing here for me."

If mass suicide were not newsworthy enough, the media were treated to an extra publicity-handle; one of the victims was Tommy Nichols, brother of Nichelle Nichols, who played Uhura in the *Star Trek* television and film series. He had been estranged from his family for years as a result of the cult's general philosophy to break family ties. He barely rates a mention in Nichelle Nichols' autobiography *Beyond Uhura*.

One unwilling "victim" of the events was Chuck Shramek. What had happened was that Shramek, on 14 November 1996, spotted a "Saturn-shaped" object near the comet and, in order to find out what it was, posted an enquiry on his own website. He never stated that it was a UFO or spacecraft. Shramek repeated his request in a radio interview, and a remote viewer (someone who is able to "see" objects out of his or her normal visible range, using psychic means) on the programme—Professor Courtney Brown of Emory University—stated that the object Shramek was asking about was an alien spaceship. Wild rumours abounded; Shramek became associated with the claim that the object was an alien spaceship, and—worse still—other rumours suggested that the suicides were inspired by "his" claim, because the cult had suddenly realized this was the spaceship they were waiting for. None of this was true, as the cult's website showed. Nevertheless, soon afterwards Shramek started receiving death threats accusing him of being the cause of the suicides.

To protect himself, clear up the rumours and put the record straight, Shramek held a press conference on 28 March which received wide coverage and which successfully put his facts across. Shramek stated:

> Like nearly all of us, I was shocked over the tragic mass suicide in California. My shock turned to horror when some wire service reports actually made a connection between me and the cult suicides. The story had me the source of an Internet rumor that a spaceship was following behind the comet Hale-Bopp. This is simply not true. I want to make it clear that I am not the source of the spaceship stories regarding the comet... Regardless of the source [of claims], one can hardly be held responsible for the actions of some very insane people led by an apparent madman... Even the cult's own Internet page stated that the cult was not convinced there really was a spaceship or "companion" near the comet. Of course I am upset and saddened by the cult suicide, but in no way do I feel I caused this tragedy.

While several Hollywood producers rejected the idea of making a film about the suicides—some only because the plot was too weak, it has to be admitted—the ABC network apparently admitted that it had signed up just such a deal. The story would be based on the recollections of the survivor, Richard Ford, according to a report in *The Independent* of 5 April 1997, which went on to say that it was to be a spiritual movie concentrating on the human angle.

The Heaven's Gate deaths are believed to be the largest mass suicide on United States soil; they are certainly the first such deaths attributed to the UFO phenomenon. There have, however, been a number of recent mass deaths: 48 people from the Order of the Solar Temple took their own lives in Switzerland in 1994, with others of the cult following in their footsteps through to the subsequent year. The fear is that as the millennium approaches there will be other cults forming or seeing the millennium as their "signal." Because the millennium is widely associated with the cultist areas of UFOs, we may yet see other extremist cults linked to perceived alien contact.

Conclusion

And the Sceptical View

The question of contact with extraterrestrial intelligence is not a simple one. In this book we have looked at the division between the statistical probabilities and success rate so far in the "Search" programmes and the conflicting reports of multitudes of alien contacts reported within the "UFO" field. Clearly there is inconsistency in the data, the statistics, or the logic being applied, which must be wrong in some part. Either intelligent life is rare, in which case the UFO reports are probably wrong, or intelligent life is widespread and able to visit the Earth frequently and with seemingly little constraint, in which case we might have expected to pick up signals from their planets.

Yet we observe around us a universe where planetary formation seems to be common and where laws of physics and chemistry seem to be "universal" in the strict sense of the word. We might assume that biology—largely dependent on chemistry in any case—is equally universal. If so, then there is logic in believing other intelligences will have developed, in which case we must ask ourselves why we have not yet located "signal leakages" from their worlds.

A number of possible caveats to our thinking are possible. Perhaps life has suddenly flourished—or been seeded—all around us in nearby solar systems, but the aliens have travelled to Earth so rapidly (faster than light) that the "leakages" of radio waves from their worlds have not yet reached us. Perhaps radio waves are simply not the signals we should be searching for, and we have yet to develop the technology that will enable us to listen. Perhaps intelligence is common, but our own is in some way abnormal, and that if we could understand the more universal version of intelligence we could reconcile our questions. Perhaps we have simply not recognized our successes to date because we expect "patterns" to have a basis in mathematics or physics, whereas perhaps they have a basis in a science yet to be discovered.

Or a host of other far stranger possibilities. To quote Haldane's famous comment: "The universe is not only stranger than we imagine but stranger than we can imagine."

Cambridge scientist Stephen Hawking offers a sceptical view of this. In an article in the *Sunday Times* of 30 March 1997 he states: "I see no reason to believe life cannot develop elsewhere but the fact that we do not seem to have been visited by aliens needs an explanation. Perhaps the most likely is that although the probability of spontaneous life is reasonably high, most life systems do not develop intelligence."

There are the claims of UFO contacts, but many—including Hawking—believe that the reports of alien contact within the UFO subject are spurious. In addition to those who believe they represent a genuine contact with extraterrestrials, there are some who believe that they are hoaxes and mistakes; others that they are genuine experiences but not representing extraterrestrial contact; still others that they are an inner, personal, experience.

If we examine the claimants of these contacts there are alternatives to be considered. Of ancient astronaut theories we may consider, but we are not yet entitled to determine, that the information we have gleaned from our ancestors relates to extraterrestrial visitation. We must consider the simpler possibility that we have yet to discover how advanced our ancestors were, based on our own abilities. When the chronological record of our history is pieced together we may not need to resort to a belief in visiting extraterrestrials to account for our own progress and development. The writings of former times could be describing visitation by astronauts, but could also be describing imagination, parable and even shamanic-type "journeys." To be relatively certain that we were dealing with a visitation from the stars we would need some information that simply cannot have been gained from the knowledge of the time. The understanding of the Dogon looks interesting, but it is possible that there has been contemporary contamination. In the modern world of high-speed communications it may now never be possible to determine what is uncontaminated knowledge with certainty.

Walk-Ins and Star People feel disconnected from people on earth and believe themselves to be alien. But there is little evidence and only their own intuition to support that contention. We do know that there are many people who feel disconnected from others around them, and we believe that to be a psychological process. Some account for this by believing they are adopted; some who are adopted attribute their feelings to this reason. Others might feel themselves mentally superior; still others construct explanations for themselves which suit their inner needs. Walk-Ins and Star People could merely have created explanations to account for inner feelings. Although they point to physical characteristics which, they believe, set them apart from "normal" people, this could be a version of the same effect. Their physical properties are not proof of alien origin; none of those qualities are exceptional for humans, and many people have them who do not believe themselves different from others around them. Upbringing, parental love, and so on seem to be factors in their thinking, which points to the likelihood that the feelings are "internal." The fact that many have this "realization" at a time of crisis suggests a need being satisfied; it compares to religious revelation. It is a romantic notion to be a "saviour from the stars," and with lack of proof to support the contention, this feeling by itself does not offer strong evidence of the existence of extraterrestrials here on Earth.

The contactees almost certainly contain claims that are a mixture of fantasy and fraud, and many of their stories are romanticized. There is sufficient evidence within the claims to suggest that a number of the contactees were genuinely explaining their belief of an experience that happened to them. But we are not obliged to take their evidence at face value even if we believe them. They could be expressing inner experiences. Two who claim to have been on board alien vessels (George Adamski and George King) describe having done so "out-of-body"; that in turn could be something akin to a shamanic journey, perhaps spontaneously triggered. The fact that the messages delivered to, and through, the contactees so perfectly meet the inner needs of the individuals and the cultural tensions of the time (cold war atomic fears, for example) must allow for the possibility that they are a human experience. We might have hoped, though perhaps we have no right to demand, that the messages given to the contactees could have predicted and assisted with identifying and dealing with AIDS, the ozone hole, and who knows what is round the corner about which we have *not* being warned. The fact that we were told what we knew already does not offer proof of superior intervention.

In Chapter 8 we considered the diversity of alien forms that have allegedly visited the Earth. Although such variety does not seem to square with the statistics implied by the Drake Equation and the lack of success of the SETI programme, we might be forced to accept that variety is present and we have not contacted it any other way. But then we are forced to account for why that diversity has been replaced with a "standardized" alien—the Gray. Nothing in the claims of the contactees or abductees explains such a change; indeed the aliens themselves, who do not seem reticent to talk, have failed to offer a convincing explanation. Since we can explain the standardization in "human" terms—in terms of media expectation, mythology and researcher intervention—we are entitled to consider this explanation strongly unless proven otherwise.

Evidence in the form of artefacts has not been forthcoming. Betty Hill did not get her book, and Betty Andreasson misplaced hers. So unsuccessful has been the search for hard evidence that we can either be cynical, or accept that we might not understand the nature of "the game that is afoot." Crash retrievals might represent that hard evidence, but its hardness has not been brought to light. There are impressive—and unambiguous—documents in existence such as those relating to MJ–12, but their history and discovery *are* ambiguous. Even discarding the possibility that they are outright fakes, they could be governmental documents issued as part of a "disinformation" exercise. Generated by the authorities or not, there is little doubt that the subject of crash retrievals has been wrapped up in paranoia and fear of, and distrust of, governmental power.

It is in the claims of alien abduction that we have what seems to be the most promising evidence. For the first time a large body of evidence has been subjected to the detailed scrutiny of a variety of researchers including John Mack, Professor of Psychiatry at Harvard. The contactees, Star People and Walk-Ins were never examined so critically when they were the predominant claims within UFO reporting. Yet we are faced with the possibility that the abductions relate to inner experiences. Consider the words of Barbara O'Brien—who is described in her own biography (*Operators and Things*—published in 1958) as a self-cured schizophrenic. She was describing the tendency of the human mind to create images it finds "appropriate."

> If your temperament were such that you would not be able to accept the fact that a Man from Mars might just pop into your room, the vision appearing before you would not be a Man from Mars. It might be, instead, the awesome figure of God. Or the terrifying figure of the devil. Or it might be a much less conventional figure. In all probability the figure, regardless of the form it took, would have three characteristics: it would represent authority; it would have superhuman powers; and its weirdness would, in some way, seem plausible and acceptable to you.

The motifs of the alien abduction experience fit O'Brien's criteria.

· Authority figure

The aliens are clearly seen as authority figures. In addition there is the "taller" being motif; symbol of dominance. They control their victims through powerful eye contact, a trait of dominance. They interfere with their victims' reproductive processes, and their activities include capture and rape, recognizably "controlling" brutalities. Multiple abductions imply that they have great power, to capture and control great numbers of people. They can pursue people through their family line, abducting the children of abductees. There can surely be no more powerless a position than to perceive that the aliens can interfere with children without the parents being able to stop or mitigate the intrusion. If the aliens can impose screen memories then they are literally controlling the way we see the world, making our own recollections unreliable. One result of this would seem to be that some people see themselves as "property," and start to refer to themselves in terms of "machinery." In summary, the aliens can control the mind and body of their victims, and impose themselves into their families. Their superiority is implied by their ability to be on our planet when we cannot be on theirs, and in addition there is a background belief in the aliens as virtual "gods." All these are strong authority figure motifs.

· **Superhuman powers**

In addition to the abilities to do the things mentioned above there are certain abilities implied by other motifs. For example, "the elevator" suggests an ability to defy gravity and move people upwards through the air under control. The several cases mentioning cures and healing suggest an ability to diagnose and deal with illnesses and diseases, against many of which we are powerless. Technologically they also have advanced abilities, implied for example by the cases of equipment failures associated with investigations.

· **Plausible**

The aliens seem plausible precisely because of the statistical probability implied by the infinity of space. The discovery of missing time seems to provide a logical time frame in which the abduction could have taken place. The sequences of aliens misunderstanding basic language, or basic Earth phrases, add to their "alien-ness." Lastly, the reports of crash retrievals and the documentations that have "come to light" suggest a plausible reality, almost as if the governmental authorities were clandestinely admitting the existence of the aliens. It is a measure of the distrust of governments that a belief that aliens and governments have entered into a pact seems plausible.

However, Barbara O'Brien worked through her visions and recognized that her mind was creating a theatre into which it projected her thoughts. There are many clues within the abduction motifs that witnesses are unconsciously "creating a theatre." For example, the emotional testing could represent the witnesses testing their own perceptions of reality; the geographical areas of the saucers—the incubatorium, the nursery, and most especially the "holodeck"—could all be literal theatres into which scenes are projected. Why should this experience be so common? It is tempting to suggest that it is so simply because it is real, but it is also possible that it is a modern mass hysteria. If the abduction scenario represents a "mass neurosis"—a modern hysteria—then these motifs may represent the beginning of self-cure.

It is also possible that the abduction represents a "spontaneous" version of a shamanic journey of self-discovery. The alien may be equivalent to the power animal which partners and teaches the voyager. And there are many suggestions of personal development in the motifs: the out-of-body travelling; the spiritual dimension of experiences; the resurgence of contactee claims in a revised guise; the artistic after-effects of perceived contact.

The abduction may therefore be an inner experience which reflects the modern-day needs of people. And those needs may be being met on a broader basis; whatever the truth of the claims of alien contact there is certainly a mythology building up around the subject. We know that all cultures need mythologies, at least that is the lesson of history. We must consider that the need for the mythology could be the point from which belief in alien contact started, rather than the other way around. We should always be wary of evidence in support of something that so perfectly meets our inner needs.

In summary, aliens probably do exist somewhere, somewhen; but we cannot be certain that they have contacted the modern human race yet. If they have, or if mankind has in some way sensed their existence in a universe far stranger than we imagine, then we may have a lot to learn about that contact before we can truly claim to be communicating with them. While listening with the electronic ears of SETI we must be open to broader "listening" possibilities.

For the moment we are still left with belief, and there is no doubt that aliens have taken a place in people's consciousness. In a Gallup poll in September 1996, around 50% of adults believed in the reality of UFOs, a constant figure in the United States for over two decades. There was, according to Gallup, a peak of 57% in 1978 coincident with the film *Close Encounters of the Third Kind*, but the figure reset to its "normal" level shortly thereafter. It was found that 72% of people believe that there is life elsewhere in the universe, but belief is clearly the factor here since only 12% claim to have seen a UFO. Despite that, 45% of people thought aliens had visited the Earth. Interestingly, only 38% think they will look like humans, while 71% of those polled believed that the US government was not telling the whole truth about UFOs.

In the end, to know the answers, we must wait for a breakthrough that is unambiguous, and we do not know what form that might take. We only know that for all the truly exciting possibilities, that breakthrough has not yet truly happened.

Were it to happen, there are some interesting hurdles to address, over and above those mentioned in this book. For example, in the United States there is a law preventing citizens from interacting with extraterrestrials—Title 14, Section 1211 of the Code of

Federal Regulations, adopted 16 July 1969. This was in fact legis-
lation enacted just before the Apollo missions, to prevent the astronauts from possibly "contaminating" the Earth environment
with whatever strange bacteria might have been picked up on the
Moon. UFO believers have tried to interpret it as blanket latitude
to detain and quarantine abductees or contactees, but it was not
intended that way, nor has it been used in that way. If actual
aliens did arrive on Earth, we would have to work through some
kind of protective measures, but we would also have to ensure
that the laws were addressed or revised if we were not to turn
First Contact into First Fiasco. Another moral argument we
would have to consider is whether or not the aliens would acquire
diplomatic status and therefore political protection from oppression, for there will be a few who would fear aliens enough to take
direct, aggressive action. Would killing an extraterrestrial be
murder? Or does murder apply only to human beings? Assistant
Attorney-General Norbert A. Schlei, of the American Department of Justice, stated: "Since criminal laws are usually con-
strued strictly, it is doubtful that laws against homicide would
apply to the killing of intelligent man-like creatures alien to this
planet unless such creatures were members of the human
species. Whether killing these creatures would violate other
criminal laws—for instance the laws against cruelty to animals or
disorderly conduct—would ordinarily depend on the laws of the
particular state in which the killing occurred." Human beings
have some developing to do.

In considering the likelihood of contact with alien intelligence, perhaps we should rely less on surveys and more on the
vested interests of the "free market." Bookmakers have traditionally offered odds of around 1000–1 in respect of such contact; in June 1997 the odds dropped to 33–1. Perhaps they know
something we need to be aware of!

Bibliography and Recommended Reading

Angelucci, Orfeo, *Secret of the Saucers*, Amherst Press, 1955

Arnold, Kenneth & Palmer, Ray, *The Coming of the Saucers*, privately published, 1952

Ballard, Robert D., *The Discovery of the Titanic*, Hodder & Stoughton, 1987

Basterfield, Keith, *UFOs—A Report on Australian Encounters*, Reed, 1981, 1997

Bauval, Robert & Gilbert, Adrian, *The Orion Mystery*, Heinemann, 1994

Beckley, Timothy Green, *MJ—12 and the Riddle of Hangar 18*, Inner Light, 1989

——, *The UFO Silencers, Inner Light*, 1990

Berlitz, Charles & Moore, William, *The Roswell Incident*, Granada, 1980

Berry, Adrian, *The Iron Sun*, Jonathan Cape, 1977

Bethurum, Truman, *Aboard a Flying Saucer*, deVorss, 1954

Blum, Ralph & Judy, *Beyond Earth*, Corgi, 1974

Blumrich, J. F., *The Spaceships of Ezekiel*, Corgi, 1974

Bowen, Charles (ed.), *The Humanoids*, Neville Spearman, 1969

——, *Encounter Cases from Flying Saucer Review*, Signet, 1977

Cassirer, Manfred, *Parapsychology and the UFO*, privately published, 1988

——, *Dimensions of Enchantment*, Breese, 1994

Clancarty, Lord, *The House of Lords UFO Debate*, Open Head Press, 1979

Davis, Isabel & Bloecher, Ted, *Close Encounter at Kelly and others of 1955*, CUFOS, 1978

Dennett, Preston, *UFO Healings*, Wild Flower, 1996

Edwards, Frank, *Flying Saucers—Serious Business*, Bantam Books, 1966

Emenegger, Robert, *UFOs Past Present & Future*, Ballantine Books, 1974

Evans, Dr. Christopher, *Cults of Unreason*, Harrap, 1973

Evans, Hilary & Spencer, John (eds.), *UFOs 1947—1987*, Fortean Tomes, 1987

Festinger, Reicher & Schacker, *When Prophecy Fails*, Harper & Row, 1964

Fowler, Raymond, *The Watchers*, Bantam, 1990

Friedman, Stanton T. & Berliner, Don, *Crash at Corona*, Paragon, 1992

Fry, Dr. Daniel, *The White Sands Incident*, Horus House (orig: 1954)

Fuller, John G., *The Interrupted Journey*, Dial Press, 1966

Good, Timothy, *Above Top Secret*, Sidgwick & Jackson, 1987

——, *Alien Liaison*, Century Arrow, 1991

——, *Beyond Top Secret*, Sidgwick & Jackson, 1996

Heard, Gerald, *Riddle of the Flying Saucers*, Carroll and Nicholson, 1950

Hickson, Charles & Mendez, William, *UFO Contact at Pascago*ula, privately published, 1983

Hind, Cynthia, *UFOs–Alien Encounters*, Gemini, 1982

Hopkins, Budd, *Missing Time*, Ballantine, 1981

——, *Intruders*, Random House, 1987

——, *Witnessed*, Simon & Schuster, 1996

Hynek, J. Allen, *The UFO Experience*, Abelard-Schuman, 1972

——, *The Hynek UFO Report*, Dell, 1977

Jacobs, David M., *Secret Life*, Simon & Schuster, 1992

Keel, John, *Operation Trojan Horse*, Souvenir Press, 1971

——, *The Mothman Prophecies*, E. P. Dutton, 1975

——, *Strange Creatures from Time and Space*, Neville Spearman, 1975

——, *The Eighth Tower*, E. P. Dutton, 1976

King, George & Lawrence, Richard, *Contacts with the Gods from Space*, Aetherius Society, 1996

Klarer, Elizabeth, *Beyond the Light Barrier*, Aquarian, 1980

Landsburg, Alan, *In Search of Extraterrestrials*, Corgi, 1977

le Poer Trench, Brinsley, *The Sky People*, Neville Spearman, 1960

——, *Temple of the Stars*, Neville Spearman, 1962

——, *The Flying Saucer Story*, Neville Spearman, 1966

——, *Operation Earth*, Neville Spearman, 1969

——, *Mysterious Visitors*, Souvenir Press, 1973

——, *Secrets of the Ages*, Souvenir Press, 1974

Leslie, Desmond & Adamski, George, *Flying Saucers Have Landed*, Neville Spearman, 1953

Lorenzen, Coral E., *Flying Saucers*, Signet, 1966

Lorenzen, Jim & Coral, *UFOs over the Americas*, Signet, 1968

Mack, John E., *Abduction–Human Encounters with Aliens*, Simon & Schuster, 1994

Mandelker, Scott, *From Elsewhere–Being ET in America*, Bantam Double-day Dell, 1995

Moore, William L. & Shandera, Jaime H., *The MJ–12 Documents*, Fair Witness Project, 1990

O'Brien, Barbara, *Operators and Things*, Arlington, 1958

Rutherford, Leo, *Principles of Shamanism*, Thorsons, 1997

Sagan, Carl & Shklovskii, I. S., *Intelligent Life in the Universe*, Holden-Day, 1966

Smith, Warren, *UFO Trek, Sphere*, 1977

Spencer, John & Evans, Hilary (eds.), *Phenomenon*, Macdonald, 1988

Spencer, John, *Perspectives*, MacDonald, 1989

——, *UFO–The Definitive Casebook*, Hamlyn, 1991

—— (ed.), *The UFO Encyclopedia*, Headline, 1991

——, *Gifts of the Gods?*, Virgin, 1994

Stanford, Ray, *Socorro Saucer*, Blueapple, 1976

Steiger, Brad, *Strangers from the Skies*, Universal-Tandem, 1966

——, *Mysteries of Time and Space*, Prentice-Hall, 1974

Steiger, Brad & Francie, *The Star People*, Berkeley, 1981

Story, Ronald, *The Space Gods Revealed*, New English Library, 1976

Strieber, Whitley, *Communion*, Wilson & Neff, 1987

——, *Transformation*, William Morrow, 1988

——, *Breakthrough*, HarperCollins, 1995

Temple, Robert K. G., *The Sirius Mystery*, Sidgwick & Jackson, 1976

Vallee, Jacques, *Anatomy of a Phenomenon*, Neville Spearman, 1966

——, *Passport to Magonia*, Neville Spearman, 1970

——, *The Invisible College*, E. P. Dutton, 1975

——, *Dimensions*, Contemporary, 1988

——, *Confrontations*, Ballantine, 1990

——, *Revelations*, Ballantine, 1991

——, *UFO Chronicles of the Soviet Union*, Ballantine, 1992

Vallee, Jacques & Janine, *Challenge to Science*, Neville Spearman, 1967

von Däniken, Erich, *Chariots of the Gods?*, Souvenir Press, 1969

——, *Return to the Stars*, Souvenir Press, 1970

——, *Gold of the Gods*, Souvenir Press, 1973

——, *In Search of Ancient Gods*, Souvenir Press, 1974

Wilkins, Harold T., *Flying Saucers Uncensored*, Arco, 1956

Wilson, Andrew, *Frontiers of Space*, Deans, 1985

About the Authors

JOHN AND ANNE SPENCER have been active researchers of the parnormal for over twenty years. John is Chairman of the British UFO Research Association and they are both members of several international organizations on the paranormal. They are at the forefront of experimental work and research into many unsolved mysteries. Both John and Anne have lectured to paranormal groups around the world, and they regularly appear in the media. They have an extensive list of publications in the UK.